my life as a SPY

my life as a SPY

JOHN A. WALKER JR.

one of america's
most notorious spies
FINALLY TELLS HIS STORY

 **Prometheus Books**

59 John Glenn Drive
Amherst, New York 14228-2119

Published 2008 by Prometheus Books

Inquiries should be addressed to
Prometheus Books
59 John Glenn Drive
Amherst, New York 14228–2119
VOICE: 716–691–0133, ext. 210
FAX: 716–691–0137
WWW.PROMETHEUSBOOKS.COM

12 11 10 09 08   5 4 3 2 1

Library of Congress Cataloging-in-Publication Data

Walker, John Anthony, 1937–
    My life as a spy / by John A. Walker Jr.
        p. cm.
    ISBN 978–1–59102–659–4 (hardcover)
    1. Walker, John Anthony, 1937– 2. Walker family. 3. United States. Navy—Officers—Biography. 4. United States. Navy—Communication systems. 5. Spies—United States—Biography. 6. Espionage, Soviet—United States—History. 7. Cold War.

UB271.R92 W3445 2008
327.12092 B 22

2008035188

Printed in the United States on acid-free paper

CONTENTS

FOREWORD

Dear Margaret, Cynthia, Laura, and Michael,

In the ancient system of symbolism called the Tarot, the sixteenth card is the Lightning-Struck Tower.

The first twenty-two cards of the deck match the paths of man's spiritual consciousness on the Kabbalah's twenty-two paths of the Tree of Life. This card shows lightning striking a stone tower, the upper part collapsing and falling. Two men, hurled from the tower, tumble toward the ground, one to die amid the falling debris, one crowned figure to live.

One interpretation of this card is that lightning will strike in everyone's life, perhaps inflicting only minor damage, or, worse: causing the collapse of one's life, livelihood, family, friends, and possessions. Each of us can react in one of two ways to the lightning strike. Build a whole new life and continue, or remain destroyed like the dead man on the card.

Those lacking self-knowledge will usually attribute their lightning strike to "fate," but I know that the fates that affected my life are the consequences of my own actions. I was ruined by my collapsing tower in 1985, but worse, I also hurled my children and closest family members onto the rocks below.

My reason for this letter is threefold. First, to give my deepest apologies to my children and my extended family for the destruction I wrought upon them. Second, to acknowledge my regrets to the nation for the danger to national security that resulted. And finally, to offer an explanation for my actions, to describe in detail for the first time what inspired and motivated me to reveal US classified material to an "enemy." My intention is to reveal exactly what was on my mind at every step and not to argue the facts or history. This is more than just a discourse on your dad's crime; it is also an attempt to relate the events of my adult life, my memoirs in letter form.

With every crime, large or small, the news media and public will clamor in a macabre frenzy of curiosity to learn why. For the police, prosecutors, and the courts, however, the reason for one's crime is irrelevant, and, indeed, they do not even ask. Reasons are, of course, invented by the media, and the government is quick to "leak" such manufactured information. The few times that I tried to explain my reasons in news interviews, my explanations were edited out while the government's opinions were featured.

This letter explains my reasons in exhaustive detail. Briefly, three milestones were the genesis of the personal tightrope-walking drama of my life as a spy:

First, after exposure to vast amounts of government secrets, I concluded that the cold war was a farce. The Soviet Union had neither the will nor the military strength to engage the United States in armed warfare.

Second, that President Kennedy's assassination was a coup d'état by powerful government officials who objected to Kennedy's domestic and foreign policies. These government entities have ruled ever since.

Third, the failure of the government and US Navy to defend the USS *Liberty* (AGTR-5) attack in 1967. That my government would put petty politics before the lives of its servicemen was a stunning realization. Allowing the Israeli sneak attack to steal Syria's Golan Heights and its water was more important than a naval attack in which 34 men were killed and 171 wounded.

As foolish as it seems to me now, so many years after the event, my intention was to discredit the fraudulent cold war that cost us so many lives and such prosperity. Oddly enough, my Don Quixote–like misadventure may have actually been partially successful. Surely I helped influence the Soviet Union into the surprise announcement to the world that they would no longer fight, that the cold war was ended.

It is important to mention my marriage in the context of my crime. Had my marriage been successful, I would now be enjoying retirement and spoiling my grandchildren, not writing about my secret life from prison. But my marriage was a failure, wrecked very early by your mother's blatant infidelity. In our first year of marriage, when Margaret was but an infant, I was faced with that classic dilemma: stay in a flawed marriage or accept reality and move on. It is a foolish master that misgoverns his household, and I was only in my early twenties. I was too inexperienced to choose wisely. Stay with the weak woman and try to build a household or obtain an adultery divorce and support a daughter. Which was the right choice? I would never know. I still do not know the answer.

Obviously, my children deserved an explanation of my activities. My original intention was to write a few dozen pages to be held by my attorney until my death, then, like the reading of a will, to release it to my children. I started writing in 1994, and the letter grew quickly to hundreds of pages. First, eye disease stopped me from writing for four years, then an attorney who was preparing a smooth version on computer disk claims to have lost the 590 completed pages. This forced me to start all over again in 2000, seriously slowed by a vision disability.

As my second attempt at a letter grew into several hundred pages, and blindness grew ever closer, I realized that I should send you, Cynthia, the complete pages and continue forwarding sections as they were completed. The finish is now a race against total blindness.

In conclusion, it is your father's wish that while I brought the lightning down upon your tower of life, you will all stand, dust yourselves off, grow spiritually from the experience, and continue your lives with success and happiness. It is also my wish that my family and the nation can forgive me for the danger I would have caused if actual war had developed between the United States and the Soviet Union.

Chapter 1

THE CRIME

It was a sparkling clear fall day in October 1967 as I drove northeast on Interstate 64. While it was too cool to have the top down on my 1964 MG, the look and smell of Virginia's autumn was effervescent, and the steady rumbling purr of the engine should have inspired pure delight. But it didn't. Inside my jacket pocket, a top-secret document burned a hole in my chest. I was on my way to become a spy.

Strangely, I was not nervous, but I knew I was walking on the cutting edge of danger. I concealed my anxiety with a too-well-controlled steadiness. Keeping the MG in the right lane and a couple miles above the speed limit, I hoped to avoid a ticket or any attention.

I loved that car, a toy in reality. I thought back to the day I bought it in Rota, Spain, in 1964. Rota was the advanced base for my submarine squadron and my boat, the USS *Andrew Jackson* (SSBN-619). A nuclear-powered Polaris missile submarine, she carried sixteen nuclear-tipped ballistic missiles. With a complement of two complete crews, one crew manned the boat for about three months while the other crew trained and led their temporarily normal lives.

My wife, Barbara, and I planned an exotic European vacation around the car. I bought it from a local dealer for $1,200 prior to a sixty-day patrol. At the end of the patrol, Barbara flew to Spain, where I met her at the Madrid airport in the shiny new red sports car.

It was a glorious summer, and we wasted no time driving straight to the Mediterranean port city of Valencia to start our casual trip along the Spanish, French, and Italian rivieras. Nothing was planned; we just gadded about, enjoying every minute. Since we had not seen each other for over three months and were still in our twenties, the vacation was more like the honeymoon we had missed eight years earlier. With Barbara's mother watching our kids in Charleston, South Carolina, Barbara enjoyed her first holiday from the children.

We quickly learned that the true charm of Europe was in the small towns and villages. At the end of the day when we finally got hungry, we would find a small inn with lodging in any small town, usually one that had never seen a tourist. Dinner might be with the family at their table, with the evenings spent wandering the town square, shops, and clubs. In the morning, we bought fresh fruit, cheese, local wine, and long hot loaves of bread. Back on the road again, we picnicked along the way, European-style, until we stopped again that night.

Leaving the Mediterranean coast at Genoa, we turned north over the Alps, into Switzerland and Germany. At Frankfort, we turned east to Belgium, then south to France, over the Pyrenees and back to Rota. We had turned slightly continental after three weeks and were not ready for the flight home. Our little car would follow by ship.

Back to reality on I-64 West, I realized that the idyllic but belated honeymoon had been just three years earlier. My marriage was now in shambles, beyond repair. That little MG now carried me on a mission far more dangerous than any submarine patrol.

This spy adventure began the day before in my capacity as communications watch officer for the Commander, Submarine Force, Atlantic Fleet in Norfolk, Virginia (COMSUBLANT). I was a chief warrant officer on the staff of the admiral in charge of all the submarines and support ships in the Atlantic half of the world.

Four officers rotated on the round-the-clock supervision of the communication center supporting message traffic between the submarines, ships, and shore. Our communication center was located in a gray, windowless building known as the Operations and Control Center (OPCON Center). This building, a graceless mausoleum, drab and cold, and HQ for the most important fleet commanders in the world, was the most secure structure in the area. It housed the war room.

The farce of the cold war and the absurd war machine it spawned was an ever-growing pathetic joke to me. Thoughts of espionage surfaced occasionally. I had no plan. Indeed, it was a spur of the moment act at about 10 p.m., a couple hours before being relieved from watch at midnight. An "Eyes Only" super-encrypted message had come in requiring personal decryption by the watch officer. A few keylists were kept in a small safe for our use, and I set up the World War II vintage electro-mechanical KL-47 machine and deciphered the message. These messages were rarely of any military interest and usually contained private and embarrassing information between the submarine skippers and the fleet commander. While the keylist might be used to privately inform the commanding officer of a death in a crewman's family, it might just as well inform some officer at sea that his wife got drunk and slapped a commodore's wife at a tea.

As I returned the keylist to the safe, a thought struck me like a bolt of lightning. That little-used but impressive keylist would be a perfect calling card to meet with the Soviets. The "cold war" is a game played by generals and politicians—and paid for by the public in money and lives. I told myself, *I play at it myself every day. Why not play at a different level?*

The keylist was hot. With an impressive orange stripe along the upper border, it was marked TOP SECRET, CRYPTO, NOFORM, and SPECAT. For access, one first had to be cleared by the FBI for top-secret access and granted by the commanding officer in writing. Crypto applies to all equipment and keylists for message encoding and decoding and requires yet another written clearance. NOFORM limits access to US citizens—No Foreign Dissemination. SPECAT, for special category, requires yet another written authorization and clearance for access to that category. In this case, it was "Officers' Eyes Only." In fact, only the communications watch officer and the admiral himself would ever see the message.

The keylist consisted of one eight-by-ten sheet of paper. The obverse side contained the "Letter of Promulgation" from the director of the National Security Agency, directing its use and safeguards. The reverse contained the keylist for an entire month. It listed the mechanical set up for each day of the month. Numbered one through thirty-one down the left margin, the sixteen settings necessary for that day's encryption could easily be read. For one sheet of paper, it packed considerable data.

As I considered that keylist, my thoughts were jolted by the scream of a klaxon in the message center, signaling the possible start of World War III. As the entire message center went into high alert in preparation for the war messages, our Morse code operator and I dashed at a full run to the door en route to the Command Center. Fifty feet down the hall, one flight down the stairs, two at a time, and another fifty feet to the Command Center door. An armed marine scanned the identification cards pinned to our shirts as we rushed in. His orders were to shoot any unauthorized persons. Inside the Command Center, the watch officer frantically mashed buttons on his communications console while trying to authenticate the emergency message. A disembodied monotone voice on some speaker droned, "NORAD has detected two hundred incoming Soviet intercontinental ballistic missiles—estimated impact on the United States in fifteen minutes." The voice—from the National Military Command Center in Washington (NMCC)—was sending the war message.

The watch officer struggled to snap open the sealed authentication system envelope to confirm the message. The four-inch-square black plastic packet finally opened to reveal a single word on each half. "Message authenticated!" he shouted. I ran to a small room behind the watch officer where my operator sat, fist on the Morse code key, ready. The submarine teletype broadcast from Cutler, Maine, rattled electronic pulses on a speaker. As custodian of "the key," it was my turn to act. I jammed the key into a large electronic device, turned it, and the speaker went dead. I had seized control of the several-thousand-watt submarine transmitter in Maine, along with the Washington, DC, transmitter and several other small stations worldwide. The speaker went dead on dozens of submarines as well, and the radiomen knew what that meant: an alert.

My operator began sending a series of V's, "VVV VVV VVV," and our station call letters, the intentional signal of a station preparing to send a message. As a chief warrant officer, my experience and knowledge exceeded that of my operator. My job was not only to seize control of the submarine transmitters but to supervise the operator and ensure that he transmitted the war message correctly. We waited for the message: Was it a Red Dot—war at last? Or a White Dot, a routine exercise?

The war message is sent in plain language, not encrypted or scrambled, but it can only be "authenticated" by the president. The short message, fewer than twenty-five words in length, could thus be faked by anyone, so the authentication code words are safeguarded higher than top-secret cryptographic material. An officer follows the president everywhere, carrying an attaché case called the "football," which contains the authentication codes for the day. After transmitting the war message, the president provides the two authentication words, which must match those at the receiving end. We had already confirmed that the message was authentic, so now we waited to retaliate against the Soviets, following our national policy of MAD: mutually assured destruction.

An officer rushed in with the message, a White Dot. My operator sent "ZUJ" to standby as I thrust him the message. I knew from my six Polaris submarine patrols that the boats were maneuvering to launch depth and were spinning up their missile guidance systems for launch. They, too, would not know if it was to be Armageddon or just another sleep-interrupting drill. An umbilical cord from the submarine's firing control computer programmed a separate target for each missile, preparing to erase the entire Sino-Soviet block.

We sent the White Dot, and I could hear the snap of some dozen or more submarine commanders withdrawing their keys from their bridge firing control panels. Just a drill.

Back in the message center, the inanity of it all struck me. *Does anyone truly believe this foolishness?* I wondered. My troops scurried about, clearing the exercise traffic and trying to return the operation to normal. The watch chief had a phone to each ear, attempting to retransmit interrupted traffic. My Morse code operator, the service clerk, was several hours behind in correcting messages. I decided then: *I'm going to copy that keylist.*

Standing, I could feel my adrenaline level begin to rise. There was a roaring of blood in my ears. I appeared calm, however—I was a submariner and every submariner sailor exhibits total composure in a high-stress situation.

Out of the bustling message center, I stepped into the online crypto-room where dozens of teletypewriters clacked away, each supported by a computerlike cryptographic device. The operators worked to clear their backlog of messages on our dedicated circuits to Cutler, Maine; Washington, DC; Naples, Italy; Holly Loch, Scotland; Rota, Spain, and many other stations. A KWR-37 crypto-machine beeped crazily; out of cryptographic synchronization, the teletype machine was spitting out gobbledygook.

The SPECAT safe was a small, one-foot-square metal box attached to the rear wall, protected by a Sergeant-Greenleaf manipulation–proof combination lock. I am told that Sergeant-Greenleaf has a transparent safe in their lobby containing $10,000 in cash that is protected by this very type of lock. The money belongs to anyone who can open the lock by simple manipulation. The money has never been claimed.

But the lock would not protect this safe.

Slipping the keylist into a file folder and locking the safe, I returned to the message center and into the small partitioned Xerox area. The machine was big, as large as a freezer on its side. Keylist on the glass, cover down, copy button pushed, I became a criminal: I was violating US Code, Title 18: the unlawful obtaining of national security information and unlawful retention of national security information.

There is really no serious protection of our national security information. No video, searches, or planting false data to trap a spy. No serious safeguards at all. But as the machine cycled, I realized that the only threat to my mission was a jammed copy machine. I was certainly qualified to clear any jam, but I also knew that my watch crew wouldn't ever let their watch officer repair a jam. If one of my crew saw any part of a keylist copy pinched between some rollers, they would recognize it and probably end my criminal career within the first minutes. But the machine ran perfectly, and with the copy in my inner jacket pocket, I returned the original to the safe.

I was relieved by the morning watch, which covered the period from 8 a.m. to 4 p.m. At the front door, I surrendered my badge to a security officer and casually walked to the Bachelor Officers Quarters (BOQ) a couple hundred feet away. The marine, who would have shot me or anyone else without a proper badge a couple hours ago, was no obstacle to the theft of a top-secret crypto-document. *No search of persons or packages was ever conducted.*

Regardless of the stolen document, I fell asleep quickly and slept soundly, as always. It was a strange ability of mine. I recall many years later visiting the parents of my girlfriend, Pat Marsee, in South Hill, Virginia, for Sunday dinner. With several guests and children, the living room was pure bedlam, complete with the annoying background noise of a blaring television. I sat on the couch with a strange child on my lap, and we both fell asleep amid the chaos. I awoke later, but with my eyes still closed, to hear Pat's mother marvel at my ability to sleep. "Anyone who can sleep through this," she remarked, "must have a perfectly clear conscience." As a successful spy for some twelve years by then, I grinned to myself. *If they only knew.*

I should have married that girl, but then I would have ruined her life.

After rising and showering the next morning, I sat at my small desk, flicked on my stereo, and pondered my next move. I had no plan. The nearest Soviets were at their Washington embassy, some four hours away by car. With the building most likely under surveillance, one cannot just walk in—or can they? Surely I would at least be photographed and maybe grabbed when I left. I recalled reading a secret intelligence report wherein the National Geographic building was used to photograph some Soviet building across the street. Was it the embassy?

Perhaps the Soviet national airline, Aeroflot, in New York, would be a point of contact? No, far too dangerous. They may use non-Soviet employees or be under more stringent observation; say, a foreign embassy, perhaps in Mexico? That seemed far too complicated. *Hell, I've had no plan so far*, I finally decided, *why form one now?* I had twelve hours before I had to be back at Norfolk to relieve the watch. Plenty of time!

Into the MG, a stop for gas, and I was on my way. I would figure out where the embassy was after I arrived in DC.

Hours later, skirting Richmond on the bypass and to I-95 North, I was about halfway there. Traffic was bad, but at least I would be going into the city when the floodgate spilled thousands of civil servants to the outbound routes. There are some three hundred and eighty thousand of them in Washington alone.

Nearing the city at last, I passed the Pentagon to my left, five concentric buildings, a skyscraper lying in pieces on its side. The home of the Department of Defense and my bosses, it was so designed to prevent its standing higher than the Capitol.

I crossed the Potomac, the gray purlieu of the city spread before me, a few monuments poking up in the distance. I exited quickly to a side street, somewhere around G and 6th streets, and parked near a phone booth not more than a half mile from the Capitol. The street was quiet, few cars and no people. The nearby Potomac and Washington channel gave off that low-tide smell.

Espionage was terra incognita to me. With no training and a dislike of spy novels, I had no guidance for making contact. I had read of failed and somewhat silly attempts in intelligence reports. One individual sought out a Soviet embassy employee's residence and placed a package on his doorstep during the night. That package contained samples of secret documents and instructions on a meeting place. The Russian saw the package the next morning and, fearing a bomb, called the police. One need not guess who made the meeting with the aspiring spy.

Another ambitious fellow was seen trying to toss a note over the Soviet embassy wall in Mexico City. The local police arrested him, ending his career before it began.

Top up on the car, driving jacket off, I slipped into a sport coat. With slacks, dress shoes, and open-collar dress shirt, I did my best to look like a Washington office worker. The phone book revealed the embassy address to be 1126 16th Street, NW. Parking in front of or even near the embassy would be foolish. Dime in the slot, I called a taxi—they would pick up from a street corner in those days. Directing the driver to the corner of the 1000 block of 16th Street, I paid the fare and strolled toward the 1100 block.

A personal axiom of mine is the principle of KISS: Keep it simple, stupid. Why not just hide in plain sight? The least likely expectation is for a prospective spy to walk right in the front door. If I was photographed, identification would be nearly impossible. The worst risk would be during my departure; I might be pounced upon and arrested as I left. Or worse, followed, identified, and arrested at my *next* meeting. I decided that the Soviets would be aware of surveillance and would advise me on how to leave the building.

I reached the 1100 block far too quickly. It was that time of half-light, the darkness was pressing down. Taut with tension, I felt the adrenaline kick in again as the stress increased. With little pedestrian or vehicular traffic, I checked for obvious surveillance while searching for obscure building addresses. Eventually I walked slightly past the embassy, a stately old gray mansion. Having passed it, I continued to the next corner searching for watchers. Seeing none, I backtracked to the building, arriving just as a car was exiting the driveway. A man walked from the departing car to the front door, so I casually fell in behind. In fact, he was startled to discover my presence as he began to close the door. I simply stepped into the twenty-foot-high entry foyer and asked to speak to "someone in security." He mumbled something to an equally surprised receptionist and quickly scurried off.

As I observed the ornate staircase and cold interior, I had a gnawing feeling of being in forbidden territory, no longer in the United States. Indeed, the embassy is technically an extension of Soviet property, so my feet stood in the Soviet Union as though instantly teleported there.

Moments later, Boris Aleksandrovich Solomatin (I would not learn his name until he wrote his book many years later) entered the foyer, shook my hand, and escorted me to an office just off the foyer. In suit and tie, Solomatin had a strong dauntless air about him and yet a rare warmth. He asked how he could be of service. I produced the keylist and said, "I am interested in supplying US classified material and I expect financial compensation for doing so." He studied the document for a moment and asked my name.

My naive intention was to conceal my identity to avoid compromise by the Soviet side. While I had confidence in their security organization, defections were common. With that in mind, I replied, "James Harper, but that's an alias I intend to work with." James is my brother's name. Harper was chosen on a whim for its relationship to my name: Johnny Walker scotch and I. W. Harper whiskey. The name would later be used as my code name, but by a strange coincidence, a US spy by that name would later be arrested.

Solomatin calmly and carefully explained that the Soviet Union was willing and anxious to work with me, but my actual identity was essential. "Why?" I asked. "It merely puts me in jeopardy by the number of your people who defect."

He spoke slowly, feeling his way. "Your identity will be known at only the highest level and to no more than three or four people. In fact, we must know your exact location at all times for *your* protection. We cannot help you if we can't find you." He continued with that coaxing timbre in his voice. "We also cannot cooperate unless we know where you obtained this document and what you can provide in the future."

Admittedly, Solomatin made perfect sense; I would demand nothing less myself. Wavering a bit, I finally volunteered my military assignment, access to classified material, and my military identification card. He asked me to wait, departing with the ID and the keylist. At that point I had violated yet another section of Title 18, US Code: unlawful transmission of national defense information.

Solomatin finally returned, but with a question. "Why wasn't the letter of promulgation signed?" He was clearly concerned about its authenticity—they probably got scammed occasionally. His question also indicated that he had never actually seen one of these keylists before, increasing its value in my mind. But frankly, I did not remember ever seeing them physically signed and told him so. With no choice but to take a chance, he shifted to the subject of money. "How much of this information can you provide and how much compensation would you expect?" he asked.

I had learned through actual intelligence reports many years before that the public's perception of espionage payments is seriously distorted. Our films and books all refer to vast sums paid for a pittance of material. One microdot or one page of a "secret plan" is worth tens of thousands or even millions. I am reminded of a popular film producer and director who said that 90 percent of what people know, they learned at the movies, and 90 percent of that is wrong. I knew that $1,000 a week, or a mere $52,000 a year, was near top dollar for routine and *continuing* information. Cryptographic information should be worth more, perhaps $1,500 per week. "One thousand to fifteen hundred a week," I answered, "and I expect payment for tonight's delivery as a sign of good faith."

He nearly gushed with agreement, "Yes, yes, of course. And you'll receive a payment this evening."

Solomatin quizzed me at length regarding the exact nature of my access to classified material. I agreed to provide most of the keylists for both the submarine shore-to-ship and ship-to-shore systems. Other channels, such as the main net that links the huge shore establishment, could only be obtained on occasion. He seemed satisfied, as well he should have been.

He asked about my family, specifically if I was married, and appeared seriously concerned by my affirmative answer. Solomatin leaned forward, emphasizing the importance of his next statement. Pointing a finger like a teacher, sure of his dogma, he explained that my wife must never know of my activity. Of course I knew he was correct, but it was Solomatin's turn to be naive. It is impossible to hide *anything* from one's wife, at least in America. Does the wife of a Mafia boss really think her husband makes his money running a fruit business? Does a bank robber's wife think her husband hits the lottery every month? I told Solomatin I would try, but thought, *Get real*. Solomatin continued, "Mr. Walker, at this point only two Soviets and yourself know of our arrangement. If your wife finds out, she will be the weak link in the chain." Those words turned out to be prophetic.

I cut short his questions about my family due to the time constraints, but inwardly objected to answering. Moving to the more important question, I asked, "This place has to be under surveillance by the authorities. How do I get out of here safely?" He assured me that arrangements had been made, and he departed again for a few minutes.

Returning, Solomatin handed me an envelope of cash containing a few thousand dollars. I do not remember the exact amount. We quickly reviewed the details of our next meeting, which was to take place in about a month. I picked the date based on my watch rotation; he selected the place and time.

The procedure for our next meeting was rather simple and no doubt hastily prepared. I was to meet with my "handler" in about one month at a Zayres store in Arlington, somewhere around Route 50 and Leesburg Pike. Solomatin asked that I commit the procedure to memory, but I did jot a few notes to be sure.

My meeting with Boris Solomatin was over, the pact was solidified, and I was ready to be hustled out. Under normal circumstances, I would have invited Solomatin out for a social drink. Having experienced his spy master acumen, I was curious to become familiar with his personal side. In fact, I was never to see him again. He now resides in Moscow, a retired KGB major general.

We rose, shook hands again, and left the office. Four or five powerfully built men awaited. Someone helped me into a huge overcoat, several sizes too large that nearly dragged on the floor, as we moved quickly down a couple passageways. A felt fedora appeared on my head. Collar pulled up, a door opened to a waiting car where I was squashed in the rear seat between two rugged guys built like beer wagons. Asked to slide down low, I could see nothing of our departure to the side or beyond the two or three men in the front seat.

This may have been the most dangerous part of the evening. If I were seen entering the embassy, FBI counterespionage forces would be poised and ready. My feeling was that they had no grounds for an arrest, so their plan would probably be to surreptitiously follow and identify the strange visitor. I asked no questions and nothing was said by my escorts, save for a few mumbles in Russian. As we drove about at normal speed and with frequent turns, I looked at my watch for the millionth time, realizing I would never make Norfolk in time. After an interminable period, we stopped. I was hustled to the sidewalk, the coat and hat stripped off en route. Without a word, the door closed and the car roared off, two red eyes swallowed by the night. I had no idea where I was, and still do not, but was able to find a phone in a small shop.

A taxi took me back to my car, and I was soon on I-95 South and pushing the little engine to the maximum. Exhausted by the experience, I was paying back my system for all that adrenaline. However, I was not too tired to contemplate my actions and the future I had cast for myself and my family. *My God,* I wondered, *how does a good Catholic, an altar boy, a dedicated father and husband, a successful naval officer with an impeccable record, end up dealing with the enemy? How would I handle my wife, described as the "weak link?" How did this happen?* How, indeed.

Chapter 2

THE TRUE BELIEVER

I could hardly be considered politically astute at twenty-two years old. However, as an avid reader of the daily newspaper and news periodicals, my knowledge of world and national events was above average. I was educated at a time when civics and government were serious high school subjects. In fact, the sisters at St. Patrick's High School in Scranton, Pennsylvania, included in their teaching a lesson on *how* to read and understand the newspaper. They instilled in all of us the need to follow world affairs.

Servicepeople tend to be politically conservative and fiercely patriotic, and I was no exception. I believed the participation by the United States in World War II was essential and correct. The Korean conflict, of which my brother Arthur was a veteran, was an important victory in stopping the spread of communism in the Far East. My opinion of politicians was that they lied to get elected and to remain in office, but that they were generally honest and motivated to do the right thing. Looking back, I was politically naive, to say the least.

In 1960 I was completing my four-year enlistment obligation to the navy, which had involved nearly continuous and arduous sea duty on a destroyer escort, USS *Johnnie Hutchins* (DE-360) and the carrier USS *Forrestal* (CVA-59). My rank was second-class radioman (E-5), equal to an army buck sergeant. I truly loved the navy but wondered how I could be an effective husband and father if constantly at sea. With one baby and another on the way, I consulted with an army recruiter, considering a change of service. The recruiter was anxious to accommodate the shift, but it would require a reduction by one rank, from buck sergeant to corporal. The reduced rank, and mostly the reduced pay, prevented me from making the move. Moreover, I had already taken the fleetwide examination for first class, or the equivalent of staff sergeant, and I felt I had a good chance for that promotion. The move I was considering would thus result in a loss of two ranks. I stayed in the navy.

A transfer to the Beach Jumpers, a small unit under the Amphibious Force, was a welcome relief for the final few months of my enlistment.

I never finished high school, a situation that both embarrassed me and lowered my self-esteem. To overcome that deficit, I resolved early on to outmaneuver my competition by studying hard for advancement. Furthermore, my high school GED tests were so high, the education officer on the *Forrestal* recommended me for the college GED, a test similar to today's CLEP tests. Successfully completing that a few months later, I went from a high school dropout to a man with two years of college. In another strategic move, I retook my basic enlistment tests, elevating my marks to qualify for officer programs. An advantage to sea duty is that it allows ample time for studying and testing.

Slipping into submarines through the back door was not that complicated. If a boat is short a crewman, you could merely approach the executive officer and convince him of your value. If the XO wants you, he can arrange a direct transfer to his boat, skipping submarine school, and in my case, the disqualifying physical examination. So, with several boats continuously nested to both sides of my ship, I befriended several radiomen and watched for a boat in need of my rank.

I settled on the USS *Clamagore*, a World War II diesel boat converted and modernized to extend her life. After meeting with her XO and arranging for a couple short cruises, I felt that I had found a home and awaited official transfer orders. But I never officially sailed on the *Clamagore*, though over twenty years later, I found her moored at Patriot Point Museum in Charleston, along with the *Yorktown* and several other ships. "My boat!" I shouted as I leaped aboard in uncontrolled excitement, showing my embarrassed and amazed girlfriend my old bunk and workplace.

My department chief yeoman on the *Gilmore* will remain nameless, but I will refer to him as "the Chief." A southern boy, hardheaded and pragmatic, he was on a personal evangelical mission for the John Birch Society. Formed just a couple years earlier in 1958 by Robert Welch, it is an avid right-wing, anticommunist organization. Named after the first

American killed by communists after World War II, John Birch was a missionary in China when killed. The objective of the society included the repeal of social security and income tax revision, but their main mission seemed to be the impeachment of then Chief Justice Earl Warren.

Like any true believer with a cause, the Chief showered me with Birch material. I was familiar with Senator Joseph McCarthy and his sensational but unsubstantiated accusations against those he termed communists. He achieved national prominence with his witch hunts in the early 1950s, but he was condemned by the Senate in 1954. The John Birch Society, however, seemed to view Joe McCarthy as their deity, quoting him passionately. I was already an ardent anticommunist, so I readily accepted and devoured his material. Even though suspicious of their pro-McCarthy stance, I found their position credible and frightening. The world was doomed to fall to communism, they preached, and the United States was doing nothing to stop the red tide. Chief Justice Warren, a hated liberal, was particularly vilified for his procommunist Supreme Court decisions.

Still somewhat in awe of chiefs, I allowed the Chief to sway me into joining the society. He was impressive and dedicated. Unmarried, he was an auxiliary police officer for the Charleston police, spending his off-duty hours in a patrol car for no pay. The Chief even found time to sell life insurance part-time, a venture I joined him in as well. Looking back at the Chief today, I see a stiff, starched, and bloodless individual with no sense of humor. Today, he would be told to "get a life." Back then, however, I was a willing pupil and finally became a true believer myself. Like the Chief, I began handing out Birch material like religious tracts to anyone who would listen. Originally right of center, I had slipped off the scale, somewhere beyond Pat Buchanan. But as I sank deeper into this anticommunist crusade, the ripple of another true believer experience ran across my mind. I had been down this road before with the Roman Catholic Church.

In my experience, I have observed that people involved in serious or important endeavors fall into one of two categories: one is the true believer and one just plays the game. A true believer is one who has total faith in the correctness of his belief. These are people who know that their side is right and the opposition is absolutely wrong. They tend to take themselves and their mission much too seriously. We have all seen them involved in polarizing issues, such as abortion and gun control. A true believer's sentiment is most usually epitomized in his career, such as the DEA agent who is saving the world from the scourge of drugs or the CIA agent who is saving the world from the latest enemy.

The majority of people, however, merely play the game. Their performance may well equal that of the true believer, but in their hearts, they take themselves and their mission far less seriously. Their motives may simply be a desire for promotion, more money, or fame. Most navy men I have met were playing the game. Indeed, when I frequently asked my superiors why we were squandering public money, or endangering people, or even killing innocent civilians in Vietnam, the response was often, "Just play the game, Walker."

Often true believers will become more informed or educated on the subject, thus losing their true belief. Now at a crossroad, they must choose either to resign or begin playing the game. Most just become game players. This happened to me once and was about to happen again.

As a child in Catholic elementary school, I had total faith in the teachings of the Church. I could hardly wait to become an altar boy like my big brother. There was talk of the priesthood. Learning all the complex prayers in Latin and the strict procedures, I was serving mass at about ten years old, even before I could carry the priest's large missal and metal stand.

Traditional Christians view the Bible as written under the guidance of God and as therefore entirely true, or at least couched in allegory. Protestants hold that individuals have the right to interpret the Bible themselves. The Roman Catholics teach that individuals may read the Bible only as interpreted by the Church, and therefore the pope was considered infallible in interpreting the Bible; he could not make an error. Catholics seldom read the Bible then, and when they did, it was accompanied by lengthy commentary regarding its meaning.

The incident that started my change from a true believer in Catholicism occurred when a group of my friends and I decided to question a nun concerning the Adam and Eve story of Genesis. Everyone knows the story. Adam and Eve lived in Eden and were forbidden from eating the fruit of the tree of life. The serpent tempted Eve, who tempted Adam, resulting in the original sin. As a result of their actions, all are born with that original sin on their souls and condemned to hell. But Jesus Christ died on the cross to absolve us of that sin, and we are saved from hell as long as we are baptized.

A great children's story, but it could not be real, my friends and I agreed. Like the Santa Claus story told to tots, the real Genesis story would be revealed to us when we grew up. Then one of my friends heard somewhere that the original sin was actually sex. Well, that made sense to us: Adam and Eve were forbidden to copulate, and hence being born and existing was a sin. We decided to test the theory on an eighth-grade nun—a real mistake.

The sister was shocked. She did not want to discuss anything relating to sex at all, but more important, she asked why we were reading the Old Testament. The Old Testament is virtually ignored by Catholics, and she wanted to know why we were interpreting it. She referred us to a priest. We were in trouble.

The priest turned out to be amiable but intimidating. He agreed that the Adam and Eve story had an allegorical component, but the original sin definitely was not sex. We were to accept the story that God's first man and woman violated God's law, requiring Jesus Christ to save us. More important, we were reminded *not* to interpret scripture and to confess our sin for doing so. If we were interested in intellectual pursuits, he suggested algebra.

My status as a true believer in Catholicism had slipped a few notches. A couple years later, I came across the Kabbalah, the mystical Jewish system of scriptural interpretation. Very deep, it is based on the belief that every word, letter, number, and even accent of scripture contains mysteries. Although I did not understand the Kabbalah's account of the tree of life, it confirmed my suspicion that all was symbolic. The tree of life is life itself, or the life principle, growing in our midst and within the planetary entity. It is drawn with three pillars, God at the center top, with male and female (Adam and Eve?) to the sides. The planets are depicted down the sides with the sun, moon, and earth in line on the bottom. In fact, it resembles a tree. Man's spirit takes a journey from top to bottom, leaving the spiritual world and entering the physical. The trip weaves between the planets, left and right, undulating like a snake. This explains the story of the serpent, tempting our spirits to taste the physical world.

Deep stuff, indeed, but then I discovered that the tree is not peculiar to the Hebrews. Every ancient race had its tree of life, including the Greeks, Norse, Hindus, Tibetans, Druids, Persians, and even the Chinese. A Hindu book two thousand years older than the Bible includes the story of the first man and woman, Adam and Eve. Christians may be surprised to discover sixteen other religions, many much older and not of Christian origin, whose saviors were crucified on a cross. Eight of those saviors had mothers whose name was some form of "Mary."

So, as a high school student, I became one of those people who played the game regarding Catholicism and organized religions. They were all lying to me. I still possess a strong faith in God but have yet to find an honest religion.

In Jean-François Revel's book *The Flight from the Truth*, he writes: "Above all and in the great majority, if not the totality, of cases, we use our intellectual facilities to protect convictions, interests and interpretations that are especially dear to us." In the vernacular of the street, that may be translated to: "Don't confuse me with the facts, my mind is made up." I have always been a skeptic, accepting nothing on blind faith. This need to be shown or convinced by facts served me well as a private investigator years later. This characteristic also destroyed my faith in the legitimacy of the so-called cold war.

On May 1, 1960, the Soviets shot down Francis Gary Powers, capturing him unharmed and recovering his U-2 spy plane. Privately grinning to myself, I knew we were technologically far superior to the Soviets. They may have launched the first satellite, but our U-2 had overflown their country with impunity for years. We knew exactly what Intercontinental Ballistic Missiles (ICBM) and rockets they had on the ground in their large space centers. Later I confirmed that the balloons *were* intelligence-gathering devices that preceded the U-2. We *always* knew what was going on behind the iron curtain. Spy satellites would now replace the U-2.

A few months later, I received surprise orders to report aboard the

USS *Penguin* (ASR-12), the submarine rescue boat in Key West, Florida. Disappointed that the orders were not for the submarine *Clamagore*, I was nonetheless excited by the prospect of a new duty station. My third daughter, Laura, had been born just a few months earlier at the Charleston Naval Hospital, so our family of five piled in the car and headed for the Sunshine State and my tour aboard *Penguin*.

Orders arrived less than six months into my tour of duty, but not for the submarine *Penguin*. To my surprise, I was to proceed to Submarine School in New London, Connecticut. So, in 1960, just in time for winter, we headed north, where I imposed upon my mother in Scranton, Pennsylvania, to house Barbara and my three kids while I continued to New London for three months of school. As a first-class petty officer, I was a bit senior and old for Basic Submarine School, but I enjoyed the privilege of rank as the class section leader.

The presidential elections occurred during my school tour, Nixon versus Kennedy, and as a staunch conservative, I voted on a Pennsylvania absentee ballot for Nixon. Of course, Kennedy won, and I specifically recall one of his campaign speeches in which he flatly stated that the USSR had a nuclear ICBM advantage over the United States. A "missile gap," as he described it, which he vowed to correct if elected president. Shocked, I could not believe the Soviets had passed us yet again. The intelligence officer on *Gilmore* assured me of our ICBM lead. *How could this happen?* I wondered angrily. Maybe somebody was lying.

Finally graduated, my class awaited our orders: what boat, what port? Excited and anxious, I waited as the personnelman read out our orders alphabetically, finally making it to "W." "Walker, USS *Razorback* (SS-394), San Diego," he read. I was to be a West Coast sailor, plying the Pacific, operating out of California.

Razorback was a World War II vintage boat with a record of war patrols and ships sunk, but she was modernized for World War III.

My wife, Barbara, was pleased by the orders, looking forward to California as much as I was. We would experience a small raise in pay since submariners received special hazardous duty pay similar to aircraft flight pay. Additionally, I had recently passed another examination for P-2, meaning proficiency pay second-grade. The navy had started a program a year or so before in which critical ratings would be used to decide proficiency pay: P-1, P-2, and P-3. Each raised the monthly pay by $30, $60, or $90, respectively, with P-2 the maximum available for radiomen. One had to pass an examination and be reexamined each year to keep the extra pay. Later, the test was eliminated and made automatic if recommended by the commanding officer, which took all the fun out of it.

At age twenty-three and with five years of service, I was off to my fifth tour of sea duty. My children had arrived far too quickly, largely as a result of endless sea duty with very short periods in port, during which one tends to neglect family planning in the heat of those short visits at home. The only semblance of normal family life was on the submarine tender where I came home nearly every day. Even *Gilmore* went to sea, although rarely and for short periods, and life was anything but normal when rotating on day, evening, and night shifts.

So in 1961, with a new three-year-old car, we loaded the family and headed for the Golden State. I had learned from experience that orders to a fleet unit usually meant that the ship was scheduled for a major deployment. Roughly every two years, each Atlantic fleet unit was deployed to the Mediterranean Sixth Fleet for six months while the West Coast ships deployed to the Pacific Seventh Fleet for six months. Somehow, crafty souls always seem to bail off their ships just prior to these deployments, causing a need for immediate replacement crew members. I reported to *Forrestal* just prior to a Sixth Fleet deployment. Worse yet, these cruises always seemed to get extended. A crisis in Lebanon extended my *Forrestal* cruise in 1959, then our relieving ship, USS *Saratoga* (CVA-60), backed into a pier and bent her screw. Her repairs delayed our cruise even more. I stayed mad at her for years, until my ship at that time pulled alongside the *Saratoga* in the Tonkin Gulf as she launched air strikes against North Vietnam. As I stood on our helo-deck awaiting a flight to *Saratoga*, I was shocked at her appearance. That lady had been on the fighting line so long without a rest that rust bloomed like a skin rash in great orange streaks along her proud gray body. I then forgave *Saratoga* for being late thirteen years earlier.

So, with my deployment experience, I was not surprised when I checked the secret Pacific submarine schedule to discover that the *Razorback* was due for a western Pacific deployment, commonly called a WESTPAC cruise. How long would *that* be extended? I wondered.

Barbara and I found a nice large apartment in the shadow of Point Loma near Mission Bay. San Diego was a friendly, peaceful city in 1961, far away from the hectic pace of neon-coated Los Angeles to the north.

My boat was moored to a tender that was herself anchored in the harbor. This working tender supported two squadrons with little help from the shore establishment, her wards tied abreast alongside. A submarine base would be built years later at Ballast Point on Point Loma, but for now, the two squadrons might as well be deployed to some advance base in a foreign harbor. The navy operated a huge small-boat service to the tender, the other anchored ships in the harbor, and the North Island Naval Air Station. The boat landing was pure bedlam in the morning and late afternoon as hundreds of sailors went to and from work on those large, open utility boats, belching burnt-oil breath. Parking near the boat landing, located just south of Broadway Pier, was impossible.

I loved my new boat and the crew. It is difficult to describe the camaraderie of a submarine crew, a tight family in which the crew's safety as a whole is dependent on each individual. Everyone's efficient performance is necessary to successfully fight the boat and to survive in a combat situation. The ninety-man crew was a single entity that would succeed or fail as one. An individual submariner does not die—if something goes wrong, we all die.

Time at home came in quick snatches and at unexpected times. One such visit home revealed a side to Barbara that I had never seen or imagined.

Razorback, scheduled to remain at sea for several more days, unexpectedly returned to port for emergency repairs. Moored to the tender at about midnight, we were to effect the repairs and return to sea by 4 a.m. The captain granted liberty (the navy term for a pass) but stressed the importance of returning on time. As a whaleboat approached to transport the liberty party, I pondered the foolishness of a two-hour visit with my wife in the middle of the night but jumped into the boat anyway. It would take an hour to get home and nearly that long for the return trip.

A convoy of taxis arrived at the boat landing, somehow sensing prospective fares. I skipped the line at the pay phone and hopped in a cab for home. The house was dark as I quietly let myself into a ransacked living room. I softly called to Barbara, identifying myself to avoid frightening her and the kids. She appeared, bleary-eyed and quite surprised.

"What the hell happened?" I asked as I flicked on more lights. "Were we robbed?" She was embarrassed but explained she was in the process of cleaning and doing laundry. I did not question her, but it was obvious the place had not been cleaned since I went to sea many days before.

Arriving, again unannounced, some weeks later to the same mess, I realized this was no anomaly. For some reason, Barbara would go on vacation from all forms of housework during my absences, living in self-imposed squalor. There was also an indication that she was secretly drinking. But then again, she was trained to drink by me, or, more accurately, by the US Navy.

The consumption of alcohol, mostly to excess, was a normal and expected factor of navy life in the 1950s and '60s. Although alcohol was very rarely smuggled aboard ship, drinking was central to the crew's recreation while on liberty. All social activity, sanctioned by the navy, consisted of food and only alcoholic beverages. One drank beer and hard liquor, or nothing.

It is difficult for many civilians to understand the necessity for a newly assigned crew member to be "accepted by the crew." While one is not treated badly, each new man is carefully watched and evaluated for normal behavior, attitude, and outlook on the navy. They are expected to join groups on liberty while partying and drinking heavily. The drunker one becomes and the worse the hangover, the better. Whoring about in foreign ports was recommended but not required, as long as one got drunk and supported his shipmates' conduct. Physical fitness training usually involved nothing more than a "beer ball game" between the crew on Wednesday afternoons. No other beverage was available. In short, the navy trained all good sailors how to drink to excess.

Acceptance by the crew became the simple matter of doing your job and maintaining your space in a shipshape manner while supporting and emulating the alcoholic rituals. To ensure nonacceptance, one had only to be a nondrinking loner who read a lot and listened to classical music in the library. Regardless of how well such a crewman did his job, the crew would probably reject such a sailor. He may even acquire the dreaded "homosexual" label, ensuring his failure.

When Barbara and I first met, I drank very little and she not at all. At parties I would get high on two or three cocktails or beers while she sipped the same drink all night. We might go to the Navy Enlisted Club for an evening, sharing a fifty-cent pitcher of beer, which we were unable to finish. But the navy trained us well, and by the time I reached the *Razorback*, Barbara had equaled and perhaps surpassed me in the quantity consumed. I never enjoyed drinking and I eventually cut it back to nothing while she got worse.

My security clearance was raised to top secret on *Razorback*, and I joined the crypto-board. All communications to and from submarines in those days were by Morse code. If the message was classified (confidential, secret, or top secret), it was received or sent in batches of five random letters. Officers were no longer available to encrypt and decrypt the message traffic due to the sheer increase in volume, so the task gradually fell to the enlisted radiomen. The clearance opened new vistas in my understanding of our naval mission and national defense in general. I read my first top-secret operations orders and operations plans, which included portions of the war plan. War plans are tabulated by sections, such as operations, communications, intelligence, weapons, supply, medical, and so on. The introduction presents an overview of the plan while the tabs are restricted on a need-to-know basis to the cognizant officer. For example, the weapons officer reads only the weapons section. The complete plan may be stored in a radio room safe, however, where total access is possible.

It was while making a routine change to an operations plan that I read some comparative figures on US ICBMs vis-à-vis the Soviet Union and discovered the United States had a considerable numerical advantage. I no longer recall the exact figures, but aerial spy photographs were referred to in which the Soviets' ICBMs were counted on the ground at fewer than five. The United States had hundreds deployed at that time, including submarine-launched ballistic missiles deployed in entire squadrons. Even our B-52 SAC bombers were capable of overflying the Soviet Union without detection by jamming their inferior radar systems. There was a missile gap, all right, a gap in our favor. Candidate Kennedy had clearly lied. As a US senator, he had access to top-secret information on Soviet military capability. Every presidential candidate is further briefed on such top-secret national security issues, so he was lying. Worse yet, the thousands of government officials and employees *knew* it. Even I knew it now. Thousands in the Soviet Union knew he was lying. Yet no one pointed out the falsehood, a vast conspiracy of silence as the Kennedy administration spent billions to correct the nonexistent gap.

These were heady thoughts for any young man. Growing within me was a rueful acceptance of the terrible knowledge that my government could be corrupt, but just contemplating it was anathema to all military traditions. Two old adages, heard a million times, passed through my mind: "All's fair in love and war" and "Ours is not to reason why, ours is but to do and die." Maybe the government simply had some agenda I could not know or understand. I had to sort out my thoughts, arrange them, impose order. But slipping into ambivalence, my conservative philosophy was decomposing.

Maybe I was still a believer, but not a true believer.

Chapter 3

THE LIES

Question: If one of our secrets becomes known to an enemy, is it still a secret? And if it remains a secret, from whom is it kept a secret?

Answer: It is no longer a secret, but it is kept from the US public.

I t was candidate Kennedy's lie and the relationship of that lie to the U-2 spy plane that challenged my true believer status. Consider the spy plane. Developed in ultra-secret at Lockheed's "skunk works" in Pasadena, California, in the mid-1950s, the U-2 was designed to fly at seventy thousand feet, well above antiaircraft range and beyond the ceiling of the best MIG fighters. Its very first flight in the late 1950s was a daring overflight of the Soviet Union's most sensitive targets: their ICBM missile bases, Moscow, and the strategic Baltic States. From the moment it reached altitude over Turkey, Soviet radar tracked the U-2, establishing her location, speed, and altitude. They watched helplessly as the Soviets' most sensitive military facilities were photographed. They had to assume the aircraft was equipped for electronic intelligence (ELINT) capability, which it was. Soviet MIGs tried to intercept, flying as high as possible and photographing this mystery plane. They watched the entire flight until the long descent into Wiesbaden, Germany, the landing site. Thus, the secrets of the U-2 capabilities were known to the Soviets within the first hours of the historic flight. So, did the US government inform its citizens? Did the Soviet government inform its citizens? Of course not! This nonsecret was kept from the citizens of both countries.

With my new military, defense, and political outlook, I was aboard the *Razorback* for her six-month WESTPAC deployment. Our proud hull number, 394, painted in large white figures on our sail, had been blacked out to prevent our identification. It added an air of danger to our mission, for we were sailing into what would be the combat zone should the cold war turn hot.

Barbara would remain in San Diego, struggling to raise our three daughters alone, along with other naval wives raising their families. These strong women, often referred to as "WESTPAC widows," fulfilled the difficult parenting roles alone as the wives of seafaring men have done for centuries. We avoided speculating on the length of an extension.

We sailed from Yokosuka at dawn in late winter, the sky a slab of lead spitting freezing drizzle on our black deck. Our line handlers and deck crew grumbled as they struggled to maintain footing on the narrow deck. We backed away from our berth, turned south into the Sagami Sea, then headed north for the narrow passage between Hokkaido and Honshu, the strategic Tsugaru Strait. Our CO's father had been a German U-boat commander, and our CO shared his father's guile. To avoid detection by Soviet agents who might have been posted to observe ship traffic, we made the transit in the dead of night with the deck awash and fake lights mounted to change our appearance to that of a fishing boat. The transit through the strait was made on the surface due to the traffic and depth, but we passed safely among the other fishermen into the Sea of Japan. Of course, we fished for intelligence.

We set a course for Vladivostok, submerged deep on battery power by day since the chance of visual detection is so much greater in daylight. Our submerged speed was kept to a minimum, conserving our invaluable battery for combat maneuvering. In the greater safety of night, we would sneak up to periscope depth, look around for the enemy, and listen for their radar or electronic countermeasure (ECM) equipment. If the area was clear, we would raise the snorkel to replace our stale air and feed our diesels. Lighting off one of our big diesels would suck the freezing air from the surface, dumping it throughout the boat. The fresh air was always greeted with pleasure, even though it plunged the temperature downward and stank of tiny decaying sea creatures that grew on the snorkel mast. The silence was broken, mainly by the roaring engine as we shifted to diesel propulsion and increased speed. A second diesel would join the bluster, its sole purpose to recharge our batteries before daylight. Soviet sonar listening ships, buoys, or submerged cables would certainly hear our diesels, and their radar would detect even the small return from our snorkel mast and antennas. But with the abundance of fishing boats in the area, we would likely blend in with other targets and be evaluated as a diesel-powered fishing boat.

Silence is golden on a submarine, for a simple noise such as a dropped tool on the metal deck can lead to detection, bringing down the wrath of the Soviet antisubmarine warfare (ASW) forces. We traveled in "patrol quiet," where certain equipment could not be used, and the crew moved about quietly. "Ultra quiet" went beyond "patrol quiet," requiring still more silence. Our CO invented a new condition, which he named "damn quiet." All shoes were removed and sailors not on watch were required to go to bed and lie quietly. I hated that, since the best things happened during damn quiet and I wanted to participate, not hide in bed wondering. We played many a dangerous game with the Russians in our hot/cold war beneath the sea.

Razorback "stood down" for a couple weeks after our return. Nestled up to the tender, we had maximum liberty, but at least a quarter of the crew remained on duty, so we only got home three out of four nights. We actually got no real rest since the boat was shortly ordered to the Naval Shipyard at Hunter's Point in San Francisco.

The navy must provide the worst possible conditions for family life. A trip to the shipyard for repairs or overhaul represents months of in-port time—shore duty, as it were. The assigned shipyard is almost always far from the seamen's homes, creating the usual dilemma of moving the family for a few months or trying to visit them on weekends—when we weren't on duty. Since I had dragged my family along so far, we packed up again for the five-hundred-mile trip north to the City on the Bay. Housing was scarce, so we moved into a Quonset hut on the shipyard for a mere $75 per month, utilities included. Barbara and I compensated for the substandard living conditions by spending our saved rent money on the city's night life. Barbara became pregnant with our fourth child.

Somewhere along the way, I had been cleared under the Personal

Reliability Program, a security clearance for those involved with nuclear weapons. *Razorback* was slated for something secret, the final atmosphere nuclear tests conducted by the United States. The boat had proven herself tight and up to the task based upon our earlier shock tests and successful special operation mission. The shipyard work included the installation of more shock-resistant equipment and safeguards.

Out of the shipyard and back at San Diego, we performed our shakedown cruise, prepared for the test with more depth-charge shock tests and deep dives. The task group secretly sailed into the southern Pacific to test the ASROC/SUBROC weapon system and nuclear warhead. We played games with that warhead on *Penguin*. I slept with it on *Razorback*. Now we would experience the real thing.

I did not enjoy duty on my larger ships, *Forrestal* and *Gilmore*. Big, impersonal floating cities, they lacked any sense of being in a "crew." On any of my smaller ships, *Johnnie Hutchins* with fifty men, *Penguin* with forty, and *Razorback* with ninety, we were dependent upon a close family-like cooperation to operate and fight the ship. Although it was impossible, I would have stayed on any of the three for an entire twenty-year career. Thus, I was shocked and disappointed when new orders arrived. Apparently, I had routinely volunteered for nuclear submarine duty—something I did not remember doing—and was now ordered to a ballistic missile boat, the USS *Andrew Jackson* (SSBN-619). I left *Razorback* with a depression equivalent to experiencing a death in the family as we packed and moved back to the Bay Area. I also felt like a ping-pong ball at twenty-five years of age, seven years in the service, and off to my sixth tour of sea duty.

Andrew Jackson was under construction at the Naval Shipyard at Mare Island in San Pablo Bay, a few miles north of San Francisco. In the Napa Valley area, the shipyard is adjacent to the little town of Vallejo, where we rented a small house for our ever-growing family. My son, Michael, was born there.

SSBN stands for submarine, ballistic missile, nuclear. Since they all fired a version of the Polaris missile at that time, they were usually called Polaris boats, or "boomers." The boat created its own oxygen from sea water, scrubbed away carbon dioxide and held a nuclear power supply measured in years. With an abundance of power, she made enough water for unlimited use, even enough to shower daily and operate a laundry. A true submarine, she could stay underwater continuously with the crew being the main limiting factor for endurance. Since a single crew could never keep up with the boat's stamina, two complete crews of one hundred thirty each were assigned, blue and gold, from separate captains to mess cooks.

Initially, I thought I would hate the Polaris duty of long patrols, hiding in the remote ocean areas away from the action, just waiting to blow up the entire Sino-Soviet Block in a war that would never happen. It seemed that my seven years of excitement was coming to an end. But, while my six later Polaris patrols were on the boring side, the building, testing, and operating of that remarkable submarine was to be the highlight of my career. While submariners were the cream of the navy, the early selection for nuclear boats was from the best of the diesel-electric fleet boat navy. Our crew was simply the best of the navy, or indeed the world.

The *Andrew Jackson* was in the early phase of her construction, really, just a shell of a boat resting on blocks. The radio room was bare walls of steel with bundles of wires and unconnected pipes going nowhere. It would be months before we would move aboard, so we operated from barracks and office barges floating nearby.

My new boat did give me greater access to classified material. Along with my usual crypto-board assignment, I helped set up the top-secret and intelligence information libraries. My clearance into the Personal Responsibility Program continued as I would have additional access to the missile launch codes.

The very month I reported aboard *Andrew Jackson*, I came across the newly promulgated rules of engagement for our military advisers in Vietnam. These rules spell out in detail exactly what conditions must exist for our military to engage in combat and the extent of combat allowed. Shortly after, President Kennedy announced that US advisers in Nam would fire if fired upon. Our military had been on the ground since 1954 and now they could shoot Vietnamese citizens.

Chapter 4

PLAYING THE GAME

E ntering the Polaris submarine program was like winning some sort of navy lottery. I went from a bare-bones budget, struggling for essentials, to a seemingly unlimited fiscal ceiling. We were able to order anything from the Naval Supply System and Government Services Administration (GSA) catalogs that might have any conceivable application. Open purchase, or going outside the government for supply items, was also routine.

I reported aboard very early in the construction, with only a couple dozen already assigned, as the third radioman of our eventual twelve. The boat was in the early phases of construction, a shapeless, unpainted steel mass covered with miles of scaffolding. Donning a hard hat that would be my headgear for many months, I climbed the stairway amid showers of welder's sparks to gaze into my new home. She was still open at the top, the keel visible in a few places, and three decks deep as opposed to the single deck on *Razorback*. Nothing resembled a fleet boat except perhaps the torpedo room forward (there was none aft). The lower portion of the sixteen missile tubes, pointing skyward, was visible behind the future control room. Next was a huge gyro, at least twenty feet in diameter and three decks high. Designed to stabilize the boat during missile launch, it later proved ineffective and was removed. The reactor vessel was partially built and many months away from receiving its nuclear fuel. The engine room was a shambles, ending in a point where our single crew would push her 425 feet and 8,000 tons through the ocean with a fuel supply measured in years.

I strode the scaffolds, excited, in awe of this dauntless and silent ghost, the world's greatest killing machine.

I have always been a frustrated engineer. The biggest regret in my life is not attending college, and had I done so, science and engineering would

41

have been my choices. Opportunities were quite different back in the early 1950s—only the top strata of society went off to college, supported by their parents. Student loans did not yet exist, and Pennsylvania offered no free state college. Of course, dedicated souls "worked their way through" somehow. Hell, I worked my way through *high school*, driving a banana truck to the New York City docks, and my poor grades reflected it. So I followed my brother into the service—an education through the GI Bill would be possible later.

While I may have failed to achieve in high school, I was now skilled in electronics, a class of physics, and would now add nuclear propulsion, missile systems, and modern submarine technology to my education. I do not recall how much the *Andrew Jackson* cost, but today's *Seawolf* attack submarines cost $1.5 billion a copy, so I was allowed to play with a very expensive monster capable of destroying the world.

Many are curious to know if my attitude and personality changed as a result of my shift from true believer to game player. It did not. My quarterly performance evaluations remained at the top, 4.0 in all categories. I continued to express a Birch-like disdain for communism, remained outwardly conservative, and condemned the Soviet goal of world domination. After all, there is no outward difference between a true believer and a game player, and I played the game well. In fact, my performance and proficiency may have improved as I realized the entire cold war was a game played by our military and civilian leadership; there was no longer any pressure. I studied harder than ever for my next advancement examination, the greatest rank in the world, navy chief. There is a mandatory period one must serve at each rank before being eligible for advancement to the next, and from first-class to chief was three years. The examination is brutal, nearly impossible to pass in minimum time, but I crammed anyway.

Our submarine was, in reality, a weapons-launching platform, where redundancy virtually ensured nothing could abort our mission. There were two complete missile computers, for example, both online and ready. If one failed, the backup took over automatically. We had a diesel engine, battery, and snorkel to operate *Razorback*-style if our nuclear plant failed. If our single-screw was shot off or fell off, a backup screw descended on a shaft like a huge outboard motor to push us along by nuclear power, diesel, or battery.

Redundancy extended to the crewman's skills as well. Every piece of radio equipment had at least two radiomen qualified to repair it—we could operate *all* the equipment. Training was thus a vital part of our pre-commission experience. Much of the equipment was so new, however, the navy had yet to create the schools needed for training. Our "shore duty" was therefore interrupted by temporary orders to navy schools in New London or factory schools, such as Collins, in Cedar Rapids, and a teletype school in Skokie, Illinois. We sailors were unusual students in the civilian schools where in-house technicians factory trained.

In early 1963, I attended my first cryptographic equipment maintenance school for the KWR-37. It was the first automatic encoding machine adopted by the navy, about the size of an average kitchen microwave oven. Up to this point, submarines still received their messages from shore by Morse code, decrypting coded messages on the electromechanical machine and typing each coded letter by hand. The new system allowed the shore station to insert a pre-punched teletype tape through a KWR-37 transmitter where it was instantly encrypted into teletype digital pulses and automatically decrypted and printed on a teletype-writer at sea.

These cryptographic devices were merely simple computers, the machines representing the hardware, the keylist being the software. The hardware had only a small secret portion, some confidential, but mostly not classified at all. The KWR-37 software was top secret and consisted of an old-fashioned IBM punch card. Each punch card was designed for a twenty-four-hour period with every station inserting its card at a precise time to synchronize the equipment.

The crypto-device was my introduction to computer maintenance, and I would accomplish many repairs over the years. Much to my surprise, the device consisted of old-fashioned vacuum tube technology. It was subminiature—about the size of a little finger—mounted on its side on small circuit boards. I thought back to my nuclear test and an effect known as electromagnetic pulse (EMP) where high-energy electromagnetic energy from a blast induces a massive electrical pulse in electronic equipment, destroying solid-state components such as diodes and transistors. It is similar to a lightning bolt zapping a computer, but much stronger. This innocuous side effect of thermonuclear war would knock out all solid-state devices and virtually all electronic equipment. All radios, televisions, automobiles, even the bedroom clock, would stop. I would hate to be on an instrument landing at O'Hare Airport only to have an EMP kill all aircraft and ground radios and navigational equipment.

Our newly launched *Andrew Jackson* was dead, just as the old *Johnnie Hutchins*, until our nuclear fuel was loaded behind a shroud of secrecy.

Our sea trial and schedule was grueling, even with two crews alternating, but fortunately, I was in port when my fourth child, Michael, was born. I felt like a ping-pong ball after six ships, an assignment to Beach Jumpers, a dozen schools, and four children, all in seven years. Our kids were all born in different states: Margaret in Brooklyn, New York; Cynthia in Portsmouth, Virginia; Laura in Charleston, South Carolina; and now Michael in Vallejo, California.

I would have been happy with a dozen children, but the navy already considered me two above the recommended limit for my rank. They were right: the more members of a family, the bigger the burden when those families must keep moving. Many of my shipmates just gave up, planted their families in a house somewhere, and visited when they could, which was rarely. I chose to keep our family together, regardless of the difficulties of military life.

Somewhere along the way, my father disappeared. He and Mom had a tumultuous relationship for many years as a result of his drinking problem. My visits home had been infrequent and short during the past seven years, and it was obvious that Dad was more absent with each visit. Mom avoided worrying me, but eventually admitted that he had left her.

Of his three sons, I was probably his favorite, the one who would help with his projects or toss the baseball around. It was Dad and I who would play casino or Crazy Eights in the evenings, one-on-one, while my brothers pursued their own interests. All kids love their dads, but mine really was special. He was handsome, college educated, charming, and very successful in his profession. As a marketing executive for Warner Brothers, he worked out of their Washington, DC, office in their huge network of distribution on the East Coast. It was the heyday of Hollywood and he was very familiar with the industry moguls and stars. Dad played the piano professionally, and with Mom singing, they did shows together live and on radio. Dad also made a lot of money.

He had a darker side, however, that devil in the bottle. His drinking became worse with time, finally causing problems with his job and family. Like all alcoholics, he lost track of time and money, and since my mother was a fiery Italian, conflict was guaranteed. There were verbal arguments when I was very young, but so what? That is normal in most marriages. It got worse when he started hitting Mom, and I hated him for that.

In 1944, when I was just seven years old, Dad was in a horrible car wreck while traveling from his DC office to our home in Richmond, Virginia. Completely sober, he plowed into the side of a car one dark night on US 1 when the driver entered the highway from a dirt road directly into his path. Presumed dead, my dad laid in a ditch for some time until a medic finally discovered a spark of life.

The recovery was slow, and he was unable to be moved, so he spent weeks in a Fredericksburg hospital. Home at last, he seemed whole again regardless of the scars, but his drinking got worse, along with the arguments. Full of ambivalence, I could not help loving the guy, but I detested him when he hit Mom. He was actually a very mellow drunk, and if Mom did not attack him at the front door like a Panzer Division, he would simply make a sandwich, plink on the piano for a while, and go quietly to bed.

Dad plodded along for a couple more years, but, heading downhill fast, he finally socked his boss (probably while receiving sound advice), and was fired from Warner Brothers. It was a financial blow, and although he worked feverishly as everything from musician to door-to-door salesman, it was never enough. He even drove a taxi—the nadir for this former executive. Money arguments prevailed, and in my childish mind, I believed I could help. I sold Cloverine Salve door to door from a comic book advertisement and felt proud at earning my own school milk money. By age eleven, I made one and one-half cents per delivery on my paper route for six bucks a week and no longer needed an allowance.

Bankruptcy finally struck our family when I was about thirteen. Although I could not define the term legally, I knew we had lost our house and all its furnishings. Shocked and furious, I knew that a strange family would move into our home, and whoever they were, I hated them. Among Dad's other money problems, the driver of the car he hit had won a lawsuit against him. Dad was found to be responsible for the accident, even though the other driver had driven directly into highway traffic. I could see that very family living in our house, laughing at it. Thoughts of burning the house down gnawed at my heart, but I settled for smashing the fireplace poker into the plaster wall. "Enjoy the hole in the wall, you bastards," I swore.

Somehow we kept the car and, loaded with our few remaining possessions of clothes and small personal items, we drove north to Scranton, Pennsylvania, back where my parents had started. We kids were split up between relatives, and Dad found work as a movie theater booking agent, the buying side of his former position. He later moved to radio, working as a talk show host and disc jockey at various stations. Working all of his life, starting as a paperboy himself, he continued in radio up to his death in his seventies.

But all I knew in 1963 was that Dad was gone for good, and I might never see him again.

Andrew Jackson completed her sea trials on schedule, and we prepared for a major event, commissioning our boat and joining the fleet. She would become a US Navy submarine at long last, or "bought" by the navy. A critical question among the crew was to which fleet we would be assigned, Atlantic or Pacific. We were the first Polaris boat built on the Pacific Ocean side, and most of us hoped we would be the first assigned to the West Coast. Among fleet sailors, the Pacific is generally considered the best, with a home port in California or Hawaii, with better liberty in Asian ports and better cruising waters.

A Pacific Fleet assignment was wistful thinking, however, since there were no real targets for a Polaris boat. Outside of Vladivostok, Petropavlovsk, and a few scattered bases, there was very little on which to waste a Polaris missile. Those targets would be instantly destroyed anyway in the first minutes of any conflict by more conventional means. Moscow and everything beyond the Ural Mountains was simply out of our range. A Polaris boat would be handy to vaporize China, but beyond her landmass, China was no real threat to the United States. No, we would be Atlantic-bound, where all the good targets are located. We were assigned to the Atlantic.

Taking advantage of our two-crew rotation, Barbara and I moved back to the East Coast while the gold crew had possession of the boat during a sea trial phase. Our ping-pong life continued with another drive across country and camping out on the floor until the moving van arrived. Based on government housing standards, the house was beautiful. Large rooms, central air, back porch, car port, spotless lawns, and wide, winding streets, our exclusive Polaris community was as gold-plated as our weapon system.

With our families settled in, we flew back to Mare Island in preparation for our commissioning. The blue crew had already been designated to sail the boat to Charleston while the gold crew moved their families east. Conditions were hectic as the boat neared the ceremony and her final departure from Mare Island.

In our rush for completion, a strange sense of urgency seemed to prevail, approaching the stress of a coming war. Our submarine was completed on time, an uncommon if not unprecedented accomplishment. What's the big rush? we all wondered. Pursuing our secret and top-secret files, nothing special was going on with the cold war or the world in general. Nonetheless, a creeping uneasiness grew within me, a terrible sense that the United States was planning the worst, and the *Andrew Jackson* was key to that plan.

Just what is Soviet and US military doctrine regarding the use of nuclear weapons, anyway? I researched the subject as best I could and as time would permit and concluded that the Soviets were geared to a defensive strategy with nuclear weapons reserved as a last resort. Soviet aims in a world war were completely unachievable and generally called for:

- Defeating NATO forces and occupying the NATO countries
- Neutralizing the United States and her allies by disrupting and destroying their military forces
- Preventing China's entry into the USSR and, if unsuccessful, neutralizing China's capability to interfere with the USSR while avoiding a land war in Asia
- Limiting damage to vital Soviet political, military, and economic structures
- Dominating the postwar world with a basic socialist, political, and economic system

Soviet military doctrine obviously employed conventional weapons, for how does one occupy the NATO countries or dominate the postwar world after nuclear exchange? Their defensive posture was not to be static, for under the principle of "the best defense is a strong offense," the Soviets would conduct fast-moving, dynamic ground attacks on several fronts to seize strategic ground objectives. These attacks would use conventional weapons by necessity.

The Soviets planned to use nuclear weapons only if war escalated to the nuclear level. However, they did envision a nuclear preemptive strike if large-scale, aggressive designs against them were detected, but that too was viewed as a defensive response. Soviet doctrine is thus similar to US doctrine: an aggressive defensive posture, the possible use of small tactical nuclear weapons in theater operation, and the use of large strategic weapons as a last resort. Both the United States and the USSR followed a policy of mutually assured destruction (MAD), the theory that neither country could launch a strategic strike without suffering a destructive retaliatory strike in return. Possession of nuclear weapons and the means of delivery guaranteed they would never be used.

I certainly viewed the United States as a peace-loving country with no desire for military domination over any sovereign state. The United States was militarily defensive and would never strike the first blow. But was that true?

During this period, I received the stunning news that I had passed the examination for chief petty officer and would advance in rank a few months hence. I was shocked, to say the least, having achieved the highest enlisted rank in just over seven years and at age twenty-six. The long hours of study had paid off. Soon I would be forced to give up the comfortable and utilitarian bell-bottoms, neckerchief, and white cap that I loved so much for the cumbersome officer's uniform.

Our cruise to the East Coast was another "fast transit," close to our maximum and classified twenty-two-knot speed. The last fast transit I made was to our spy and nuclear torpedo mission off Vladivostok on USS *Razorback. What was the rush?* I wondered. The navy had fourteen operational Polaris boats in its arsenal by 1962. Counting the short turnaround time and occasional maintenance periods, the United States had eight to nine Polaris boats on station at all times and they were now armed with the A-2 missiles. Still, something unusual was going on. My sense of foreboding grew.

Chapter 5

THE CIA GETS A WAR

The blue crew got a much-needed break following the long transit from the Pacific and the feverish pace at which we had tested our missiles. The gold crew took the boat for further exercising and the cruise to our home port, while we flew to our families in Charleston. I had not been home since we moved east many months before.

Life was great. I finally made enough money to afford a few luxuries, and my raise to chief's pay was a few weeks away. Our little Polaris village had a nearby movie theater, commissary store, and navy exchange, all offering significant discounts. We enjoyed church services at our own chapel just a few blocks away. Most important, I was guaranteed to be home half of the time, thanks to the two-crew rotation, an average that exceeded my previous sea duty. Aside from occasional distant school assignments, the off-crew had very few duties, allowing us to enjoy our families.

One item we added to our furnishings was a small four-stool bar. Situated between our living and dining rooms, and next to the latest stereo sound system, it complemented the drinking patterns we followed during those years. Alcohol was quite inexpensive at the navy exchange package store, and I kept the bar stocked with dozens of the usual hard liquors and mixes. Our little bar was the focal point of many great parties, but it also provided an all-too-easy source for before and after dinner cocktails. Our drinking increased, and with it, the real start of Barbara's drinking problem.

The ease of off-crew is perfect for personal improvement projects, so I set up a study program for my next advancement examination. The navy had decided to eliminate the warrant officer ranks and replace them with enlisted "super chiefs," two new ranks known as senior chief and master chief. The plan did not work when they realized the essential role of warrant officers, who not only possessed technical skills but had the power

51

of a commissioned officer as well. So, the navy ended up retaining the warrant officer program plus the two new super chief grades. Although it was another three-year wait before I could take the senior chief examination, I started studying.

Polaris off-crew was paradise. While the gold crew completed their final torpedo and missile training, we enjoyed a couple months off, a needed rest before our first operational patrol. Our duties were essentially nonexistent, a condition I had never experienced before in the navy. There were no-duty days when we manned a certain station, remaining there for twenty-four hours every fourth day. We mustered two or three times a week, a process that took fifteen minutes or so, but otherwise we were off every single day. I planned two more years on *Andrew Jackson* and realized I would spend half of that, or one year, at home with no serious disruptions; it would be like having a six-month vacation. My career up to that point had been a series of emergencies, pressure, and danger, separated by short periods of peace.

One of the worst consequences of the life of a seafarer became painfully obvious when I finally got to know my children for the first time. At that time, their ages were from seven to one, and it never occurred to me how little I knew of them until I was able to spend every evening and much of the day at home. We hiked the local woods, paddled the swamps in my homemade canoe, went to church, and visited historic sites together. Dinner every evening was semiformal—stimulating conversation well into the evening with no television. It was family life as I had imagined but never experienced. In retrospect, the damage done to the family of a seaman is appalling.

Unfortunately, Barbara and I drank more, including before and after dinner cocktails and often wine with the meal. Barbara's capacity increased to my level, then beyond. Drinking would never become a problem for me, and she seemed to be able to control her drinking at that time. We were also sensible, never driving after drinking and celebrating New Year's at home parties or those within walking distance.

At the height of my first off-crew vacation, I was ordered to another two-week school in New London. Rather than ruin the vacation, we decided to drive the family north to visit our families; Barbara and the kids would stay with her mother in Boston while I attended school. It was that fateful month of November 1963, when we drove north, hoping to avoid those early winter snowstorms.

My promotion to chief petty officer took place within a couple days of starting school, so with an inadequate clothing allowance, I trudged off to the uniform shop to pick up the huge purchase. Out of the enlisted barracks, I moved into the chiefs' quarters and into a new world. In my new, large quarters, I slipped into my dress blue gabardine uniform, white shirt and tie, and CPO hat. At twenty-six and looking twenty-one, I neither looked like nor felt like a chief. In all the movies, chiefs look about fifty years old, like Ernest Borgnine in *McHale's Navy*. The big thirty-dollar hat was heavy and uncomfortable, a far cry from the ninety-cent white hat easily stuffed in one's waistband and tossed in the washer when dirty.

The Kennedy assassination had been a terrible shock to everyone and especially to those of us in the military. And so, it was back to Charleston. Our long trip home was gloomy; even the children sensed an important event had occurred. Kennedy had become a hero to me in the past several months, most likely because I had met him so recently. I saw him as the man who would abandon the US covert war–making policy of foreign intervention and replace it with something useful to humankind, like his quest to the moon and maybe to the stars beyond. His improved relations with the Soviet Union may have even ended the cold war. Just a few weeks ago, I fretted at missing the Vietnam conflict due to Kennedy's plan to withdraw and now, ironically, I wondered if the CIA and Pentagon could prolong it until my next transfer in two years.

On top of the loss of our president, I also learned that my father remained missing: no address, no phone number, and no contact. My thoughts drifted to my Uncle Joe Prinsky, an air force officer, married to my mother's sister, Marie. He was never popular with my mother's side of the family. While driving with his family to Scranton for a visit a few years earlier, my uncle's car experienced a blowout and my aunt was thrown to the pavement and killed in a wild skid. Uncle Joe, totally unhurt, was somehow blamed, even called a murderer. After the funeral, Joe told my brother Arthur that he would never again speak to his in-laws. Keeping his promise never to be heard from again, he completely disappeared. I wondered if my dad had done the same.

Chapter 6

THE COLD WAR MYTH

Our Polaris home port doubled as an ammunition dump for the navy. Its vast, well-groomed acres contained strange grassy humps of partially buried bunkers full of ordnance. They also contained our missiles and nuclear warheads.

At home, a deep gloom slowly fell upon the Walker household as the date for my first patrol neared. The kids became less playful, either understanding or sensing that Daddy would be leaving again. Missed holidays and birthdays were planned, sometimes celebrated once with Mom and then again when Dad came home. Conversations between Barbara and I declined into discussions on how she should handle the usual emergencies, from car breakdowns to medical problems. Sex became more frequent in anticipation of the long dry spell but less enjoyable. Perhaps like the last meal of the condemned, the expectation diminished the pleasure.

Hugging the wet-eyed kids and getting back into the car, Barbara and I reenacted that all-too-familiar drive up the pier. The boat stood ready, so sleek she seemed to be running even when tethered to the pier. Her big white hull numbers, 619, had long before been blackened out, never to be seen again. We parked amid other cars where crew members and wives performed the sailor's departing ritual. Barbara and I hugged and kissed, always strangely awkward for me at such times, and soon I was aboard, watching her drive away. Long departures were always very emotional, and in my earlier years, produced a welling in my eyes, noticeable only to me. It is something a sailor gets used to, but it was always painful.

Thrust into the activity of my radio shack, I was fully aware that the separation would be harder on Barbara. She would lose whatever help I contributed to the house and kids. Managing the house alone seven days a week with no rest and no change was not a role I would choose. Meanwhile, I had a million-dollar radio room to play with on a submarine costing in the billions while heading for a port call and liberty in Spain.

Busy with my radio, I could only guess at the topside scene as a tugboat thumped alongside to help us back into the Cooper River. We sailed downriver, past the navy base, downtown Charleston, and into the bay. I peeked a quick periscope glance at Fort Sumter where the War between the States began a hundred years earlier as we slipped into the Atlantic and submerged. We were leaving our home port for a period of years, en route to our advanced base.

Now on my sixth ship, I was aware that I had entered a new confrontational level in the cold war. Thus far, every real and potential challenge between the United States and the USSR was at a conventional weapons level with only small tactical nuclear weapons in reserve. Our elite, a handpicked and exceptionally trained group of professionals, now operated a weapons system designed exclusively for massive strategic nuclear destruction. The fun and games when US and Soviet fleet units taunted each other was no more. This was deadly serious business now, and we all realized our Soviet counterparts were equally trained and dedicated. I knew the Soviets to be militarily second rate, although few shared my view, and their inferiority made them particularly dangerous. If recklessly provoked and sensing a US attack, they might launch a preemptive missile attack simply to avoid total destruction. It seemed obvious to me that the USSR was afraid of the United States and in a defensive position.

Having evolved into an insufferable skeptic by this time, I did not believe that our medical community or government had rigidly followed ethical guidelines in conducting human radiation experiments. I even felt relieved that my personal experience in an atmospheric nuclear test was from a submerged submarine. As for those at the CIA, my growing perception of their lack of ethics made me shudder at the thought of their sordid experiments.

As a professional military man, I supported strong armed forces and knew that our strength was the best way to prevent war. As George Washington said in 1790, "To prepare for war is the most effective way of making peace." His wisdom was repeated by John F. Kennedy in 1960 when he said, "It is unfortunate that we can secure peace only by preparing for war." Trained and prepared for battle, I believed in the concept of meeting the enemy with overwhelming firepower. If the Soviet military was weak, all the better. I liked the Soviet strategy of avoiding a nuclear war with the United States based on our strength and wanted them to keep thinking that way. What I found troubling was the obscene exaggeration by the CIA, which produced misleading, doctored, and erroneous information in which the Soviets were shown as superior to the United States, or at least at parity. It should be no mystery why that was done. To support a big military, we needed a big enemy. And big military machines—like my shiny new submarine—cost a lot of money. The contractors got very rich.

Chapter 7

A COUPLE OF GOOD YEARS

Time does not fly on a Polaris patrol. My speculation a few years earlier proved to be true. The patrol operated in the doldrums. While on the cutting edge of importance, we lived in the backwater of boredom. On other fleet units, whether submarines, aviation, or surface, there was always some exciting event taking place. To relieve our boredom, the captain would sometimes stop in the middle of the ocean for "swim call," allowing the crew to splash about for a couple hours. Or maybe we would break out the small arms and let the crew take turns sinking old boxes tossed overboard. It is exhilarating to blast holes in the ocean with a tommy gun or M-1 rifle. Then there are the big guns, target practice at towed surface targets or aircraft-towed sleeves. We might shoot at unmanned aircraft drones, which were not to be actually hit, but everyone tried earnestly to shoot them down, cheering wildly when we blasted one from the sky.

Johnnie Hutchins had a skipper who enjoyed night gunnery practice, a wild show for a ship still possessing those wonderful World War II guns. We would fire a "star shell" from a five-inch gun, approximately a 127-millimeter cannon, which would burst high overhead to trail a bright flare below a small parachute. Then the light show would begin. Our two five-inch guns firing antiaircraft exploded rounds, bursting in bright flashes around the flare. The five 40-millimeter twin and quad mounts fired rapid tracer rounds, set to explode at altitude, punctuating the big detonations. Meanwhile, our six 20-millimeter twin machine gun tracers hosed down the sky with arcing points of light. The little target was followed down to the surface, where the sea boiled with exploding rounds. Great fun for teenagers and old vets alike.

For a real water show, one has to experience a destroyer practice depth-charge attacks. This means chasing a simulated submarine at twenty knots then dropping a depth-charge pattern of twelve from the stern racks and fired from the side-launching K-guns. Each shock wave reverberated through the ship as we raced away from our own blasts while geysers filled the sky. The navy really is an adventure.

Adding to our boredom was the lack of mail, both incoming and out-going. While the rest of the fleet enjoyed frequent mail deliveries, we were limited to three short messages from home, just three or four lines long, sent amid our usual broadcast message traffic. They were received by Morse code like all of our traffic, and we prepared family telegram (famgram) message blanks and envelopes to resemble Western Union telegrams. They were eagerly awaited by everyone and talked about regularly as the crew exchanged clever lines from their wives and families. Of course, serious problems and family deaths were sent by separate "CO's Eyes Only" messages, encrypted in a keylist with very limited access.

Posted in every workspace on the boat was a countdown record of some type, usually a simple packet of sheets marked seventy through zero days. Spirits rose steadily as each new day saw the numbers lower. By the time single digits were reached, spirits skyrocketed in anticipation. The boat crept ever westward toward Rota, retargeting missiles as another inbound boat assumed our targets. Through the strait, into the Atlantic, we surfaced at last off Rota with a blast of unmanufactured outside air, always smelling slightly of decaying sea creatures affixed to our super-structure. After two months in our sterile environment, the smelly air was a delight.

The gold crew stood waiting on the tender's rails, as impatient to climb aboard as we were to leave. The relieving process began immediately, and although the formal relief would take place two or three days later, the relieving crew always assumed the duty to allow us to go ashore that night. A cold beer, restaurant food, and a show in town was a welcome and relaxing treat for all.

Chartered planes carried the assembled blue crew on a nonstop flight to the United States. In an odd departure from the norm, our wives, loved ones, and families met their seafaring men not at a pier with our brave ship in the background but at the Charleston Air Force Base terminal, our ship five thousand miles away. But, while the background was odd, the universal scene was the same as it had been for thousands of years for returning sailors.

Barbara positively glowed. At five feet two, she remained trim and chic with alluring raven hair. The kids looked like they just stepped out of Saks Fifth Avenue. I tried unsuccessfully to hug and kiss everyone at once, then we piled into our big Pontiac and headed home for one hundred days off, the first thirty days of totally free R&R. Life was sweet.

A separation of only three months was long enough for major changes in my children. They were still so young, at one, three, four, and six years old, that I was pressed to get to know them again between each cruise, if indeed I ever could. They all talked at once, telling their little stories, vying for attention. I loved it, just hearing their squeaky, excited voices, regardless of what they were saying.

Years earlier, I had developed a simple savings plan resulting from each promotion and raise of pay. We were living well enough on our current income, I reasoned, so why not save half of the raise and use the rest to improve our standard of living? The plan worked with each of my promotions, including two levels of proficiency pay and submarine hazardous pay. Consequently, our savings swelled, allowing us to speculate in the stock market. We bought high-tech electronics, a major food conglomerate, and pharmaceutical stocks. The pharmaceutical was selected specifically because of its research and development of birth control pills.

Barbara and I were naturally frugal, a quality that developed in our childhoods. Barbara's woeful background was particularly unpleasant, as her father had died while she was still a child, plunging her family into poverty. Living in the Waterville and Skowhegan area of Maine, her widowed mother probably did the best she could, but the family remained impoverished. Her mother eventually remarried a ne'er-do-well worse off than herself who rarely worked and sexually abused the youngest daughter. Barbara escaped, dropped out of school, and ran to Boston, where she boarded with a family in East Boston and found a bank job in the downtown financial district.

My childhood was far better. Our family was upper-middle class, and even after its collapse, life for me was still much better than Barbara ever experienced. Regardless, we both learned the virtue of hard work and the value of a dollar.

In actuality, my childhood was never as difficult as some might have thought. The negative psychological impact of seeing our home lost and family scattered simply drove me into believing I should earn something to help. But none of us starved, suffered, or went without clothes. Our relatives were all working middle class and well equipped to help in our time of need. Someone should have grabbed me by the collar and advised me that I had a job, which was to work hard in school. Anything that took me away from that job, such as working at silly little jobs for mere pennies, was more detrimental than beneficial. Although I may not have believed that to be true, it was never once explained to me by anyone.

To the thrifty, however, pennies do build up. When I started selling newspapers from the corner, my nightly take was just over fifty cents. I saved the half dollar and spent the remaining nickel or dime on myself. But slowly I built up my customers by wandering to some nearby bars, a fraternal club, and local restaurants and businesses to increase my savings to nearly a dollar per night. While it may sound amazing in today's society, in the 1950s, I could leave ten or more papers in the three-sided wooden box placed on the corner by the *Scranton Times* when I left to cover my route. Upon return, change would be loosely tossed atop the papers for each one missing, including tips. Such conduct today is unthinkable. The money would be gone, the papers stolen, and I would probably be jumped and robbed while passing some dark alley.

Life improved dramatically for me as a movie theater usher at a salary of twelve dollars a week. A fellow usher suggested that I needed a car, but at age fifteen, I had yet to receive any driving practice and thought him to be crazy. Nevertheless, we took a bus downtown to shop the car dealers. I was soon hooked on a 1949 Ford, about four years old and in good shape. My friend agreed to teach me to drive. So, still a few days shy of my sixteenth birthday, I put a deposit on the car, which the dealer promised to hold until my father approved the purchase.

Dad was stunned, as was the rest of the family, when I asked if he would accompany me downtown to pay off my car. My brothers, both of whom squandered every penny the moment it crossed their fingers, were equally shocked. The cost of the car was $590, and with cashier's check in hand for the remainder, I became the owner of a paid-for car on my sixteenth birthday. Of course, the car became transportation for the family as much as my own personal car, but I felt good about it. In a strange case of position reversal, however, my dad would ask if he could borrow my car for the night. Normally he brought it back on time and full of gas.

Characteristically, I was always easygoing and probably cheerful to a fault. As a kid, I was nicknamed "Smilin' Jack" after the old comic book character. While I was respectful of elders and authority, and sobered by real tragedy and pain, I was entertained by most of life's conflicts, which I found to be comical. Navy boot camp was a perfect example of manufactured drama and seriousness, which I saw as absurd and delightful. The more oppression and misery the recruit staff created, the more I had to suppress my grins. Life was a play: I could do an impersonation of the perfect recruit so well, I was promoted to platoon leader.

To say I had found a home in the navy would be an understatement. I was one of those strange recruits who not only enjoyed boot camp but chose the navy as my career while still holding the rank of seaman recruit (at a salary of about fifty dollars per month). My tormented shipmates at the Naval Recruit Training Center in Bainbridge, Maryland, gave me strange looks when I mentioned my plans. Was Smilin' Jack joking again? they wondered. What most did not realize was that I not only enjoyed the experience but deduced that if this was the worst of the navy, the fleet would be exhilarating. And it was. After two promotions, graduation from radio school in Norfolk, Virginia, and a year of sea duty under my belt, my opinion and goal had not changed.

I met my wife-to-be, Barbara, at a dance one Friday night at Revere Beach. A skating rink featured dancing only one night a week, which proved a popular spot for those of us too young for the bars and too old for roller-skating. She was perky and lighthearted, but a bit haughty in a delightful Bostonian way. Both teenagers, we dated and soon became inseparable. Barbara dismissed questions about her family, and, since it was obvious that she was on her own, I stopped asking. I was quite proud of this eighteen-year-old, self-sufficient woman who rode the subway every day to work in the big city. Most of my shipmates in the same age bracket dated either shiftless girls who lived at home or unemployed barflies. We were married a year later, she at nineteen and I at twenty, and since she needed parental permission to wed in Massachusetts, we drove to North Carolina for the ceremony. Shortly thereafter, I met her family.

Barbara was abnormally glum when she told me that we should meet her mother and family—people she had declined to even acknowledge in the past. She was obviously upset by the prospect; I found it ominous. Worse, I felt betrayed by the belated revelation. That Barbara was hiding the skeletons of her family in the closet had been obvious, but there are only two options when one has skeletons: either reveal them early on or keep them interned forever. To spring them on a new spouse is not only unfair but can also be destructive to the marriage.

We drove to a run-down business district of Boston called Scully Square, a dismal, soul-stifling part of town with smelly sailor bars, small, cheap storefront shops, and bleak apartments three and four stories above. It was walking distance from the naval base, and since I had wandered those bars with my altered ID card before, I wondered if I had already met my in-laws while on liberty.

Into one of those obscure doors that no one notices, squashed between a couple small businesses, we climbed the rickety stairs to the apartment of Oscar and Annie Smith and two of Barbara's five siblings. Annie gushed with cheerfulness, but her blithe manner was thin disguise to her normal born-to-worry nature. Oscar was cheery, old, and gnarled, seemed to live in bed, and had the expected pallor of a hospital patient. Annie drew Social Security widow benefits and worked part-time as a cook at nursing homes and schools. Her husband seemed totally disabled, had just undergone major brain surgery, and probably drew Social Security supplemental income. Barbara's brother Frankie, about fifteen, was a pleasant, gangly youth, the most intelligent in the apartment, with an aspiration to become a writer. Cynthia, the youngest, was rosy cheeked, fresh, and in the bloom of youth at about thirteen, but morose and sorrowful of spirit. Two older brothers and a sister lived in Maine, one of whom refused to even speak to any family members.

These people were poor, dressed in thrift-shop clothing. Aside from Frankie, they were beaten people, living life in the last lane. We rarely visited.

So it was just a few years after our wedding, by working hard, shopping carefully, and saving, that we reached a point where life was good. On paydays, I would toss my check in my dresser sock drawer where there were always three or four uncashed checks. Barbara's friends would be stunned in disbelief when she slipped the oldest check from the stack as they prepared for a shopping trip. We actually dressed for dinner at home. I would not know it then, but that short period of time somewhere after 1963 would represent the best part of our married life. In fact, in our nineteen-year marriage, we would enjoy only a couple good years.

Like any 1950s high school student in a Catholic school, I was required to take Latin. Every Latin curriculum includes translations of Cicero, the great Roman orator and philosopher, unsurpassed in the mastery of Latin prose. In one of Cicero's more famous quotes, he said, "The first law for historians is that he should never utter an untruth." History cannot be driven by propaganda or prejudice and it must be applied to current events. But Franklin Delano Roosevelt lied about the attack on *Greer*, a lie that helped propel the United States into World War II. That historical untruth would never be exposed and thus not applied to the attack on the *Maddox* and *Turner Joy*. The politicians would give us a history of lies built one upon another. Had the public known of the *Greer*'s true role, Americans may have been less prone to accept the government lie about *Maddox* and *Turner Joy* and our phony entry into the Vietnam War.

Because of my dad's position with Warner Brothers in the 1930s and 1940s, I would learn about propaganda at a young age. Roosevelt needed a war to bolster America's military buildup and get people back to work making war machines. The film industry was seen as the premier propaganda tool to broadcast a hatred of Hitler and the need for the United States to save Europe. Theaters attracted fifty million, or over one-third of Americans to the movies at least once a week. The Pentagon sought to lure moviemakers, executives, and actors into uniform to better control the film industry in its war-making plans. My dad was offered a commission as an army officer, which he refused, since he was making far too much money to accept the paltry pay of the army. Dad knew many moviemakers, such as Ronald Reagan, who eagerly accepted commissions and got their tickets punched without ever leaving Hollywood. Uniform or not, Warner Brothers turned out pro-British and prowar films with Dad's assistance. As I became older, he explained the hidden messages in many of the productions. The 1941 Warner Brothers release *Sergeant York*—the rousing story of a pacifist turned war hero—was typical of the propaganda blockbusters of the era.

With little to do during long stints at sea, I shared with shipmates my observations and opinions of government trickery in creating wars. Many just shrugged off the government lies as normal or said that the government knew what was best. A few were positively enamored by the government's cunning ploys that drew the enemy into action, just as long as communists were injured in the process. If it resulted in limited war, all the better. As military men, most yearned for a chance to experience combat, and we all expected the Vietnamese conflict to last a long time, two or three years.

My interest in international and military affairs was far from the most important thing in my life. Had it not been for my access to top secrets and firsthand experiences, I may have been as apathetic as the general public. And why not? We pay our elected officials huge salaries with princely perks to do what is right for the country. Since they all take an oath of office, the public should be protected from wrongdoing on their part.

My growing family was my main concern, and our marriage was so strong, it seemed beyond harm. For our second off-crew, Barbara and I planned a European vacation without the kids. During my thirty-day upkeep in Spain, I was introduced to auto racing at a small local track. Using small sports cars and little British Morris Minors, we raced in modified G-class on complex tracks where speeds rarely reached ninety miles per hour. Racing was slow, safe, and enormously exciting. I was smitten and joined local and international sports car clubs and vowed to buy my own car. Barbara loved the idea of touring Europe in our own sports car and avoiding those organized tourist traps in cosmopolitan hotels and antiseptic tour buses full of elderly picture takers. We had no need for a second car—Barbara knew it was my personal toy.

Barbara arranged child care with a shipmate's family a couple blocks from our home, and we would pay them back in kind by watching their three kids while they vacationed later. The unhurried trip around Europe was the first time Barbara and I spent more than a few hours together without the children since we courted seven or eight years earlier. It was truly a belated honeymoon, and people we met along the way actually thought we were newly married.

We enjoyed one more trip together after my third patrol, a free flight to Rio de Janeiro, Brazil. The air force had a scheduled MATS flight between Charleston and Rio twice a week, and like all such flights, military personnel and their families were allowed to apply for space-available seating. The hazard was the return trip, for if there were no seats available, we would be forced to finance our return on a commercial flight. But we could afford that emergency. We farmed the kids out in the same arrangement and experienced the vivacity of the city that defined entertainment.

The golden quality of our marriage would begin to slip during this period. While our drinking had increased over the years, mine reached a level somewhere short of intoxication while Barbara's just continued to grow. She started drinking during the day while I was at work or at sea. While Barbara had always smoked very sparingly and with the utmost grace, her smoking increased to the point of positive annoyance. She felt smothered by the kids and the nonstop around-the-clock role of mother. I could appreciate her frustration, for I would never choose such a vocation. The thought of managing as a single parent was inconceivable to me, and were I to assume that role, I would surely choose to work and leave child care to a hired professional.

On a more alarming note, Barbara burdened the children with jobs that were clearly beyond their ability and punished them for failure. Barbara stopped doing dishes and most of the cleaning, and the kids suffered through those projects for hours, only to be beaten in the process. Barbara and I were both quick to administer corporal punishment, something I shall regret to my dying day, but Barbara was frightening in her level of discipline. If drunk, she was a terror who could lose control. It was time for a serious talk, so I planned dinner and a show away from the kids where we could talk in a relaxed atmosphere. I realized she worked prior to our marriage, and if she chose to return to work, I had no objections.

Competent babysitters were everywhere, and if she made enough to cover that expense, it was satisfactory to me.

I broached the subject when the time seemed right, but to my surprise, she interrupted with an idea she had been planning for some time. She wanted to start and operate a business, a hunting lodge in Maine. In fact, she had gone so far as to find the perfect building for sale at a reasonable cost. The building abutted prime hunting land, and the owner had agreed to allow access to his land by lodgers for a small percentage of the profit. I was impressed—the idea seemed viable. Her figures were a bit rough concerning overhead and marketing, but she had done quite well without my help. The downside involved family separation, which I had vowed would never happen. With my family living in the wilds of Maine, my thirty days' annual leave from distant duty stations would quickly reduce me to a stranger. Just nearing ten years of service, I could retire in ten more years, but I planned for a thirty-year career.

I had told her something along the lines of "you can get a job or be a mom, but you cannot do both." With motherhood seeming to drag her down, I hoped she would jump at the thought of a small, unstressful job. I did suggest a bank job, but she refused to consider working for a poor bank salary. Whatever her choice was, it was obvious to me that a major change in her life was necessary. Less obvious was the downhill slide of our marriage.

Chapter 8

HEADING DOWNHILL

As we drove north to Maine, my excitement grew at the prospect of opening a business. While neither Barbara nor I had any business experience, I was confident that my organizational and managerial skills, acquired as a navy chief, would serve me well. We had the money to start and the income to support mortgage payments. I studied my children in the rearview mirror with ambivalence—they were just babies, between three and eight—and I wondered if I would know them in the future. It was already a struggle to make up for my frequent absences, trying to fill in the blanks in their growth.

We dropped the kids off with Barbara's mother in Boston and traveled on alone. Our business target population would be upscale Boston urbanite hunters interested in operating from a comfortable hunting lodge as opposed to the trunk of a car on some muddy logging road. The ease of driving out of Boston was therefore an important part of the plan, but we found the trip to be very smooth: it was a straight shot north on Interstate 95 as we passed quickly out of Massachusetts, through a corner of New Hampshire, and into Maine. The scene slowly gave way to vast miles of wilderness forest, a place where one could get away from it all. Less than one hundred miles from Boston we exited on Route 201 northwest to Skowhegan. We entered the rolling hills and valleys of a mixed forest with oaks, elms, and birch amid the green pines and spruce. We were in the land of real Down East people with complete Yankee accents. I am no hunter, but it looked like perfect country to me and surprisingly uninhabited for an area less than two hours from metropolitan Boston. My spirits rose.

Our first stop would be visits to Barbara's two brothers and sister whom I had never met. The eldest was George, described by Barbara as noncommunicative and hermitlike. He and his wife lived in a small residential enclave of modest bungalows. George ushered us into his simple living room and sat quietly. Barbara and I are both exuberant by nature, but we were unsuccessful in developing any conversation. Embarrassing gaps lingered between our questions while George answered with grunts or one-word responses. The only time he spoke was to complain that something had killed the germs in his septic tank and he had to buy a new bottle of germs in town. His wife, sharing his antisocial behavior, hid in a bedroom for most of our twenty-minute visit. Finally appearing as we prepared to leave, she was a spiritless person, gray and distant.

Annie and her husband lived like pioneers of old, their home one step above a log cabin. Up a dirt road and into a tiny clearing, it was like stepping fifty years into the past. The yard was packed dirt with clumps of tortured grass. A couple dogs dozed under the porch, a few chickens clucked about. Annie's husband was the picture of a backwoodsman, comfortable when chopping at something. Gracious living for him would be to visit a Holiday Inn. Annie was a perfect country wife, unglamorous, appearing older than her years, a few teeth missing. She fit seamlessly into his life.

We sat in their spartan living room and discussed hunting and the cost of lumber. They seemed baffled by my life, submarines, missiles, technology, and our recent European trip. Like communicating with people from a distant planet, it seemed impossible to establish common ground. As we talked, the threadbare carpet seemed to move, but no one noticed. It finally bellowed up several inches in the center like some sort of animal was materializing from below. Like the phantasm of a ghost, invisible to everyone else, the apprehension was ignored. As it bellowed up again, I finally had to ask. They explained nonchalantly that the wind was simply blowing under the house, through the gaps in the floorboards, and lifting the carpet. Here was this house in the refrigerator of Maine with an insulation value of R-zero.

Tom was last on our list and a refreshing change from George and Annie. He and his family were a perfect example of a middle-class couple, living in a nice house with many handyman improvements. Tom was clearheaded, ambitious, and energetic with a practical nature and great sense of humor. His wife was pleasant with refreshingly ingenuous warmth. They had done much of the research for Barbara and paved the way for us to see the property. First, however, I would go deer hunting with Tom and his friends the next morning as part of my indoctrination.

With borrowed boots and clothes, a shotgun thrust into my hands, I drove with Tom and his buddies into the forest in predawn darkness on rutty dirt roads. These guys knew the best spots, and we parked our two-car convoy and started into the woods as dawn broke. Wandering through the woods in the brisk fall weather was enjoyable, although I dislike hunting and had no intention of shooting anything. Our group did kill a buck around midmorning, and by the time we followed the shots to a clearing, the deer was already gutted and ready to drag out. The heart, still warm, had been removed and was cooking over a small fire. Part of their ancient ritual was to cook and share some part of the game on the spot, and, admittedly, it was not bad.

The experience was educational, and later that day, Barbara and I met with the property owners. The building was large, three stories high with more than ample rooms. The living room with a huge fireplace would be furnished in English or Early American and serve as a common area for the guests. Space for the family's privacy was plentiful. The place seemed perfect and affordable; Barbara was thinking along the lines of a "bed and breakfast" before the term was ever invented.

Vital to the plan were the hunting grounds that abutted the property, allowing the guests to wander out the back door and into prim forest areas. A farmer named Mr. Nagle owned the land. It was a huge tract of heavily wooded acres, ideal for deer and spacious meadowlands, perfect for bird hunting. Nagle was agreeable to the use of his property, which was not posted anyway, for a small compensation.

I would never see any of Barbara's Maine relatives again. While no loss in the case of George and Annie, I would have enjoyed the friendship of Tom and his family under different circumstances.

We left Maine faced with the mathematical problem of estimating the probability of success. Our expenses were calculated as accurately as possible, including utilities, mortgage, legal, accounting, insurance, labor, maintenance, household, and food. With the overhead costs established, it was a simple matter to calculate the room and occupancy rate necessary to meet that overhead. Our break-even room rate was very low, and according to our estimates, the lodge should turn a modest profit. Missing from the equation was marketing—how to advertise and attract customers. As we drove toward Boston, I thought of my dad, the marketing expert, now missing for years. Was he even alive? I wondered. I needed Dad now with his wisdom, his vast marketing knowledge. I said a silent prayer, and, most amazingly, it was answered almost immediately.

We picked up the kids in Boston and drove slightly out of our way to visit Mom in Scranton the next day. The moment we walked into the house, I could see Mom was troubled, and she soon called me aside. She had learned of Dad's location just the day before in a very strange way. Her brother, my Uncle Frank, was driving north from Florida and had decided at the last minute to take the long way up Route 13 through the Delaware-Maryland-Virginia peninsula. As he neared Salisbury, Maryland, he heard my father's voice on a local radio station doing a commercial. Somewhat stunned at hearing that familiar voice, he jotted down the station letters and told my mom.

I was totally exhilarated and realized I was driving south, saying my prayer, just as my uncle was driving north through Maryland. Exhausted by the long drive, I barely slept that night and paced around, unable to relax the next day. Salisbury was a two-hundred-and-fifty-mile drive, but after lunch I knew I had to go. We were to visit for several days, but Barbara and Mom understood when I jumped in the car alone and drove off. I arrived in Salisbury at about sunset with no real plan but found him listed in the phone book. There was stunned silence on the other end when I asked for directions, but soon I was with Dad, crushing him in a bear hug. He had a new wife, Dorothy, and a daughter, my half sister, Cheri.

It had been five or six years since I saw Dad, and then only infrequently for years before that. We had never spoken adult-to-adult in our lives, and one evening would not be enough time to even scratch the surface. We poked around town that evening and drank a few beers while he bubbled over with pride as he introduced his chief petty officer son from the nuclear submarine force. He naturally agreed to help with our hunting lodge project, and, after a night on the couch, I sped back to Scranton after promising to never become separated again.

Back in Charleston, Barbara and I continued calculating the business prospects as Dad furnished new unexpected problems to overcome. Dad's brother and my Uncle Jim had recently bought a Miami travel agency and provided valuable information on advertising and promotions, all of which were becoming more expensive. Our lodging rates were less than expected, but the worst part was the seasonal aspect. The hunting seasons would not provide year-round occupancy, and that economically depressed area of Maine offered no alternative attractions; Skowhegan had never seen a tourist. In the final analysis, we could never sustain the occupancy rate necessary to break even. It was a great idea, but, regrettably, it would not work.

Barbara became despondent, and with her mood came an increase in drinking, smoking, and watching television. The household was sinking into disarray, and like all depressed people, she would stage major house-cleaning projects, all done at breakneck speed. Eight hours of work simply cannot be jammed into a couple hours, regardless of the hectic pace. The kids would be terrorized as they tried to meet demands beyond their ability and would get pounded in the process. Alarmed and feeling helpless by her conduct, I urged her to just get a job and hire a sitter. But she did not want a low-wage job and was embarrassed at not having a high school diploma. Suggestions of adult GED classes were rejected. We were getting nowhere and she was sinking fast. Then for some unknown reason, she took out her wrath on Cynthia, our second-born. That child received beatings that would put Barbara in prison today. Cynthia's little legs always seemed to be bruised, often with tiny red loop welts made from wire coat hangers.

Barbara was finally appeased a bit by my suggestion that we pursue a less ambitious business venture. Our little submarine community was definitely in the boondocks, the nearest town being Goose Creek, population less than ten thousand. But growth was occurring, property prices were reasonable, and zoning laws were nearly nonexistent. A major interstate highway, I-26, was under construction nearby, connecting Charleston with the capital, Columbia. I focused on the planned interstate exits and found the Route 78 interchange to be very promising. The three-mile stretch between the ramp and Summerville was nearly barren, mostly solid with trees on both sides, but growth seemed guaranteed. As I prepared for my fourth patrol, I assured Barbara we would make a business decision when I returned. Her spirits rose, but only barely.

The navy's error in canceling the warrant officer program was recognized during this period and reestablished with great fanfare. A flurry of applications were submitted the first year from first-class petty officers and above for what in the past had been one of the finest ranks in the navy. I did not apply, considering my new super chief rank to be unparalleled, but many of Barbara's friends were excited by their husbands' applications. Barbara could not understand why I would ignore the program, a promotion to officer. The husband of her closest friend had taken the first test and made the alternate list for possible selection later—nearly guaranteed the following year. His wife was so certain of his impending officer's commission that she bought him a beautiful officer's sword for a couple hundred dollars in anticipation of the event.

Barbara became obsessed with becoming an "officer's wife," which increased the pressure for me to apply. I had many reasons to oppose the warrant program. Money was one consideration—my salary already exceeded warrant pay and it seemed senseless to reduce my pay just to increase my prestige. Also, there were no warrant billets on submarines, so a warrant promotion would "surface" me, ban me from submarine duty forever. I was near the top of the enlisted ranks and enjoyed the advantages; why would I go to the bottom of the officers' ranks to remain there forever? But Barbara goaded and coerced until I gave up and applied for testing the following year.

My next cruise was a period of soul searching as I considered my time away from home, measured in years. The rotation plan for shore duty had always been two years at sea followed by two years ashore. In 1965 I had nine years of continuous sea duty of my own choosing, a record nearly unheard of. The experience had benefited my career, since my meteoric advancements had been equally unusual. My drive for promotions had come at the expense of my wife and family, however; I had put my career ahead of family. Now my marriage was feeling the strain. I needed shore duty, bad.

Servicemen do not need a sixth sense to deduce that things are wrong at home; their incoming mail tells it all. My three famgrams were no exception. One bland message was received early in the cruise, then nothing until the hastily written final two near the end. I thought back to the one other time my lack of mail had set off alarm bells. I was just twenty-one in 1958 and cruising the Mediterranean on *Forrestal*. Barbara and our first baby, then just a few months old, stayed with my mother during the seven-month cruise. My mail dropped to zero for a couple months. Sailors can send inexpensive Western Union telegrams from sea, but I was too embarrassed to have my fellow radiomen read my distressful message home. So I slipped ashore in Naples and sent a short but frantic international telegram asking what was wrong and demanding a wire reply. A week later I received a short letter saying everything was okay, she was just "busy." She would explain when I got home, but every serviceman knows what that means.

When I finally picked up my family months later, she had no real explanation, just evasion and silence. But I noticed an element of distress in my mother and Aunt Amelia, both of whom were hiding anger. I pressed my mother, who put me off but promised to tell me later. That Barbara had been unfaithful was obvious, something I knew when I sent the telegram. I just needed to know how bad it was. Finally Mom admitted that she and Aunt Amelia had stumbled upon Barbara and one of our relatives "in the act."

Mom would not tell me who the man was, probably because she knew I would kill the bastard, and I just assumed it was one of my cousins. I said nothing to Barbara at the time, intending to confront her later, but I ended up dropping the issue entirely for reasons I still do not understand today. In fact, if she reads these pages, it will be the first time she realizes that I ever knew her secret. Years later I would learn why my Aunt Amelia was so angry: it was her husband she and Mom caught, my Uncle Bill. I had lived with Amelia and Bill when our family disintegrated, becoming the built-in sitter for my baby cousin, Patrick. They divorced shortly after Bill's incident with Barbara, and since both Amelia and Bill are now dead, I guess no one else can be hurt by revealing their indiscretion.

What was now going on with Barbara some seven years later, I could only guess. Hopefully, it was just her growing disillusionment with motherhood.

I took the examination for senior chief radioman, a test I had studied hard for but still found very difficult. The electronics were deep and the test covered geopolitical and international treaty items previously found only on the officer's battery tests. I was not hopeful. Nevertheless, I was informed that I had indeed passed and was selected for advancement some months hence. Another stunning promotion after the minimum three years as a chief; I would soon affix a star above my chevrons, a super chief.

It was during this last patrol on *Andrew Jackson* that my executive officer approached me with a transfer proposal. He was to assume command of a new Polaris submarine, USS *Simon Bolivar*, and wanted me to join him. He was assembling a handpicked crew, a fairly common practice, and wanted me to run the radio shack. I was flattered, but I told the XO I was ready for shore duty, now long overdue, and the *Bolivar* was still under construction far away in Virginia. He pressed, explaining that the boat's construction was near completion and it would be stationed in Charleston. Further, she would carry A-3 missiles and would not operate from Rota, so our thirty-day upkeep before patrols would be spent at home. He promised I could leave after one patrol. Shore duty billets for senior chief radioman were not that plentiful, and since I wanted to stay in Charleston long enough to finish Barbara's business project, I accepted his offer.

Walking down *Andrew Jackson*'s gangway in Rota for the last time was a gloomy moment for me. Orders in hand, I flew home in the company of men I had known for three years, a superb crew of professionals. The arrival rites at the air force base for my fourth and last time were a bit strained. My children were as joyful as ever, but Barbara was in the more doleful mood she had recently assumed.

The house looked good, and I hoped the kids had not suffered too much in the cleaning frenzy. After a few days of relaxation and becoming reintroduced to the kids, Barbara and I sat down for our final meeting on the business plan. I had located excellent property on Route 78, about three miles from the I-26 exchange, with five acres of land and a large four-bedroom house. It had over two hundred feet of highway frontage, about one acre wide and five acres deep. The building sat in a front corner, so there was ample space for a road to the rear or even a second building on the highway. The first significant building project was already under way, a huge Baptist college complex at the exchange.

My mother had received her private pilot license when I was a child, so we kids all had the chance to ride in small aircraft, even hold the wings level under Mom's strict care. Getting my pilot license was always a dream, so I decided to take my first lesson while checking the property from above. Flying a small aircraft may well rank as the most exciting of my many exploits, and I could barely calm myself long enough to study the land along Route 78 as arranged with the instructor. It was a desolate six miles of two-lane road to the town of Summerville with I-26 under construction exactly parallel. Then I saw the unexpected signs of an interstate exchange about a mile beyond my proposed property. It seemed to serve no purpose other than supporting Rural Route 535, which seemed to be gravel. The highway plan at the Berkley courthouse did show a planned exchange at 535, but no one could fathom its purpose. Like the railroads of old, the interstate highway system brought commerce and increased land values. Something was planned for Route 78, something big. We had the opportunity to buy a nice piece of land with a building while it was still affordable and to grow with the area.

Barbara was excited, and I will admit to being attracted to the project. The property's back acres did not seem to have great commercial value, but the land was well suited for a simple mobile home park of about thirty units. The nearby air force and navy bases created demand for rental lots, guaranteeing business. Sewage and county water were on the way, so we decided to start by converting the house to a restaurant and building mobile home lots slowly using our own water and septic system to start. The long-range plan was to build our home on the property later. But this would be Barbara's business, with minimal contribution from me. I was already absent a great deal of the time from my role as a husband and parent, and when I was transferred away from Charleston, my contribution would be nil. So I made my final appeal, asking Barbara to consider the difficult task and long work days. She had three choices: be a mom, get a simple job that paid enough for a sitter, or build a business. She emphatically chose the business—it was unnecessary to tell her it would be "none of the above."

I sold our stock, all of which had gained, especially the investment in the birth control manufacturer. We bought the property at about $30,000, a low price even for the 1960s. With a respectable down payment, our mortgage payment was a mere $95 a month. We built a large septic system, improved our well capacity, and installed our first mobile-home facilities. We bought and set in place the largest available mobile home, which would be our first rental unit in the future. Unfortunately, Barbara and the kids would have to live in that four-bedroom unit temporarily while we started renovation for the restaurant. It would take a few months before the work would start, after I returned to my new boat.

The PCU *Simon Bolivar* (SSBN-641) rested in the ways at Newport News Shipbuilding and Drydock Company, the largest employer in the state of Virginia and a major defense contractor. Her construction was not as advanced as I had hoped; she was not even launched. My blue crew first-class radioman had the radio shack under control, and since I had gone through this very routine three years earlier, there was far less challenge and adventure. *Bolivar* was a newer class of Polaris submarine but identical in outward appearance. She was built for the three-warhead A-3 missile, for which the entire fleet would retrofit at the very first opportunity.

I would be stuck in Newport News for about six months and far enough from Charleston to make visits very difficult. Norfolk to Charleston was a laborious eight-hour drive each way: the limit I would tackle for a weekend drive. Newport News would add an hour or two, making the trip a rare event unless a four-day weekend could be arranged. I had done what I swore would never happen—I was officially separated from my family. They would have their roots sunk in South Carolina while I would be stationed around the world for the next ten or twenty years. There was a small communications center at the Charleston Naval Station, but it had only one billet for a senior chief radioman out of the hundreds worldwide, so my chances were slim of ever landing that post.

Dad and his family did live close enough for frequent visits, and I finally got to know my father on an adult basis. He answered every question with candor, even the embarrassing ones, and told the stories of his childhood that I had never heard. I realized how close I had come to never knowing my dad or experiencing the depth of his wisdom. Knocking around the Eastern Shore, we got a little drunk together and even raised a little hell.

He had never driven a sports car, and after one evening of us both drinking a bit too much, he insisted on driving the MG. He was fascinated with my small experience at racing in Europe, and since my car was modified slightly, he had to try. Dad quickly got the feel of the gears and steering, and was soon roaring around those winding rural two-lane roads of the area. I was impressed—this guy could drive, taking sharp corners at nearly top speed. Hanging on the dash strap, bouncing in the double shoulder-strap belts, I was glad we had a roll bar.

We were interrupted by the glowing red sky of a nearby fire. Dad pointed without slowing and rushed to the scene of a blazing grain storage facility. The silos and elevators were fully engulfed, and Dad wasted no time assuming his news reporter persona. After a quick interview with the police and fire marshal, he was on the pay phone filing an Associated Press story and giving live coverage to his radio station. When Dad drank, he developed a slight British accent and a deeper, more resonating voice. Like a true professional, he never missed a beat, and I wondered if drinking improved his performance. (As children, we called him "Lord Johnny" when he drank, due to his changed accent and tone.)

As the crisis came to an end, Dad wandered back to the car, ready to go home. But first he put a hand on my shoulder and said, "Son, it's a nice car, fun to drive, but it doesn't have any guts." I admitted she could never beat a Detroit muscle car, but he had to admit it did well on tight, winding roads. "Dad," I pointed out, "you were taking those curves at well over eighty miles per hour." He seemed startled, and I finally realized he had been looking at the *tachometer*, not the speedometer, thinking the car was topped out at under fifty MPH while reading the tach near the five-thousand RPM red line. That was sobering, but, admittedly, he could drive. God, I miss that guy.

The testing phase did give us off-crew time as the gold crew exercised, so we were able to open the business during one such period. The family moved to the mobile home, a wretched form of living I swore my family would never experience again after our short rental experience in Key West many years before. But that was the plan, and we viewed it as temporary. The crew pitched in to save us a fortune by ripping out the interior walls, installing a couple of load-bearing beams, and patching the floor and ceiling. The kitchen remained for freezers, sinks, and stowage, and the bathroom served as one restroom. We had professionals build a second restroom and the counter. Furniture, grill, fryers, and ovens followed, and we were ready to open. To save money, we covered the unsightly interior walls with rolled bamboo sheets, an Asian motif, and applied for our license.

The plan was to obtain a beer and wine permit as soon as possible, but the state would not issue a permit unless the business had been established for at least ninety days. To show we were a restaurant and not a café or bar, we were licensed as the Bamboo Snack Bar but commonly referred to as the Bamboo Shack. It was a difficult three months with our major customers coming from the Baptist college. College kids neither have nor spend money, and we prepared for the loss. A pool table, juke box, and several pinball machines helped. Our beer and wine permit was issued, officially making us a café, as construction began for a huge General Electric turbine generator–manufacturing plant directly across the highway. The construction workers supplanted the college kids and the business took off, at least enough to end the losses. The area was growing, and we were on the ground floor.

The business actually started with a partner, my first-class radioman, Bill Wilkinson. Barbara and I felt it was best to develop profit from the unused land as soon as possible, even in temporary ventures. Wilkinson invested a small amount, about $1,000 to start for a small percentage of ownership. He envisioned something simple like a putt-putt golf course, which I did not favor. We eventually agreed upon a simple automobile storage lot, a new idea in the area. Single Polaris sailors treasured their precious cars and were animatedly against leaving them unprotected during their long patrols. The property was fenced, and we could store up to one hundred vehicles safely, although in the open, for a handsome monthly profit. All the owners asked was that we keep them safe, start the engine once a week, keep the battery charged, and have the car ready to drive away. We found a small used Airstream trailer to serve as an office and planned for a low-salaried local to operate the business, including free trailer accommodations. Wilkinson eventually dropped out of the partnership due to pressure from his wife, and I returned his money.

My brother Arthur arrived in Charleston during this period. At that time, he was a lieutenant aboard USS *Grenadier* (SS-525), a diesel electric submarine. When asked if he was interested in assuming Wilkinson's business investment, Arthur immediately contributed a couple thousand. My first *Bolivar* patrol was rapidly nearing and Arthur's boat would be in Charleston for a few months, so we agreed to explore the storage lot idea when I returned. We had just recently received our beer and wine permit, and Arthur's crew naturally took over the Bamboo Shack as their personal submarine bar. As I left for sea, the shack was generating profit, albeit small, but the situation would eventually create a tragedy that would play out over several years and spell doom for many.

There was little change in my fifth patrol, my first on *Bolivar*. We sailed from Charleston for a seventy-day cruise, going alert and ready to launch while still in the Atlantic and far from any possible Soviet opposition, thanks to our new, longer-range A-3 missiles. We cruised into the usual waters of the Mediterranean where our missiles could penetrate even farther into the hidden strategic bases deep in Siberia.

Barbara's famgrams were bland and lacking any real information, but at least I received all three. We surfaced off Charleston and cruised up the Cooper River to the ammunition dump pier where the gold crew and our families waited. Barbara was unemotional, quiet, and not very forthcoming with news. Her business was just breaking even, a situation that was still expected and easily afforded. I should have been ready for a rest, but I instead threw myself into the business as a real challenge. There was a long list of problems, from the heating and air conditioning to the customer parking lot, all normal growing pains. The children seemed unaffected by the change and even seemed to enjoy having their mom own a restaurant. They had their lunch at the counter, they drank from the soft drink dispenser, and they could snatch an occasional candy bar or bag of chips when no one was looking.

Grenadier and Arthur had returned to New London, leaving our construction workers and a few locals as customers. I was not particularly concerned, since the auto storage lot seemed potentially very profitable. Word of mouth inquiries on my boat and half a dozen others operating from our Polaris base generated far more interested customers than we could ever accommodate. Most did not realize they could cancel their liability insurance while their cars were parked and not in use, a savings that would more than pay for storage. The business needed only a little to start, just a battery charger and tire inflater. The most serious concern was the security measures, a way to keep out crooks. There were already a couple of locals fighting for the manager position. I contacted Arthur to discuss some security ideas, but he responded by saying he wanted to drop out of the agreement. This was the second time I had been left holding the bag, and I was livid, but I returned his money. Arthur would not say why he was backing out, but he implied it was pressure from Rita, his wife. I heard something more dire in Arthur's voice and would find out later that he had a more serious reason to withdraw.

Ruefully, I had agreed to a second patrol on *Simon Bolivar*. My detailer in Washington had fantastic shore billets, including Japan and Naples, Italy. Under normal circumstances, I would be packing up the family for a two- or three-year stint in Naples, but I prepared for sea instead. There was no foreseeable shore duty opening for me in Charleston.

The off-crew period flew by, and I knew my contribution to the business would be missed. As free labor, I helped keep us in the black. Barbara spent long hours at work, the norm for any mom-and-pop business, but her drinking increased precipitously. In hindsight, it was ludicrous for a potential (or actual) alcoholic to be engaged in the bar business. I was shocked to discover she kept a bottle of hard liquor behind the counter, a violation that would instantly cancel our beer and wine permit in that dry state and destroy her business. Unconcerned, she chain-smoked and drank cocktails while the customers drank beer. Worse, she usually had a paid employee behind the counter doing most of the work. One person could normally handle the business, and Barbara often had both a waitress covering the bar and a sitter watching the kids while she sat on her reserved bar stool and "managed." I sensed the first sign that she would not make it, more so after the loss of my skittish former partners. The auto storage lot did require some pavement, fencing, and security lights at a minimum, and my commitment to the café went beyond my ability to finance another business. Thus, the easiest and best income source was abandoned when it was needed the most.

I never felt prepared for my advancement examinations and I always worried that I had done badly. The warrant officer exam, however, seemed fairly easy, the standard officer battery examination, several parts long and taking most of a day to complete each section. I had not studied, and since

I found the test to be easy, I figured my assumption was wrong and I would fail. But my marks were excellent, and I proceeded to the next step where my marks and detailed application went before a formal officers' selection board in Washington. I was slowly being drawn into a program I really did not want to be part of, but it seemed too late to withdraw.

My second patrol on *Simon Bolivar*, my sixth overall, would end ten straight years of sea duty. I had submitted my shore duty request, asking for Charleston, Jacksonville, and Norfolk as my three choices. Each town was selected so that I could stay as close as possible to my family; I turned down several sweet stations where openings existed. This all became irrelevant, however, with the surprising news that I had been selected for promotion to warrant officer. The news brought mixed emotions. On one hand, I had achieved officer status from the ground up and been called a "mustang" in the navy, an accomplishment realized by less than 1 percent of enlisted men. With hard work, I had eclipsed most of my peers. But on the downside, I would move from the top of the enlisted ranks to the bottom of the officer ranks. As a warrant officer, I should make less money, but the law said that could not be, so I would continue to draw senior chief pay. My proficiency pay was gone forever and, of course, my submarine pay. Worse than the money, however, was to be surfaced—off submarines forever, where no jobs existed for warrant officers. And paradoxically, the chief who applied for the program the year before was not selected. It was that chief's wife who had encouraged Barbara, who in turn berated me to apply. I wondered what they did with the officer's sword.

My famgram situation on that final patrol was worse than ever with no mail received throughout the first two months of the cruise. My radiomen politely refrained from discussing the unusual absence as they compared the clever and slightly risqué love notes from home. Submariners are a close bunch who eat, sleep, work, and fight in a group. We shared everything, including our feelings and news from home. By my silence, everyone knew I had problems with Barbara. Then in our final ten days at sea, I received two nearly back-to-back famgrams but never the third. The messages were uninspired and furnished no information. It was as if she had awakened at the last minute and dashed off three quick notes. The navy received the third one too late to transmit.

Barbara was excited about my promotion, but otherwise gloomy. The café's business fluctuated in earnings but showed an overall slight loss. I dove in to help, but felt sure my off-crew period would be short. Barbara seemed locked into her pattern of being onsite but doing very little work. I thought of my Aunt Lina who owned the Victory Grill in Scranton and her nonstop work pace. My brother worked there as a kid, and we all learned young that you have to love the restaurant business, because to succeed, it must become your life. It was the calling for a workaholic, not an alcoholic.

Every officer had a detailer in Washington, a personnel specialist who assigned all the officers of a specific specialty. My designation was operations, and instead of waiting for a random set of orders, I drove to Washington to personally meet my detailer. It was a wasted trip. The submarine force commander needed four warrant officers qualified in communications, and I would be so assigned, regardless of my preference. On the upside, we were technically an afloat command, so I would qualify for submarine pay.

Barbara was sullen, but I reminded her that I would be more available than if she had opened a business in Maine. I did not ask if she was ready to back out of the business, and she did not suggest doing so. Selling the business would be easy and would probably return our investment with a profit. Leasing seemed easier and a way to retain ownership. As a last resort, just locking the door was an option since the mortgage at under a hundred dollars a month was an affordable payment on valuable property. I had been saving more than that each month in the past, and the real estate would appreciate faster than common stock. Just let it run its course, I thought, since we cannot lose.

We celebrated my transition to the officers' ranks over a fancy dinner at the Naval Station officers' club, an elegant but quiet venue frequented by those of high rank. Arthur had something to say, and I simply expected him to apologize for dropping out of the business. Finally, in a quiet corner of the bar, he pulled his mouth in at the corners, and with the distress of a condemned criminal, he told a sorry story about Barbara.

It was a weekend night at the Bamboo Shack, and *Grenadier*'s crew had taken over with an uproarious party. Barbara's stash of liquor was augmented by several bottles, which had been brought in by Arthur and others. The party continued until after closing hours, and with the outside lights off, the partiers escaped the scrutiny of any roving state ABC (Alcohol Beverage Control) inspectors. Arthur admitted to getting quite drunk, but his fellow officers had a designated driver for the old used car they had jointly bought for their stay in Charleston. When the party finally broke up, Barbara insisted that Arthur should sleep on the couch. That made no sense, since they had a sober driver to get him back to his submarine. But she, too, was stoned, so no one argued when she locked up and led Arthur to the mobile home. There was no haze; I could clearly see where this was going as Arthur continued in a tormented voice: "She just made a move on me and I was so drunk I just let it happen. Being drunk is no excuse, I just don't have any excuse."

My temper should have flared, but I had known that something was wrong for a long time, all the way back to Uncle Bill. I was angry with my brother, not for what he did to me, but for what he had done to himself. "So what do you want from me, Art, absolution?" I grumbled on. "Okay, you're forgiven." I started to add, "But don't expect me to forget," but Arthur was so relieved and pathetic that I stopped short.

"It gets worse," Arthur continued, as he complained that Barbara now telephoned frequently as though they had entered into some lovers' pact, asking when they could get together again. While Arthur considered it a one-time mistake, she saw it as a continuing relationship. Barbara also bragged about another lover, one of the amusement equipment men (who will remain mercifully unnamed). I assured Arthur that he was not the first (or even second once the amusement equipment operator was counted) and told him how she and Uncle Bill had been caught in flagrante delicto years earlier. "Christ, John, the whole family knows about Barbara and Uncle Bill," Arthur said. "Aunt Amelia divorced Bill right afterward and everyone wondered if you would do the same."

Every act of infidelity builds a wall. Whether one is caught or feeling guilty, it is better to confess, call it a stupid error, swear it will not happen again, and ask for forgiveness. It is always worse when the offended party finds out on his own. Perhaps I should have smacked Barbara in the face

or just divorced her after her first "stupid error." Before Arthur returned
to Connecticut, he asked what I planned to do.

"I'm already a class-B brown-bagger, Art. She can stay in South Carolina and I plan to get on with my life," I said. Arthur understood, a class-
B brown-bagger is a naval expression meaning a married sailor separated
from his family and acting single. The bigger question was what Arthur
would do. Shared sex creates an instant and mysterious link, like two con-
spirators with a criminal secret. Arthur needed to break that link. I pointed
out that Barbara and his wife, Rita, disliked one another, and someday
Barbara would tell Rita just to enjoy Rita's pain. I suggested he end his
problem by confessing his one-time mistake to Rita. We both agreed that
Rita was unforgiving by nature, and I could see he would foolishly hope
that his secret was safe.

I have always been one of those overly organized people who made
lists prior to any important decision. When I bought the sailboat, I used a
sheet with a line down the center, left side marked "pro" and the right
"con." The fun of sailing weighed against all the negatives, such as slip
rental, annual maintenance, trailer storage, sail repair, and replacement,
registration, insurance, and so on. In the quiet of my BOQ room, I wrote
out the most important list ever, titled "Options." Which path would I take
in my destroyed marriage? It looked something like this:

1. Divorce; try for child custody.
2. Divorce; forget custody, pay support.
3. Stay married, live apart, pay support, create a new life.
4. Resign from navy, grab the kids, take ARAMCO job in Saudi
   Arabia.
5. Resign navy, take ARAMCO job without kids.
6. Kill the bitch.
7. Do nothing, be a wimp.

The last two options were rejected immediately as unthinkable,
although I felt that Barbara did deserve at least one slap. The job as a
radio operator for the Arabian-American Oil Company (ARAMCO) in
Saudi Arabia was viable. I had taken a complex electronics correspon-
dence course a few years earlier, which led to my obtaining a second-

class FCC radio telegraph commercial license. ARAMCO was hiring, and the pay was very high due to the poor and isolated working conditions. Kidnapping the kids was a bad idea, even though the idea of saving Cynthia from hundreds of future beatings made it tempting. Quitting the navy, my life and my career, was also rejected.

An old navy proverb advises, "Never own more than you can fit in your seabag." I heard it many times in my teens as the old salts warned me about marriage and family, items that do not fit into a navy life. While I did not agree with the adage entirely, I knew for certain that after my failed marriage I would never start another family. Child custody awarded to the father was practically unknown in the 1960s, especially to a father facing sea duty, so such a fight would be futile. Further, the conventional wisdom at that time concerning custody taught that it was better for children to be raised in a single household rather than remain in an unloving marriage. The concept of "joint custody" had not yet been invented. Divorce became a moot point. Barbara would raise the children, and I would be obligated to pay regardless. Therefore, I chose option 3, stay married in name only, create a new life, support my family, and try to maintain a relationship with my kids. With luck, Barbara's business would succeed and she would remain in South Carolina forever.

The parallel between my father and me became obvious, now that I was faced with the choice of walking away from my family and starting a new life as he had done. But when I mentioned my brothers and Mom to my dad, I could tell by his pained, wounded expression that he still loved them. He was always anxious to hear about them, thankful for the small link I provided. Once I asked him if either of my brothers had ever contacted him since I had long before given both his address. They had not, so I asked him why he didn't just call them. "It's the children's responsibility to contact the parent," was his wistful reply. I thought of Dad's hopelessness and realized that I, too, faced a similar devouring gulf with my kids. They, too, would become strangers, and I wondered if years later I would wait for telephone calls that would never come.

The confrontation with Barbara would be done face to face on my next visit, the mere thought of which brought on a sense of foreboding similar to a heart seizure. That night on the mid-watch, I slipped into the lounge and television room for a vending machine sandwich and sat with a WAVES officer who worked next door. She was a watch officer at Ocean Systems Command, the operators of the secret SOSUS system, and we had been meeting during watch breaks for several weeks. A sun-washed blonde ensign with shining eyes, in her early twenties, she had been prodding me to take her sailing. She smiled with open delight when I agreed to pick her up that afternoon.

Chapter 9

THE NADIR

I was remarkably composed on my next trip to Charleston, even though I was faced with the dreaded confrontation. My feelings toward Barbara were strangely placid; I had no desire to punch her out or exact some revenge. It finally occurred to me that I felt nothing for her. We are told that the opposite of love is hate; even psychologists use a test of rapidly fired words in which one must sing out the antonym: hot-cold, up-down, love-hate. However, I feel that the opposite of love is not hate but rather indifference. When I saw Barbara for the first time, I did not hate her; I did not even know her, I was indifferent. Slowly, we had fallen in love, and now love had vanished, replaced by the original emotion, indifference.

My brother had not confessed his mistake to his wife, and I realized at the last minute that I could not reveal my knowledge to Barbara since she would know that Arthur was the source. If I did so, Barbara would waste no time informing Rita, destroying their marriage and punishing Arthur for revealing their secret. I did not owe this to Arthur, but I decided to give him time to muster the courage to save his marriage before it was too late. It was a wasted effort since Arthur never would tell Rita, thus allowing Barbara to later enjoy the final act of her drama by shattering Arthur's family and much, much worse.

It was past midnight when I arrived at the Bamboo Shack, which was still open with a few customers. The kids were asleep without a sitter, since Margaret, at ten, was considered mature enough to assume the duty. My plan was to accost Barbara in the morning when we were both more alert, but the thought of spending the night in anticipation drove me to the café's back door, where we waved hello and I drained a cup of old coffee from the urn. The last customer soon left, and as she locked the door, I announced, "We gotta talk," while waving her to a barstool.

It was not much of a fight. Like our confrontation years earlier, after my seven-month *Forrestal* cruise, she remained blank, unresponsive, and unemotional. She showed no response at learning that I knew of her tryst with Uncle Bill, pointing out that it was common knowledge among my entire family. Arthur was not mentioned, but I was able to name her local lover whom she had bragged about to Arthur, leaving the details of that knowledge a mystery to her. There was no name calling between us, my only belittling remarks involved her excessive drinking, chain-smoking, and abuse of the kids. She asked only one question. Did I want a divorce? I explained that a divorce was irrelevant and I would continue to support my family. She had her business, I had my career, and we should both pursue our own lives. If she wanted to remarry later, we would then divorce.

We slept separately that night, the norm for the future, and I left the following day after spending some time with the kids. My hope was that her business would succeed to the point that my financial burden would be eventually reduced to child support. That proved to be wishful thinking.

I have always thought about the world geopolitical situation and once, when asking myself what really made the world so dangerous, an idea germinated. What kept us on the brink of World War III for the past twenty years? To me it was obvious: a third world country with nuclear-tipped missiles, the USSR, was surrounded by a far more powerful enemy, the United States and NATO. If the USSR were ever cornered and genuinely expecting a preemptive strike by the United States, the real danger to the world was that a misread provocation or accident by the United States would trigger a nuclear response by the Soviets just to save themselves. The Glassboro Summit was a feeble attempt to prevent misinterpretations and panicked responses. The error was that the United States planned no such action. The earlier ravings to invade the Soviet Union by people like General Curtis LeMay were just that: ravings, not national policy. So how could this truth be revealed to the Soviet Union?

I did not have extensive training and experience in intelligence, but I knew that a one-time delivery of sensitive material to the other side was of no real value. Every intelligence agency is chiefly concerned with the reliability of its source and is constantly on the alert for faked and planted information. Intelligence agents frequently approach one another, pretending to have secrets for sale in an attempt to sow false information upon an enemy. This technique is most useful as a prelude to an attack by lulling the enemy into a false sense of security or luring their defenses away from the attack point. The Soviets, long expecting a US invasion, would be particularly cautious of such an old ruse. To be confirmed as a true and reliable agent, one must provide a quantity of verifiable material over a long period of time. And even if one important document could be validated, its usefulness would be short-lived and of limited value. A war plan today indicating no intended aggression could change tomorrow to one of invasion preparations; in a volatile world, plans may change quickly. No, a one-shot release of one or more classified documents would accomplish nothing, and the thought of a long-term career in espionage was overwhelming. I pushed the thought to the limbo of my mind.

My unofficial divorce offered little relief from the stress of marriage. Barbara carped at her workload, whined about money, and generally terrorized the kids. But while the visits home were often agonizing, Barbara and I could be oddly cordial, even to the point of enjoying activities with the kids. Still, even though money was her constant complaint, her bookkeeping declined to the point of chaos. Receipts and invoices were missing, making it impossible to produce a monthly profit-and-loss statement. Business seemed to run at a slight profit based on the daily receipts available, but she denied that this was the case. I suggested she relieve herself of the burden by leasing the business and staying on as a salaried manager. She fumed at the suggestion, probably because I did not suggest a rescue like moving her back to the old life and buying a house in Norfolk, but I had no intention of making that offer. Then her behavior became bizarre.

On my next visit, there were no indications of problems and Barbara seemed untroubled and normal. One morning I helped her set up for business as usual, but I noticed the cash register tray was missing. Only then did she announce that we had been robbed the night before. She had already taken the cash tray and paperwork home, but she returned to the café for some reason. Someone had grabbed the tray while she was away, she explained, resulting in the loss of a couple hundred dollars. Oddly, she told the story smugly, implying the dangers she faced bravely, attempting to make me feel guilty. In fact, I did feel guilty, subjecting my children to such dangers.

Later that day, while the kids and I played in the back acres, a twenty-dollar bill floated past, carried by the wind. Astonished, I went on to find more bills scattered far and wide, nearly one hundred dollars, most of it stuck to a fence. Either we had been robbed by the world's stupidest crook or Barbara had experienced one of her drunken outbursts. I chose the latter. The kids knew what happened but were scared nearly silent. Barbara had no comment, but I deduced she had tossed the tray and money into the windy field while cursing her absentee husband. She started referring to the café as "my" business, not hers or ours, as though she had never thought of it, as if the trip to Maine never happened.

A few weeks later, she telephoned me at work to explain that she had pawned her engagement ring and needed to pay the loan in two days or lose the ring. I wired her the money immediately, but the symbolism of her stunt was not lost on me. I could visualize a cheap tabloid article titled "Ten Ways to Win Back Your Estranged Husband." Item 1: See if he'll bail your engagement ring out of hock; save the ring, save the marriage. She tried that one twice.

My plan had been to move into a small apartment, for although the BOQ room was free, it had the amenities of a cheap motel: a single bed, small closet, tiny table and chair, and a sink. The common showers and toilets were down the hall. There was simply no space for important property, much less my uniforms and clothes. Most of my possessions were packed in a large wooden storage shed that came with the Charleston property. It contained all my professional books, some uniforms, tools, and a large amount of electronic gear and test equipment. Those irreplaceable mementos, photos, and souvenirs—those priceless, nostalgic trinkets from seven ships and countless foreign countries—were carefully stored in that shed.

Barbara burned it down.

Like the missing money story, Barbara seemed blasé, almost self-satisfied, but she offered no explanation. The kids again knew more than they would say and indeed were starting to look shell-shocked. They more than implied that Mom had burned down the shed, and it was then I realized she had won. Her actions were becoming more and more destructive; eventually she would hurt the children or herself. Her drinking was completely out of control to the point of blackouts. Find someone to lease the place, I told her, and I'll move the family to Norfolk.

Back in Norfolk, I wondered what I had done to myself. Did Barbara think that my moving the family to Norfolk would end our informal divorce? More stressed out than my usual exuberant work style would imply, I remained cool and unemotional, the normal behavior of a sub-mariner in times of tension. I was hiding my depression and after a bad day on the pistol range, I finally realized how far I had sunk. Pushing cleaning pads through the barrel of my .45 pistol in the quiet of my BOQ room, I had the strange urge to pop a round in my forehead. That incident may have finally snapped me out of my gloom. The divorce would remain in effect, and if I could not afford a separate apartment, the BOQ would do just fine. I would not be a slave to a broken marriage and if I needed a bit more cash for my pilot's license or a bigger boat, I would just work more hours at my part-time Yellow Cab job. Yeah. The spring returned to my step.

I started thinking again about the world situation vis-à-vis us against the Soviets. Do people actually follow a calling to become a spy? Do people plan a lawless career of pilfering material, picking locks, stealing lock combinations, sneaking around with fake IDs, running surveillance, tapping phones, meeting secret agents, and creeping to dead drops? From my extensive security training, which included espionage and counterespionage techniques, I had a good handle on spy operations. I also had access to the secret and confidential publication *Guide to Security Training*, which included a section on counterespionage and showed photos of actual operations and arrests. The public's perception of the business, gleaned from movies and fiction writers, I knew to be generally wrong. All those perfectly timed and complex plans, secret spy gadgets, and frequent murders come from the fertile mind of the screenwriter. One of the biggest myths concerns the enormous price paid for such services—millions of dollars for a single sheet of paper containing the "secret plan." In reality, two or three thousand a month is a more likely salary for a spy, and then only after a proven record of providing valid material and a measure of sustained performance.

One would think that physical security would offer the best protection of classified material, such as silent alarm systems and hidden cameras. Simple hidden trip switches that record the exact time vaults were opened could show illegal access. For more sensitive targets, such as the cryptographic room, cameras used in banks, either in plain sight or hidden, might be employed. But in actual practice, I never encountered either alarm or camera security in any cryptographic center during my twenty-one years of military service. In fact, the obvious lack of security led me to the private and amusing speculation that we exercised only the appearance of security since everything was compromised anyway—already leaked by the government or sold by spies. There is an entertaining story relating to Nikita Khrushchev's visit to the United States, which included a tour of Midwest farms. A wheat farmer spoke of the disastrous drought the year before and the poor crop yields, much to the surprise of Khrushchev. "It was no secret," the farmer pointed out, "it was in all the newspapers."

"That's the problem," Khrushchev replied. "If it had been a secret, I would have known about it."

In reality, physical security was excellent at preventing penetration from the outside, for example, a common burglar bent on stealing military secrets. But anyone familiar with business theft at any level, from manufacturing, shipping, wholesale, and retail, knows that the major source of theft is *internal*, by employees, not external, by burglars or shoplifters. Security experts estimate that as high as 90 percent of theft is internal. Oddly, physical security in the navy ignored the internal threat, where the real danger existed. After my arrest for espionage, I was quoted as saying that "K-Mart provided more security in protecting their toothpaste than the government provided in protecting their top secrets." That oft-repeated quote was not meant to be flippant but was based upon my broad experience with government and retail store security. Our accountability of classified messages was comparable to a bank in which the money was never counted and the bank never audited. Imagine a bank where the teller loses a hundred-dollar bill and is allowed to make a replacement Xerox copy. Yet that is how the message center worked— need another copy? Make one. Moreover, when the hundreds of messages were distributed to the various departments, their copiers ran what extras were needed. Top-secret messages and cryptographic material was inventoried and accounted for, but that material was also vulnerable.

There is a wide range of available security measures, such as paper that will not reproduce on a copy machine and paper with secret markings that can be traced to a source. I never saw such security practices used, which again casts doubt on the value of the material. Also, security systems were never tested for leaks to the public or the Soviets. One simple test is to plant a fake document of seemingly high importance and interest at a specific office. If it ends up in the newspaper or if the Soviets respond, the guilty party can be easily identified, a simple trick that was never tried.

The government's physical security system threatened little hazard for internal theft of any material by the officers, enlisted men, or civilians who worked with secrets. Security was so lacking, it discredited the material it purported to safeguard, reducing the system to a sham.

Overclassification then and now remains a major problem in maintaining security. I wish it were possible for every reader to have before him or her the one-year supply of secret messages that passed over my desk in 1967. For those who have never seen a military secret, the opportunity may seem an exciting adventure, but after the first few hundred, and with thousands more to go, one would not only learn very little but also would surely question *why* the information was secret. Most messages are mundane, unimportant events that would put a Soviet analyst to sleep, to say nothing of the reader. They consisted of minor maintenance problems: some ship movement that every wife and bar girl knew about for a year; endless dribble on exercises and training; and constant changes to everything, such as changing a few words in a training schedule that should never have been secret in the first place. I estimated that far more than half of our classified messages should have been unclassified, perhaps as high as 75 percent. Two years later, I was not surprised by a report on secrecy by the Defense Science Board that called for a 90 percent reduction in the amount of classified material and a complete declassification of information after one to five years. The recommendation was never adopted, and indeed, overclassification increased and continues even after the end of the cold war.

Such material, usually classified for political or bureaucratic reasons, has a long history of secrecy classification for notoriously frivolous reasons. Secrecy is second nature to bureaucrats as they resist sharing their information with the public or other agencies. They affix secret stamps by reflex or out of habit, and by adding thousands of unnecessary secrets to the system, they undermine accountability and damage national security.

A second area of overclassification abuse is political: secrecy imposed for purely political objectives where no threat to national security exists, such as hiding blunders and misconduct or avoiding embarrassment. Why are the details of President Kennedy's assassination classified? Why, when a high-level diplomat mispronounces a foreign name during an overseas address, was the speech classified secret? Why has the report on environmental damage by jet fuel and paint at the secret Groom Lake Air Force Base been declared a state secret? The Soviet Union did not care about any of these secrets, and as an ally of the United States in World War II, they already had the secret US invasion plans for Europe. These political secrets are classified to keep them from the American public.

Obviously there are secrets worth keeping, such as cryptographic and code information, weapon technology, and some war plans. Disclosure of such secrets could threaten the nation and require vigorous protection. But in instances where the most sensitive secrets were compromised, there have been no harmful consequences. For example, I learned that the Soviet Committee for State Security (KGB) had electronically intercepted the most highly classified messages from and to the US embassy in Moscow between 1952 and 1964. This brilliant operation conducted at the most dangerous period of the cold war caused little or no damage to US security. The United States was not invaded and did not collapse as a result. Similarly, while the United States intercepted for decades the private telephone conversations between Soviet officials as they rode around in their limos, the Soviet Union did not collapse as a result of those massive disclosures. Those who created and propagated the cold war were quick to point out that the damage would certainly be felt if war broke out, whereas disclosure of US secrets would give an advantage to the enemy. But that theory raises the larger question: What was the actual prospect of war with the Soviet Union? In my opinion, that prospect was zero, provided the United States did not start the war or threaten the Soviets into a protective response through some warlike provocation.

No doubt my "zero invasion prospect" assessment will cause resentment and confusion in many, particularly the cold warriors, but before slamming this book closed, let me issue a challenge. Demand the declassification of all classified documents—everything through the cold war. Those documents were bought and paid for by the American public, and if they no longer serve a valid national security interest, they should be available to those who own them—the taxpaying public. Then read those documents and make your own assessment, which I contend will be similar to mine. I would even suggest going a step further and finding the authors of the documents, particularly the CIA analysts, and taking them to task for the exaggeration, lies, and nonsense they wrote. Was it institutionalized, were they ordered, or were they just plain stupid?

Everyone sees the world through a different set of lenses, which are ground by our personal life experiences and knowledge. We thus develop our personal opinions and biases, and so it was for me in late 1967 as I contemplated doing something bizarre, dangerous, and very illegal. In my view, the federal government was given very little power under the Constitution; its most important task is to defend America from invasion. With a method available to increase their power, federal politicians steadily expanded the claim of impending dangers from various enemies, real or imaginary. The United States slowly became a "national security state" with the government and public always on high alert for hobgoblin attacks. Since no one ever invaded, the United States carried our defense to third world enemies by attacking them when the United States had a "legitimate national security interest."

Up from my desk, I took the first step toward the little top-secret safe on the wall of the online crypto-room, the first step of my eighteen-year journey. I knew not what the future would hold, only that my life would not be the romanticized version of Hollywood myth. My final thought was that if the United States could enter into a pact with the USSR granting license to kill third world people (the Glassboro Agreement), why shouldn't I enter into a pact with the USSR that might prevent *everyone* from being killed?

Chapter 10

THE SPY

Flashing back to my entry into the world of spies and my heart-thumping trip to the Soviet embassy, I thought about my feelings.

My high-speed drive from Washington to Norfolk may have set a record, but I was still two hours late for my midnight watch. The off-going warrant officer had been understanding, even though minor car problems had made me late a couple times on those long drives from Charleston. I owed him at least four hours and was scheduled for a full eight-hour shift later in the week, an arrangement he did not expect, but I insisted I would make it up to him. He left appeased, as my section chief snickered in the background at my lame excuse (submarine chiefs can get away with needling officers). Had I told the chief that the KGB had made me late for watch, he would have really howled.

Settling into my job, I should have suffered immense exhaustion from a very long day, but a lingering exultation kept me alert; I was almost enjoying the danger-excitement of surviving the evening. There remained a gnawing prospect of arrest, however. My exaggerated concept of FBI invincibility prevailed in those days, particularly within the counterespionage departments. Surely I was photographed entering the embassy, and their tracking and surveillance would have ensured that the lone KGB car did not escape into the night. Would I be arrested later? Was a search warrant being written at this very moment? The court-martial would reduce me to something below dog meat. Without question, the Soviet Union was our archenemy, hated with the same intensity the United States felt toward Germany and Japan during World War II. The propaganda against the "Reds" started before World War II, and while it took a brief hiatus during the war when the Allies needed the Soviet Union's help in defeating the Axis, the cold war propaganda started immediately after the surrender. By the mid-1960s, fear and loathing for the "Red Menace" was ingrained into the US psyche.

Wondering about the effectiveness and subtleties of propaganda, my mind wandered back to my usher days at the Roosevelt Theater and the movie *High Noon*.

We wore regal uniforms in those days, light blue and adorned with ornate gold sleeve designs like a banana republic admiral. Made up of a two-piece suit jacket with brass buttons and a white cardboard collar and dickey with a clip-on tie, the uniform was incredibly uncomfortable. As I leaned on the ticket-collecting machine watching the film for the fourth time, my dad walked in to join me at my lonely post; as an executive for the chain that owned the theater, Dad could do such things. The 1952 United Artists film was a commercial and critical success with an Oscar won by Gary Cooper and others. There are only a few Western "formula" formats, and I considered it a typical but excellent "town-tamer" film. Dad, an expert in propaganda, agreed with my assessment in overall form, but he challenged me to find the deeper message.

The film, now a classic, was simple enough in my sixteen-year-old mind. The sheriff of a small town, Gary Cooper, had just retired and married his Quaker wife, Grace Kelly. As the newlyweds prepared to leave town, they learned that the man who previously terrorized the town had been released from prison and would return on the noon train with his gang, seeking revenge against Cooper and the town. Cooper is unsuccessful in rallying the townsfolk to defend themselves; his deputy goes fishing. A meeting is called, and the frightened townsfolk vote not to fight the gangsters. The progressive little town would handle the problem peacefully, as Cooper reminded them that he was no longer sheriff. As the clock neared high noon, everyone urged Cooper to leave town, including his wife, but he chose to stay and fight, badge or not. Of course, he defeats the gang alone, helped only by his antigun, antiwar Quaker wife who shoots one of the bad guys in the back. Aside from the belittling anti-Quaker message, the deeper message was lost to me.

Had I been more politically astute, which would be highly unlikely for a youth my age, I would have seen *High Noon* as the embodiment and the aggrandizement of the American culture, the American psyche. And that was the courage of the independent American. The Westerner with a strong conscience who would stand up against the toughest odds for a principle. The principle here is the rugged individualism so prized by the new race of people called Americans.

Dad then explained the film was a right-wing allegory from a cold war prospective. Totalitarian Nazi fascism had been defeated in World War II, and now the new aggressive totalitarian communism was "returning" to threaten the United States. The democratic town meeting represented the failure of the general public and of the Truman administration to meet the communist threat. Basically, Dad saw it as Hollywood's caving in to McCarthyism, showing that a few public servants crusaded against the communists alone while a weak public worried more about domestic and economic progress. Knowledge of current events was important, for Senator McCarthy was at the peak of his communist witch hunt, while President Truman was under attack by the Republicans for being weak on communism.

Propaganda is cunning to the point of being subliminal, the message existing below the threshold of conscious awareness. I could see why Dad, like Ronald Reagan, was urged to join the military service and contribute by making these films for Hollywood, the premier vehicle of propaganda. After a twenty-year diet of thousands of books and films on the Red Menace, the public had long ago been persuaded that "the Russians are coming!" Propaganda embalms the mind. Once so conditioned, any military misadventure against communism could be justified to the general public in the name of national security. No matter how illegal, atrocious, or wacky a government operation, one can always find pious defenders among the public. To these people, I would become a pariah if caught. I also realized, somewhat ironically, that I had become a part of the very covert elements I complained about so angrily. I was now a secret agent.

Little work was getting done at my desk, so when the WAVES from down the hall phoned me to meet her in the TV lounge for a snack, I turned the watch over to the chief. The lieutenant had prepared an elaborate picnic fare in several Tupperware containers, perfect for a guy who had eaten nothing but a few scraps of highway junk food in the past eighteen hours. She was fishing for a boat ride later that day, but I had a twenty-four-hour watch to stand, a new experiment we warrant officers were trying when one of us went to sea. As we strolled along the empty halls back to our offices, she pouted, and I scheduled a cruise for later in the week.

Since no one can work effectively for twenty-four hours straight, we were permitted to sleep a few hours between midnight and 5 a.m. So I left the chief on watch and wandered across the hall to our makeshift bedroom in the office of our boss, the chief of staff for communications. A rollaway bed and sheets were stored in a small closet; one just unfolded the rig in the empty office and grabbed a couple hours if and when possible. The others normally laid on the mattress fully clothed, like firemen, ready to run in an emergency. I did it right, however, slipping on clean sheets, fluffing the pillow, and stripping down to my boxers. "Call me in two hours," I instructed the chief, "or if a war starts." Of course he had to call me in the event of war. I had the key that *started* the damn thing.

Barely dozing, the light of the hall flashed as someone quickly opened and shut the door. Was the chief screwing around or looking for something? "That you, Chief?" I called. No answer. "Just turn on the light," I growled. No answer, no light. Clothes rustled, then the sensually soft fragrance of Shalimar lightly touched the air. She silently slid under the sheet, wrapped an arm around my waist, and pressed a naked breast against my chest. A warm wave of breath brushed my neck. A perfect ending to a wild day. I had never been a fan of James Bond movies, finding them to be total Hollywood fantasy and sophomoric at best. But lying in the commander's office with a beautiful blonde in my arms just hours after a secret meeting with the KGB, I could not help thinking of 007.

Americans have an inordinate need to know the exact reason behind every crime. It is not enough that someone goes berserk and murders several people; there is a drive to know the reason as the news media digs ever deeper in the exhaustive search for "why." After my eventual arrest, I submitted to interviews with two writers and the reporters of three television news programs, but not once did anyone grab me by the collar and simply ask: "Why the hell did you do it?" The question was oddly skirted, nibbled at around the corners. Reporters focused on sensational questions, such as "How do you feel about your wife and daughter turning you in?" Endless streams of government experts, psychologists, neighbors, police officers, and friends were paraded across the screen, babbling their opinions of "why he did it." But the fundamental question was never asked of *me*, even by the Soviets.

The prosecutors and government always describe the motivation for crimes in the simplest and most demeaning terms possible. In my case, their general answer to the question was "greed" or a remark like "He sold out his country for the money." In fact, the money was the least important motivating factor, if it was a factor at all. One writer and friend, George P. Morse, asked me to write the foreword to his book *America Twice Betrayed*. Mr. Morse discussed the government's failure in building an effective system to safeguard the nation's secrets, and I agree with his premise. In the foreword, I briefly mention four reasons why one would resort to espionage, which were: Ideology, or allegiance to another country; Venom, or the disapproval of US policy; Money; and Ego, or the intellectual challenge to beat the system. The author delves into these categories in detail and includes other reasons such as coercion by foreign agents and lust, where one is enticed by sexual favors. I clearly stated in the foreword that my personal reasons had never been explained, and if they have not been gleaned by the readers in the foregoing chapters, they are expressed here for the first time ever.

If asked to list my reasons and evaluate them on a scale of one to ten, I would rate them as follows:

1. Bring about an improvement in US-Soviet relations with a view toward reducing the prospect of war. As long as the United States maintained a war footing and continued its saber rattling against the Soviets, no improvement in US-Soviet relations could be negotiated. Ten on the scale.
2. Disgust with US government deception, the cold war fraud, and covert misadventures. Black budgets and most covert actions are in violation of the Constitution and are illegal. Most of the government's classified material is made secret to hide illegal activity from the Congress and the American public. A nine or ten on the scale.
3. Adventure. At about eight on the scale, I will admit it was an adventure, although not at the level of Hollywood scriptwriters.

My private detective agency and European aircraft delivery service was far more adventurous. The Soviets did not recognize the adventure factor, however.

4. Psychological pressure. Had my marriage remained strong, I would never have dreamed of so irresponsible an action. I could have and should have simply walked away from my marriage, surrendered the kids to their mom, which was the norm back then, and enjoyed my naval career. In one respect, it was a matter of timing. My old life as husband and father had ended, and the espionage adventure became part of my new single life. This pressure rates about six on the scale.

5. Money. The lowest motivating factor, it rates about three on the scale. I knew espionage paid poorly and, were I inclined to get rich in crime, I would have chosen a career as a pilot-drug smuggler. As it was, I had no financial problems but certainly expected to be compensated for my services and expenses. In fact, the pay is so poor when weighed against the severity of the crime, money provides nearly no motivation at all.

At my initial meeting at the Soviet embassy, the KGB was interested in the type, quantity, and classification of the material I could supply. My access to material was so extensive, however, that they seemed somewhat overwhelmed, at a loss to ask for specific items. To simplify matters, I agreed to supply what I considered the most useful material and included a list of items available—a "shopping list," so to speak. A meeting with a KGB handler was scheduled for a couple weeks later, the date and time suggested by me and based upon my watch schedule. The list was easily prepared, and I began assembling the best material for my next meeting— the top-secret, crypto-keying material.

The KL-47 cipher machine—and the first keylist of which I compromised—was very similar to the German three-rotor Enigma. A six-rotor machine was later invented, and finally the US military settled on the KL-47 seven-rotor system, in which the rotors were selected from a box of ten and arranged in the machine in a particular order. The six-rotor machines would produce over one hundred million letters before it repeated the sequence.

The KL-47, with more rotors and other variables, would not repeat the sequence until beyond the quintillion mark. So, as with Enigma, a cryptologist who had the keylist for that day could decrypt all the enemy messages using that key, but no others. If the key for one day, say, June 6, was deduced through some compromise, the enemy could decrypt all messages for that day but not for the fifth or seventh or any other day. Further, there are dozens of different keylists, even hundreds, and the compromised key would work for only those messages ciphered in that key. By having one keylist, one has not "broken the code" of an entire cryptographic system.

In my case, I had compromised a KL-47 keylist for the entire month of November 1967. All messages transmitted in that key could be decrypted by the Soviets, although the KL-47 and the key were very narrowly held and rarely used. Messages encrypted by the KL-47 were called "off-line," since the cipher was performed separately; they were then placed on the line. The KL-47 was a World War II relic, mostly a backup system by the 1960s, long replaced by "on-line" equipment. On-line is encrypted and transmitted automatically at the speed of light.

Modern on-line equipment is not as complicated as most people imagine, and in fact, the simplicity of the transmitted signal leaves the crypto-analyst little to work with. The US military's first on-line machine was the KW-37 system, a vacuum-tube device about the size of a large microwave oven that was introduced in the early 1960s. The keylist consisted of a single hole-punched IBM-like card that was inserted into a card reader. The keylist was good for twenty-four hours, with each card date-stamped. It was a one-way system with the KSW-37 (transmitter) ashore and KWR-37 (receiver) at sea. At precisely the start of the crypto-day, say, exactly midnight, the man ashore and all the radiomen at sea would simultaneously mash their start buttons. Everyone's pseudo-random "cipher chains" would all start for the day in perfect unison. If the enemy or anyone with a receiver and teletype machine tried to print the radio signal, only a garbled string of letters would appear. At sea, the crypto-equipped teletype printers would remain idle, smart enough to ignore the cipher chain. When it was necessary to send a message to one of the ships, a radioman would punch a teletype tape of the secret message and place it on a tape reader. The plain-text message would first go through the KWR-37, however, where the plain text would be combined with the cipher chain. Assume the first letter of the message was "A," in teletype code, 11000. The "A" is combined with the cipher chain transmitting random bits, perhaps 10010. The two digital signals meet at the logic circuit, similar to the one used in a commercial system called XOR Vernam cipher, which is:

Logic Circuit
0 and 0 = 1
0 and 1 = 0
1 and 0 = 0
1 and 1 = 1

The logic circuit uses simple algebraic multiplication where the "A" would change into 10101 or into an "R." On the ship, the 10101 would combine in the KWR-37 with the cipher chain of 10010 and automatically print 11000, or an "A."

Letter "A" = 11000
Cipher chain = 10010
Encrypted letter = 10101 or "R"

Letter "R" = 10101
Cipher chain = 10010
Decrypted letter = 11000 or back to "A"

The enemy would still receive an "R," but even worse, the enemy would never know when a message was ever sent or if the transmitter was just in idle. There is simply nothing for the crypto-analyst to attack. And while "A" may become "R" in this case, the long cipher chain would randomly change the next "A" to some other letter or number.

The reader should understand that equipment security is the least important aspect of a crypto-system. Much is said about the algorithm of a system, that it is the pseudorandom cipher chain building and logic circuits—although that is not the heart of a cryptographic system either. What is needed to decrypt a message is the keylist. Think of the equipment as simple dumb hardware and the keylist as its software. The hardware can be vigorously copied, stolen, removed from downed aircraft, or captured in battle. It is the keylist software, however, that makes it work, and without it, the enemy has nothing. The commercially available XOR cipher uses a 512-byte key where all the work goes into generating an unpredictable cipher chain. The XOR is unbreakable, for like any cryptosystem with a long and random cipher chain, it is impossible to decrypt without the keylist.

Electronics have gone through at least four generations, starting with the vacuum tube. Tubes are delicate, consume great power, and burn out routinely, like lightbulbs. The KW-37 used such technology with hundreds of subminiature tubes. (The Soviet Union never seriously moved past the first generation, and indeed, today Russia is the world's only manufacturer of vacuum tubes.) Second-generation, called solid-state electronics, used the transistor; smaller, less fragile, they are about the size of a pencil eraser. This technology was used in the second-most important on-line crypto-device, the KW-7. This device is about one-third the size of the KW-37, and with hundreds of transistors, it can both send and receive crypto-messages between ships, shore, and aircraft.

To put these crypto-computers into perspective with the present, electronics have passed the third generation of integrated circuits in which thousands of transistors could be placed on a circuit board. The fourth and current generation uses tiny silicon chips with millions of transistors in each one. The world's first computer, called ENIAC, for Electronic Numerical Integrator and Computer, was built in 1946. While it weighed thirty tons, used eighteen thousand vacuum tubes, and filled a room thirty by fifty feet, ENIAC could be replaced today by a fingernail-size silicon chip. Today's crypto-devices are easily the size of a laptop or palm-size computer.

The KW-7 (now probably retired) was transistorized and set up in the daily key by inserting about fifty dangling plugs on its face into an equal number of jacks. The operator followed the sequence, something like: "A-23," which directed wire "A" into jack "23." The complete keylists for each month were on two sheets with each two-by-four-inch daily key torn off along perforations.

I did not agree to spy for the Soviet Union with the intention of playing a game of deception, eking out a few old documents while stringing them along for maximum income. My intention was to allow them to read the military strategy of the United States, to understand with total certainty that our country had no plan to invade the USSR. They would be given the best top secrets, the cryptographic ones.

I focused on the keylist for the KW-7 and KW-37 on-line systems and the old KL-47 mechanical off-line machine. The KW-37 keylists would allow the Soviets to decrypt the submarine broadcast to all Atlantic fleet boats, less the spook boats on special operations. About six or eight land-line circuits to our facilities in Europe, Africa, and the United States were covered by the KW-7, and if the Soviets could tap these lines, they could read that traffic as well. Two or three KL-47 keylists, one month on single sheets, were rarely used but contained important special category information. As best as I can recall, I copied some used material for November and December, plus a few random days of future material for December.

Accountability of the crypto-material was fairly simple, and since each system's keylist was packaged for an entire month, it was issued to the watch a couple days before the start of the new month. At that time, the registered publications officer would gather the new material from his walk-in vault and have the current watch officer sign a receipt for the new month's issue. This mass of about a dozen IBM-card packets and an equal number of keylist sheets were placed in a small wall-mounted safe for the operator's use. Several watch standers had access to the small safe, while I had access to even more, including the walk-in vault. Making copies was not complicated.

The new crypto-day started at exactly midnight Greenwich Mean Time (GMT), when every circuit in the world went dead a few minutes before midnight as operators jammed new key cards into readers or rushed to arrange the new plugs into proper order. The old cards and little tear-out sheets were returned to the same small safe, to be destroyed later. It was a simple matter for me to copy the old material on the Xerox machine. Normally I would simply carry an empty file folder to the safe, slip the cards or keylists inside, and carry them to the copier during slow periods. The cards were in a tear-out packet, much like a pad of paper with a glued strip along the top. The old cards were stuck back in the packet in order, and I would just slip three at a time into a clear document protector to copy all at once. The unused cards became stuck fast, and since removing them might have been noticed, they were usually avoided.

I viewed my first real delivery as a sample of my access, so it included several pages of the equipment manuals and a few pages of our operations orders and war plans. The crypto-equipment maintenance manuals consisted of the complete electronics construction of the equipment, and a complete manual in the hands of any technician would be enough to build an exact copy. I did not consider the dumb equipment to be an important item, which turned out to be true.

As I assembled the material, I had but one concern: compromising the future crypto-keys. Every government intercepts, tape-records, and stores away every shred of the cipher communications to and from prospective enemies. Even if there is no chance of decrypting these messages at the time, there is always the hope that the old key will be found someday and reveal some old stored-away secret. Perhaps like Enigma, some human error in encryption could be exploited. Regardless, the United States, the USSR, and nearly every other country files away tons of encrypted messages on tape, filling massive warehouses. I had no problem with the Soviets joyfully reading our old messages for November, but revealing our future keys was a different matter. With future keys, the Soviets could start their equipment at midnight like everyone else and decrypt our secret messages as they were sent. In spy talk, that is called "real time" intelligence. I wanted the Soviets to read about our benign and nonaggressive operations after they occurred but did not want them on the scene before they happened. While I still felt completely confident that war with the Soviet Union had a prospect of nearly zero, I did not want them to have advanced information about the exact time and place of our operations and plans. The main vault had the keys for at least two months in the future, and while breaking the seals, copying, and resealing was dangerous but technically possible, I viewed that material as off-limits.

Gathering the material was probably the easiest part. A copy machine jam—a partially copied top-secret keylist ground up in the gears—was the worst potential risk. I did experience jams a few times over the years but quickly cleared them myself before a helpful subordinate pulled and recognized the illegal copy from the mechanical maze. The second-most serious potential hazard would be the discovery of a missing keylist page or book of cards in my temporary possession, but I could easily talk my way out of that with the explanation of a legitimate inventory or page check. That never happened anyway. Storage of the purloined documents presented the most serious obstacle.

Since copying any keylist or card is forbidden, those copies had to be kept out of sight and necessarily removed from the message center immediately. While I was never searched leaving the building, that disastrous prospect always loomed, so I devised a simple trick to make the removal seem legal. I had been designated as an Armed Forces courier years earlier when promoted to chief and had been redesignated regularly. Why not wrap the stolen documents to look like a normal courier delivery?

Courier material is enveloped like a normal letter with from and to addresses but stamped to show the classification of its contents, normally top secret. It is then placed into an outer envelope, addressed, but not classification-stamped. Finally the whole mess is carefully sealed with nylon-reinforced tape. The courier carries a simple five-by-eight-inch authorization card, a copy of which is held on the sending and receiving end. Normally I would address the package from COMSUBLANT to my old Beach Jumper unit at the Amphibious Base across town. Since I always assembled the material during the midnight watch, my departure after 6 a.m. seemed perfectly normal for a courier delivery. The only item missing was my sidearm. So, package and courier card tossed conspicuously into my cheap government-issued attaché case, I marched confidently out of the most secure building of the compound, directly to my BOQ room a couple hundred feet away, and to bed. The courier package and authorization card could be checked, but the card was perfectly legal. If the faked originator of the package was asked to confirm the delivery, I would have been caught. But I had never been so challenged in the past while on actual courier deliveries and knew of no other such security checks. As it was, my fake courier packages were never challenged, and indeed, my attaché case or person was never inspected. Eventually, I just jammed the top-secret crypto-copies into a pocket and carried them out.

All of the illegal copies were carried to my room and hidden as soon as possible. No exotic tricks were used and, following the principle of Keep it simple, stupid, they were just stuffed into the inner pocket of some obscure uniform hanging in the closet. If the security force never searched individuals leaving the Operational Control Center, they would never dream of searching the rooms of the BOQ.

A part of all deliveries included important secret messages that crossed my desk. As watch officer, I received a personal copy of every incoming and outgoing message from the command. These were screened for routing and content and then tossed into a burn bag for later destruction. So it was a simple matter to keep the important copies as part of my delivery. They were kept in my personal drawer under some arcane label, hidden in plain sight, lost in the avalanche of secret messages. Making a personal copy of top-secret messages invited no danger, and the copies were carried out daily to be stored in my room.

It was time for my delivery and meeting, and like any impending danger, the few weeks since my embassy visit seemed to fly. The long weekend scheduled for the trip was upon me, and I finally realized that the FBI would have never arrested me before now. They would wait to arrest me during my next spy meeting. Heavy surveillance would be established, and I would be arrested in the act, the foreign agent also captured to embarrass the Soviets. This realization made for an uncomfortable evening as I prepared for the trip. First, how to carry the documents to avoid suspicion? Drugs were becoming an ever-increasing problem, and with drug couriers routinely moving north on I-95 from Florida, any package was suspect. My delivery consisted of about three inches of standard-size paper, mostly junk secret dispatches mixed with the truly valuable and fewer cryptographic keys. Adhering to KISS, I placed them in an empty bond paper box as writers do and marked it "manuscript." One would have to carefully inspect the sheets to realize that the top secrets, crypto-material, and secret markings indicated something more than a simple manuscript.

The second problem was surveillance. How could I determine if I was being followed? All I knew about detecting a tail came from Hollywood, and I was one of the few who realized that everything I learned from that medium was wrong. No, I would be forced to use guile and common sense. Driving my own car was out of the question, since it would by then be equipped with an elaborate tracking device. A rental car would foil that trick, so I decided it would be safest to fly to Washington, rent a car there, and stay off the phone. Advance reservations were impossible since telephone taps are probably the best source of FBI intelligence.

The next afternoon, the delivery day, I casually drove off the compound. It was a Sunday, and since the government seems to shut down on weekends, the base was a ghost town. There were no signs of surveillance or tailing vehicles, but would they be so obvious? Making a few unnecessary turns, I drove to Norfolk International Airport and parked at the Piedmont General Aviation Terminal, where I had started my flying lessons in earnest. Still I seemed to be alone. With overnight bag and manuscript box in hand, I strolled among the parked aircraft and finally slithered along the tie-down area and taxiway to the smaller general aviation service, Cavalier Flyers. Having gone between the flying services from *inside* the gate, I was sure I had not been followed.

Cavalier Flyers was a Cessna dealer, air taxi, and student training service. Years later, I would fly air taxi for that very company and form a small European aircraft delivery business with the current owner's son, Carl Baker. But before that day, I had never set foot in Cavalier. Inside, I explained an urgent need to attend a funeral in Washington, and since flight instructors always seem to be in abundance "hangar flying" with one another, I was soon in the air, the lone passenger of a small four-seat Cessna. Using an assumed name and paying a couple hundred in cash, I felt I had escaped any counterespionage teams. A couple hours later, with a thump and a squeal of rubber, we touched down at Washington National, and soon a smiling girl handed me a car rental agreement and keys. The District of Columbia was much less dangerous in 1967, and one could still land small aircraft at Washington National, rent a car without reservations, encounter far less traffic, and drive around without getting shot.

I then made a stupid mistake. Convinced I was clean, my concern turned to my contact, the KGB agent posing as an embassy employee but probably well known to the FBI. Would he be followed to the meeting? I had received no instructions for handling the delivery material and would never carry it into an FBI trap. It had to be hidden until after the meeting proved safe. I shoved the manuscript box into a twenty-five-cent airport locker and drove my bug-free rental to the meeting. Behind, a mass of cryptographic top secrets sat protected by a two-bit lock.

The meeting was to take place at a Zayres store somewhere around

Falls Church near the Lee Highway or Arlington Pike. I peeked a look at the store before the sun went down; it was a discount pharmacy chain expanded to sell everything. It occupied a corner in a quiet residential outback, a few miles from the mix of Washington's stately buildings, disfigured slums, national shrines, and urban squalor. I was still inside the Beltway, that loop of I-95 and I-495 that girdles the District, home to thousands of organizations and businesses that live off government contracts.

I killed time by watching kids play soccer at a local park and over a slow dinner. A few minutes before the 9 p.m. meeting, I parked on the residential street and walked the last block into the brisk, invigorating air, certain I had not been followed. A *Time* magazine folded in my hand as identification, I entered the nearly empty business and wandered the spacious aisles picking out a few random items. Within ten minutes, a well-dressed and totally nondescript gentleman passed nearby and, using my code name, James Harper, he asked me to pay for my purchases and follow him outside.

Once outside, we walked in silence into the neighborhood of sidewalks and manicured lawns. The agent finally spoke, asking about my safety, the security situation at work and en route, or any signs of surveillance. I answered negatively, that conditions were normal. The question of safety put to rest, the agent asked what I had brought. My description was detailed, and when he asked for the material, I explained it was safely stored nearby.

The agent's face dropped and then twisted into an expression of disbelief and frustration. It suddenly occurred to me that I would be viewed as either a nut case or an FBI plant if I failed to deliver the goods on the spot. I quickly explained that I had been given no instructions on handling the material and thought it best not to carry it to the meeting until our safety was ensured. When I told him where the package was stored, his tension rose a few more percentage points. "You can't ever store material in rental boxes," the agent nearly moaned with an edge of desperation in his voice. "The authorities constantly open and check those boxes." Of course, I thought: something stupid I had learned in the movies.

The return trip to the airport did not take long on a Sunday night, and in the light traffic of almost forty years ago, and I was soon back at Zayres where the agent patiently waited for my return. The box was as I left it, and he presented me with a package of cash in exchange, my payment arrangement of a thousand dollars a week having been accepted.

The most important part of our meeting was the response to my shopping list when it was carefully explained in relation to my difficulty or ease of success. I considered lying about the reserve or future crypto-keying material but decided to be honest even though I generally objected to furnishing it. The reserve key cards were sealed much like a package of cigarettes in cellophane. To open the package and reseal it without creating suspicion was possible. The old, mechanical KL-47 keylist sheet was sealed in the envelope. The KW-7 keylist sheets were not sealed at all. Much to my relief and surprise, I was advised to avoid the reserve material, play it safe, and concentrate only on the old. Also surprising were my instructions to avoid a major system called AUTODIN, a world-wide network linking the entire military establishment on telephone company–leased wires. The equipment, the KC-13, did cut the key card in two when it was placed in the card reader and the two halves were stapled together and placed in the small safe after use. Pulling the staple to copy and restapling in the same holes was not that difficult, but I shunned that system entirely. I was flatly told not to copy the maintenance manuals, confirming my suspicion that they had long ago been compromised, although they had been useless to the Soviets before now without the keying material.

The Soviets clearly did not want every classified item possible, and in some cases, that made perfect sense. One area of top-secret material that we guarded so closely, the Emergency Action (war) Message System, was of no concern. All the war messages and authentication codes that follow the president and provide the reason for the existence of our war room were of no value. From the Soviet perspective, the Emergency Action Message System was for retaliation against the USSR for an attack on the United States, and since the Soviets planned no such attack, knowledge of that system was superfluous.

The final items discussed were the various codes, one-time pads, numerical codes, and authenticators. These systems troubled me because they were mostly used in tactical engagements such as air strikes and patrol instructions. These codes offered less security and were less valu-able, so it may seem silly to the reader that I worried about low-level codes after giving away the cryptographic crown jewels, but I had marine and navy friends in Vietnam who used those codes when operating in the bush and river patrols. So while I wanted the Soviets to read our long-range strategic plans, I inwardly objected to their having any current or future codes. Like the reserve crypto-cipher keys that would give them real-time intelligence, I could not know with whom they might share these codes—perhaps the North Vietnamese. The Soviets had no interest in those systems whatsoever, and I wondered if the KGB agent heard my long exhalation of relief.

We then reached the final phase of the meeting, the plan for our next and future exchanges. From then on, we would use elaborate and much safer "dead drops," the next to take place in about a month. The agent explained that face-to-face meetings were far too dangerous as he handed me a thick envelope containing "the procedure," as it was called. I was always to pick the date for the drops while the Soviets supplied procedure containing the times and all other details. We briefly flipped through the clearly highlighted maps, handwritten driving instructions, and at least twenty photographs of each drop site and checkpoint. The instructions were clear, and with no further questions, the agent gave his final advice: "Do not let your wife learn of your cooperation."

Fat chance, I thought, without replying.

Then came the final surprise. At my planned drop some four weeks hence, I would be setting the date of the next drop, and it was to be some six months later. We obviously could not set the date then due to my rotation days off, but he gave me a time frame for the primary date and a couple alternates.

We separated with a warm handshake and wishes for good luck. As we walked our separate ways into the night, I realized that I might never again see or meet the agents in our future dealings on the dark side.

I had made reservations for a late commercial return flight to Norfolk under an alias, and as I jetted south, I had much to contemplate regarding this strange world I had entered.

First, the spy exchange procedure was to take place only twice a year. This stunning time interval between the deliveries of top-secret cryptographic material seemed unbelievable. *Amazing*, I thought, *they're going to pay me fifty-two thousand a year for two days' work.*

I had always been told, and firmly agreed, that these keylists were near the top of America's most vital secrets. From the Soviets' reactions, I felt certain that there was no other supplier of most of this material. Yet they seemed satisfied to decrypt our intercepted transmissions as many as six months late. Surely I was capable of more-frequent drops, perhaps every sixty days, and I had expected a demand for monthly drops. Further, if my material was as valuable as advertised, should not the Soviets arrange for much more-frequent drops in Norfolk through another agent? Under this schedule, each delivery would contain keylists at least a few days old and up to six months old. My fear of a Soviet demand for reserve keying material was totally unfounded, since they seemed perfectly happy with six-month-old decrypts and did not care at all for real-time intercepts. Why would they settle for such old material and infrequent deliveries? What did this tell me about Soviet military doctrine?

I could conclude only that I had been right all along. Any nation planning an attack against the United States would want the most current military information available. Determining the enemy's weak points through troop levels, deployments, and defense structure were vital in planning an invasion. Reading six-month-old secret US messages was no way to assess the current US defense structure. No, the Soviets were content to glean US aggressive policies, which could be deduced through older material. There would be no invasion by the Soviets, and interestingly, if such a Soviet invasion of the United States were anticipated, I might be one of the first outsiders to know. They would need more current intelligence, and that would probably create a greater demand upon me for reserve material and more-frequent deliveries.

The Soviets' satisfaction with old material, combined with the complete lack of interest in tactical codes, also confirmed they were not sharing the tactical intelligence with the North Vietnamese and other communist states. Reserve crypto-material could reveal tactical troop and ship movements, and the codes could disclose battle communications. But the Soviets wanted neither the reserve crypto-codes nor tactical codes, verifying the Soviets' low level of cooperation with petty communist states. They may send arms to North Vietnam and other client states, but not their high-level intelligence.

I was also right about the crypto-equipment maintenance manuals, which contained the complete plans to reproduce the equipment. The Soviets simply did not want these plans, so the equipment was obviously compromised, sitting somewhere in Moscow, waiting for the crypto-graphic "software" keylists to make them work.

As my flight started its late-night descent into Norfolk, I felt a twinge of guilt. Who the hell was I to conduct a one-man think tank on US-Soviet relations? How could I presume to know more than the thousands of highly educated politicians, diplomats, and government employees who dealt with this problem daily? Were they all wrong while I was right? Per-haps I *was* wrong, but I knew without question that those in power inside the Beltway were definitely wrong.

There was one thing I had learned. The government did not work. One government program after another had failed miserably, but rather than eliminate them, they were "fixed" over and over again with more money as they grew ever larger. Prior to World War II, President Roo-sevelt's New Deal was a colossal flop as unemployment remained at an alarming 17 percent. Then a ghastly new government program was intro-duced: war. And like all government programs, America's intervention in that European war seemed to work. Industrial production rose dramati-cally, and after World War II ended, US unemployment was near zero. Then, like any seemingly successful program, the politicians, industrial-ists, and generals decided to perpetuate what seemed to work. Maintain the "gunfighter nation" mentality and keep the United States in a state of continuous war.

After eleven years as a government employee, I knew that govern-ment intervention never solved problems, be they domestic or military. Government just makes problems worse. The job of the Defense Depart-ment and military should be to keep us *out* of war, not endanger and kill American citizens by perpetuating a state of nearly continuous warfare. Most defense treaties and pacts actually make our lives more dangerous by forcing our youth into foreign conflicts in the defense of some treaty partner. If the United States is not threatened, why should we intervene in any foreign conflict? Would our weak and distant treaty partner send its youth to America if we were threatened? I think not. The military's job should be to keep the peace. But the military is a government program that must justify its existence and continue to grow like every other government program. While the United States has no legal, moral, or defensive reason to seek out and take sides in the world's trouble spots, it continues to grow by exaggerating the danger to the United States and creating endless conflicts.

American shores have not been threatened since the War of 1812, when the British burned Washington, but still our troops are stationed around the world. The most dramatic change in foreign policy occurred in 1917 when the United States entered World War I, forever abandoning America's neutrality. That war was of no concern to the United States, and since then, all foreign conflicts are declared to be of vital US interest. The United States entered two world wars to "make the world safe for democracy" and failed on both occasions. The US military has been highly successful in performing its mission, however, since its purpose is to kill people and break things. The government in general cannot solve domestic problems, and likewise, the military cannot solve foreign problems.

Still, I could not shake the dread of having made a tragic mistake. As the lights of Norfolk drifted below, I slumped with morose musings. What if my actions did not bring about any noticeable improvement in US-Soviet relations? What if I was wrong? What if everything became much, much worse?

Chapter 11

WOULD THE WORLD CHANGE?

The complications I had imposed upon my new single life left me unprepared for Barbara's return. She had quickly found a lessee, not a difficult task: it was her lover from the amusement machine company. It was common for these companies to lease or buy marginal bars and restaurants to ensure spots for their equipment. The constant search for businesses among the competing amusement companies often resulted in gangsterlike turf battles between competitors, so Southern Amusements of Walterboro was quick to gobble up the Bamboo Shack, guaranteeing their territory.

Leasing had been my first option, so I was grateful. In my heart, I could never sell the property, and had we left the building abandoned, it would soon have been destroyed. The payments on the entire property were about $95 a month, and Southern Amusements was quick to lease for a mere $150. The mobile home payments were even less, and they agreed to rent it for about $100 more. They had already located a sub-lessee to assume the entire package, and the business would change hands without closing for even a day. This arrangement would continue for almost twenty years with the lease rate increasing only slightly and remaining ridiculously low. I could never complain, however, since monthly profit and the overall appreciation of the real estate would yield a greater profit than the stock I had sold in the first place.

The real problem was how Barbara would complicate my life, a life with one foot in a burned-out marriage and the other in the semi-single life, navy career, emerging flying career, and—oh, yeah, my part-time job as a spy. I most definitely did not need this burden, but my kids were looking so pathetic; they resembled trailer-park trash. They needed normal living conditions and decent schools. Barbara would be satisfied to drink vodka and watch television all day, so my hope was to keep one foot in each world and try not to go crazy in the process.

The Algonquin House was a lavish apartment building about a mile from the gate of my workplace. Located on the branch of the Lafayette River and complete with a uniformed doorman, its luxury, space, and graciousness was the exact opposite of a trailer on South Carolina Route 78. The navy still owed us a free move and also travel expenses. We were soon settled into our elegant four-bedroom apartment off a warm, carpeted hallway that resembled a five-star hotel. The rent was a bit high, but my intention was to limit my tour to two years, so we would be moving again in slightly more than a year. I owed this small piece of luxury and class to my family. The apartment was equipped with a small private marina, and I bought a Sunfish sailboat for the kids. I did not give up my BOQ room, however.

Oddly, I spent much more time with the family than expected, usually joining them for dinner and even sleeping over. We continued to enjoy family activities together, with Barbara even occasionally slipping out of her doleful moods. Sex remained out of the question, as it had for about a year. Barbara soon found a lover down the hall, however, which concerned me not at all. She had taken to drinking straight vodka in full-sized tumblers, which I stupidly thought was water for many months. While she slipped deeper into alcoholism, I cut further back and vowed never to drink to excess or become drunk.

My other life remained very active as I completed my private pilot course and started on my commercial license on the GI Bill. I hoped to trade up to a bigger sailboat. A couple WAVES officers and a college coed more than adequately filled my social life, and it seemed my peculiar triple life of bachelor, husband, and secret agent might just work. Barbara did notice the extra money, but I explained it was income from my Yellow Cab job, which I had not given up entirely. She seemed suspicious, and I thought back to that good advice from the KGB. It was a mistake not leaving them in South Carolina, but I was too weak to put my kids through that life, perhaps too weak to make it as a spy. One must possess a certain level of ruthlessness to succeed in crime and have the ability to do what it takes to avoid detection. But I lacked the ruthlessness to abandon my kids to an alcoholic mom and a life stuck in a trailer behind a juke joint.

My first dead drop was smooth and uneventful, and compared to the world of fiction writers, rather unexciting. The fear of arrest still produced that haunting uneasiness, but I was becoming more convinced that I had won, that I had somehow never been remotely detected.

The dead drop procedure had been prepared in excruciating detail to avoid any chance of error. In fact, the procedure was described in three different ways: a narrative description; a series of hand-drawn maps and carefully cut local maps, all marked with arrows and times; and a dozen or more photographs, painstakingly marked with hand-drawn maps on the back of each. Any of the three instructions would be adequate to follow the procedure.

My contact was surely an employee of the Soviet embassy and therefore had diplomatic immunity from arrest or prosecution under US law. As a Soviet official, his car would bear a distinctive diplomatic license plate, clearly identifying his Soviet citizenship to all police, and he would be required to remain within a certain radius of Washington—twenty miles, I believe. All of my drops, which numbered over twenty-five, took place near the edge of their limit and in the most remote, unpopulated areas possible. Most were near Fairfax and Vienna, Virginia, but they were also done in Maryland around Wheaton and east of Washington beyond Andrews Air Force Base.

The key to the procedure was that the agents would never meet during the drop and would probably never get closer than five miles from each other. This obvious safety factor would probably protect one agent if the other had been followed. The entire route was traveled by automobile and took about three hours to complete. But since the route had to be driven at least once in advance to spot the drop and signal points, it made for a long night.

The drop was scheduled for a Saturday night, and I casually drove to Dulles Airport where I picked up a rental car. Certain I had not been followed from Norfolk, I was even more confident that no one could have stuck with me after my complex moves through the airport.

My first drop signal was scheduled for about 8 p.m., or well after sunset on a winter night. I arrived in the drop area in early afternoon and drove the route in segments, often in the reverse direction to throw off any tailing vehicles. Each drop and signal location was positively identified, and I estimated, as best I could, how they would look in the dark. Finished at about 5 p.m., I ate dinner slowly and then wandered around a shopping center until it was time.

At a totally pitch-black intersection on a dirt road in the middle of nowhere, I dropped an empty 7-UP can from my car window and drove as the map directed. At that exact moment some miles away, I knew that my contact dropped a similar can, and the game began. I would drive to his spot, and he to mine, both of us following routes that would keep us miles apart. Some thirty minutes later, I arrived at a dark, desolate intersection to see his can on the ground and I knew he would view my signal can at the same time. These cans signaled our readiness to make the exchange as we drove to the next phase, the actual material drop.

Another forty minutes or so later, I reached my drop point on a forlorn stretch of dirt road that had not seen a car for hours or even days. The drop point was behind a large tree six or eight feet off the shoulder, and slamming the car into park, I bounded out the door and dropped my half-full grocery bag behind the tree while a tightening portent of doom gripped my chest. My big .45 pistol was in my hand, hammer back and safety off, but in all honesty, if the lights had snapped on, I do not know whom I would have shot—them or me. But there was no movement, not even the whisper of a sound. Into the car and away, I relaxed for the first time in hours, since, for a short period, I would have no incriminating evidence in the car. My contact had just dropped his delivery behind an obscure pole an hour away, and we would again drive our complex routes, staying miles apart for phase three—the pickup.

These routes followed none of the major, or even minor, highways or roads. Even when a highway with a fifty-mile-per-hour speed limit paralleled my route, I would follow a series of secondary and dirt roads where twenty-five miles per hours was an excessive speed. It seemed to be a tradition in America to destroy all rural route and street signs, so getting lost was an occasional hazard on those black, lonely roads. As I neared the pickup point, the subtle tightness of an impending heart attack returned, for this was a near repeat of the most dangerous act in the play, picking up the KGB drop. If my contact had been followed, I would walk into an ambush. I had measured the distance from an intersection to the pole earlier on my odometer, and as the number turned, the pole suddenly materialized, like a ghost. Gearshift in park, .45 in my fist, penlight in my mouth, I raced to the pole and grabbed what looked like a bag of trash. The roar of absolute silence filled my ears as I crouched and panned the darkness with the big pistol, but I was quite alone. Bag on the floor, I drove at least two miles before relaxing enough for phase three of the drop.

The drop procedure ended by signaling the other agent that the pickup was successful. So, about twenty minutes later at yet another obscure and forsaken intersection, I dropped my final 7-UP can while hopefully my counterpart did the same many miles away. My last act was to check his final can, for if something went awry for him, I would be forced to retrieve my package and try to deliver it again on the next alternative date. This forty-minute drive was always the most annoying part of the procedure. The adrenaline and excitement had subsided, and after a long day involving close to twelve hours of driving, I was always slouched out, bleary-eyed, and weary. I was ready to go home and find a cheap motel but had to drive the maze of black roads to spot his final signal. But at last it glimmered in the glare of my headlights, and the drop was finished. Too exhausted for the drive home, I crashed in one of those rural El Ranko motels.

As we entered into 1968, I will admit to entertaining a fantasy. I pictured several grim Soviet generals gathered in a bleak Kremlin office sifting through my material. As they read through the US war plans, they acknowledged with relief that the "US is not going to invade!" I continued to pore through the international news and my secret dispatches for some sign of US-Soviet warming, secure in the belief that tension in the Soviet Union would surely be relieved. This was 1968, however, one of America's most tumultuous years, and it would start with a most depressing event. The United States would lose yet another spy ship, this time USS *Pueblo* (AGER-2).

I drew a few important conclusions from the *Pueblo* catastrophe, and once my shock wore off, I realized I could not have caused the tragedy. Indeed, my actions should have *prevented* the attack. The following was obvious:

- The Soviet Union did not order the attack and capture of *Pueblo*. Two months earlier, I had offered to disclose the equipment diagrams for the very equipment carried aboard *Pueblo*. And even though the Soviets implied they already had reproduced the equipment, I sent them the wiring diagrams anyway. The Soviets therefore did not order *Pueblo*'s seizure in order to capture the equipment, *since the United States would simply modify the equipment after its capture*. To capture the crypto-equipment would be totally counterproductive.
- The North Koreans did not obtain Soviet permission to attack and capture *Pueblo* and would have vigorously advised against any such action for the same reason.
- The Soviet Union had very little influence over North Korea's conduct. While the United States may have avoided retaliation against North Korea for fear of angering the Soviets, the Soviets were far more angry at North Korea for wrecking their newest intelligence source (me). I was finally going to give the Soviets copies of the keying material to allow their equipment to decrypt US secrets, and now the United States would make changes to all that equipment.
- The North Koreans did not seize *Pueblo* to capture its spy and cryptographic material since it did not board the ship until an hour after firing the fatal cannon round. *Pueblo* was only then ordered to proceed under escort to the North Korean port of Wonsan. Following the North Koreans into port, *Pueblo* destroyed nearly everything and communicated with the Navy Intelligence Station at Kamiceya, Japan, until she was eventually boarded an hour later. So, while the North Koreans did remove over a ton of smashed equipment from the communications space, the attack was not to capture US intelligence and communications equipment.

I had met many of the intelligence spooks over the years and scanned the list of captured crewmen for a familiar name. Sailors from the Security Group had rode *Razorback* with me on my spy mission and I had drank with spooks from the spy ship USS *Muller* in Port Everglades, but I recognized none of the captured. They would suffer badly in the hands of the North Koreans. If only the North Koreans had first spoken to the Soviets, I thought, they would have never been allowed to attack.

My mind wandered to my imaginary Soviet generals and admirals sitting in a drab, wood-paneled Kremlin conference room, smoke-filled, vodka glasses scattered about. A KGB general bellows, "How could those *stupid* Koreans grab a US spy ship without checking first with Moscow?"

A low-level officer feebly volunteers, "Well, at least the Koreans will give us their crypto-equipment."

The general roars, "The equipment is useless—the Americans will change it!"

So, while 1968 was off to a bad start, I knew with certainty that *Pueblo* was a tragic mistake, and had North Korea made a simple phone call to Moscow beforehand, my act of espionage would have *prevented* the torture and injuries of those captured as well as the death of one crew member.

The reality of *Pueblo*'s loss had barely sunk in when the navy would again be shocked by another loss, this time a submarine. The submarine force is a small community where everyone seems to know at least one crew member on every other boat. Old career salts appeared to know everyone. The loss of a submarine is thus more than a piece of iron and a small crew of strangers; it is a personal loss to the entire submarine force.

Above my desk was a black felt status board where all the units of the Atlantic submarine force were listed with white plastic-slotted one-inch letters. The communications status of every boat and surface ship was its main purpose, for that was how we knew where to forward their messages. Our many submarines and surface ships would show the message routing for those at sea, the location of those in the shipyards for repairs and those in port. Next to the submarine USS *Scorpion* were the simple words CHOP CLF. Everyone in communications knew exactly what that meant: she had changed operational control to commander in chief, US Atlantic Fleet (CINCLANTFLT). She was a spook boat. All of *Scorpion*'s communications were sent and received from the building next door, from their intelligence department. During *Razorback*'s spook patrol years earlier, a similar status board in Hawaii would have read CHOP CPF (CINCPACFLT).

Communications to *Scorpion* were encrypted by the intelligence people using exclusive KL-47 keylists, then sent to us for actual radio transmission. They were transmitted on our normal broadcast, encrypted again on the KWT-37, or "super-encrypted," as it was called. Only spook boat intelligence personnel could decrypt the message. Outgoing messages from *Scorpion* were similarly super-encrypted, usually sent on a "burst" transmission of a few milliseconds long, then forwarded by us to CINCLANTFLT intelligence for final decryption. We at the submarine force had no idea where *Scorpion* was or the nature of her mission.

The first sign of trouble was a slightly stressed phone call from CINCLANTFLT on the secure telephone: "Ah, you heard anything from *Scorpion*?" We had not—a very bad sign indeed. We later learned that *Scorpion* had been lost.

My new but limited dialogue with the Soviet Union indicated that the election of Richard Nixon was viewed as a welcome change. When Nixon spoke of entering an era of negotiations with the Soviets in his inaugural address, the Soviet response seemed enthusiastic. While the Soviet invasion of Czechoslovakia had delayed the Soviet peace negotiations, it seemed the United States would end its Vietnam misadventure and enter into serious talks.

But Nixon would not end the war. Secret dispatches reported upon Nixon's remarks to Republican congressional leaders that "I will not be the first president of the United States to lose a war." While Johnson would quit before facing that prospect, Nixon would expand the war into a larger, more bloody disaster. His rate of US troops killed in action would increase to five thousand a year for his first three years as commander in chief of the armed forces. South Vietnamese casualty rates would also soar. Laos and Cambodia were openly within the combat zone as the war was enlarged. In a sense, Nixon did end the Vietnam War—he converted it into the larger Indochina war.

By the end of 1968, I made my third dead drop somewhere in the Washington area. The Soviets had furnished me with the famous German-made Minox camera and a large package of film on the previous exchange. The camera, seen in countless spy movies, was black, about three inches in length, and the film manually advanced after each shot by snapping the body closed and open. It was totally manual, did not even possess a light meter, and required some skill in selecting the shutter speed and f-stop for ambient light; there was no auto-focus. The camera's main claim to fame was its excellent and unique ability to photograph documents from close up. A thin chain attached to the body was actually a measuring tape with beads at various distances in inches. To photograph a standard sheet, the camera focus was set to twelve inches and the twelve-inch bead was pressed next to the page with the camera held taut above the document, guaranteeing the camera was at the correct distance.

I only received one other spy gadget during my long employ by the KGB, a custom-made electrical device to read the rotor wiring for the KL-47 crypto-machine. The rotor was about three inches in diameter and a quarter-inch thick. There were thirty-six numbered contacts around the face, with an associated pin on the reverse, but they were internally wired so that the current entering the contact on one side would come out at some different point on the other side. The internal wiring could be easily traced using a simple continuity device or ohmmeter, a common procedure for any electronics technician. It was a slow process, however, and the KGB device allowed me to drop the rotor on a shaft and spin a rotating arm to each contact, which would give me an instant reading on thirty-six tiny lights. It was much quicker and therefore safer in one sense, but with it came the danger of carrying it to and from work. But no one was ever searched, and the small innocuous device was carried through security with no difficulty. About the size and appearance of a woman's small compact, it contained two tiny watch batteries and cleverly folded open on miniature hinges.

Cameras of any type are totally forbidden in any crypto-center by regulation. In many cases, however, the Minox was much easier and safer in copying material at work. So I carried the camera to work on most days, casually slipped into a pocket or buried in my attaché case. The camera was most useful in copying bound publications, such as the equipment maintenance manuals and operations orders. My methods followed the principle of KISS, and rather than carry sensitive material to the Xerox machine, I instead photographed it in the main walk-in crypto-vault or the commander's office across the hall. The desk lights were bright enough, and with the steady hand of a pistol shooter, I just stood at the desk, twelve-inch-bead under my left thumb, camera in my right hand over the document. Always done during the quiet part of the midnight watch, preferably on Sunday nights when the cold war rested, surprise visitors could be heard before they arrived. Normally I would leave the desk drawer open a few inches, and when someone came near, I would calmly slip the camera into the drawer, slide it shut and cover my work with a sheet of paper. No one ever showed the slightest sign of suspicion.

As a result of the *Pueblo* incident, the KW-37 broadcast receiving equipment was slightly modified by the replacement of a wiring plate. The plates resembled a circuit board about six by four inches and were made of insulation material with embedded wiring patterns. I wondered how best to copy the plate and finally realized the conducting portions were slightly raised above the insulation. By laying a sheet of paper on the board, I was able to scribble across the paper with a pencil to make a perfect copy, much the way a child would scribble over a paper-covered coin. It was not a major equipment change, but I included the rewired plate copy on my next delivery along with the minor degree of equipment modification. The other most important crypto-device, a two-way ship-to-shore KW-7, was not modified at all. This further illustrated the real value of the actual equipment hardware. Even when captured by the enemy, the KW-7 remained unchanged but still secret.

The six-month span between deliveries did not create an unexpected problem in material storage. All the crypto-keying material, operation plans, and other large publications were photographed on the job, and the small Minox film cassettes were easily carried and stored. The huge masses of secret messages were too numerous to be photographed. Hundreds crossed my desk on each watch, and I set aside only those that appeared to have some value. But even if I selected as few as twenty a day, many multipage in length, they would build up to a stack of thousands between deliveries. I estimated it would take well over one hundred rolls of film to photograph the six-month supply, or far more film than was available. The Soviets expected my delivery drop to fit into a single soft drink can, as would their return cash and instruction drop. It became obvious that I had more material than they expected, and a soda can would not do.

As the stash of secret messages grew, it became necessary to get them out of the message center every few days. Storing stacks of secret documents in the BOQ seemed far too dangerous, since the rooms were cleaned daily by enlisted orderlies. It seemed safest to store them at the apartment—a real mistake.

Officers and senior enlisted men, like all managers, will usually take their work home. I had set up an office at one end of the massive master bedroom, and it had always been normal for me to take home such projects as writing enlisted evaluations, recommendations for awards, and general reports to my boss. An unused cabinet in the master bath had been commandeered earlier for storage of office supplies and basic junk files. It was there that I secreted the small but growing stack of secrets in a common grocery bag.

The dead drops had become almost routine, the frightening prospect of arrest much diminished. Slowly I began to accept the fact that I had somehow made it, the invincible FBI and military security had totally failed. If cautious, I should be able to operate indefinitely. Unless a tree fell on my car during a drop and the paramedics found a bag of secrets, I would never be detected. I looked back in amazement. Naval security was so ineffective that anyone could walk out with reams of secrets, and spies could carry cameras, film, and KGB electrical gadgets in and out of the most secure buildings. And worse, the one place in the entire United States where a spy could "fence" his stolen booty, the Soviet embassy, was similarly wide open. There was simply no security.

Sometime that year, I was promoted from warrant officer (W-1) to chief warrant officer (W-2). An easy promotion and a far cry from my enlisted days of cramming for examinations. Officers are promoted automatically, unless they screw up.

In selecting the best top-secret and secret messages for delivery to the Soviets, I almost felt guilty at subjecting them to the mostly boring, inane, and useless information. A great deal of the messages was generated by exercise, or training missions. Another large category involved maintenance, repair, and supply problems in keeping the fleet on alert. Even the routine operational messages were uninteresting, predictable, and of little value. The Soviets delicately suggested I discontinue furnishing the bulk messages entirely, presumably duplicates of what they could decrypt themselves from the stores of intercepted tapes. I continued to deliver them regardless, since I wanted to be sure they knew exactly where the Soviet Union stood in relation to US might. The *real* message of those hundreds of dispatches was not in the words themselves but the deeper meaning that they implied. The US military was on a war footing at a level that would suggest a Soviet invasion was imminent. Training exercises simulating different Soviet invasion scenarios were endless, often involving the other services and US allies. Response to any equipment failure that could threaten a ship's combat readiness was treated as a major emergency, as though the ship was actually engaged in battle. Operational dispatches were likewise treated as actual combat movements, defending the United States from Soviet attack but carrying the battle aggressively to the Soviet homeland.

The vigorous posture of America's defense must have surely sobered the Kremlin generals and admirals. The level of US exercising and training had built the most professional, effective, and deadly military machine the world had ever seen. US supply and logistic systems were unparalleled, responding to every minor casualty instantly, keeping the military machine at maximum combat posture. Operationally, the Kremlin knew the United States would take the fight to the Soviet heartland at the first hint of Soviet aggression. The absurdity of all these emergency dispatches must have struck the Soviets, for they had no invasion plans against the United States. But more important, these messages made it crystal clear that the United States harbored no invasion plans against the USSR. The United States was poised on the Soviet borders (and only sometimes beyond) purely as a defensive measure. I wanted the Soviets to read these insane messages and to understand—and the evidence was that they *did* understand, at long last.

As I reviewed 1968, I felt certain that I had helped influence the Soviets to begin serious negotiations with the United States. Glassboro did make the world safer by reducing an accidental World War III. That the Soviets would agree to anything with President Johnson is surprising, since Johnson's Vietnam War was growing so dreadfully at the time. That the SALT talks would unexpectedly start under Nixon, the president who would end the Vietnam War, but instead expand it even further showed a clear indication that the Soviets could actually trust the United States. Perhaps a degree of sanity would return to the world, and in my small way, I was sure I had helped.

Chapter 12

THE WEAK LINK

I had been warned. Within the first hour of entering the Soviet embassy to commence my life as a spy, I had been clearly advised not to let my wife learn of my choice to become a secret agent. This advice came from an organization that had handled thousands of agents throughout the years and spoke with the confidence of extensive experience. I would violate that sound wisdom within my first year as a spy and live to suffer the consequences.

What is particularly agonizing is that Barbara and I had separated long before my embassy visit. I had chosen a naval career path with the frequent moves to new assignments. Barbara had chosen a business path, sinking roots and staying put in South Carolina. Our marriage had soured irreversibly, and we were separated by conscious career choices. The marriage was technically over, so any chance of her finding out about my new life had been eliminated; I only needed to maintain the status quo. A career as a spy would seem to dictate the need to remain unmarried, to live alone. Security must be paramount since it is impossible to conceal a secret life with wives, children, girlfriends, or houseguests. The slightest suspicion that one is hiding something will titillate their curiosity, turning them into very dangerous snoops. That is precisely why I did not build a secret room, install a safe, or lock anything. Hidden in plain sight, the secret messages were in a grocery bag among paperwork files, and the vital exchange procedure was simply stuck in a book no one would ever read. But separation from one's wife is far easier than separation from one's children. So my decision to rejoin my family was based on more than pity for the kids living in trailer-park conditions; I also wanted to be at least a small part of their lives.

Life in the luxury apartment was a welcome change for us all. I was spared those miserable drives to Charleston. Barbara enjoyed the doorman who also carried her groceries and packages to her door. Her allowance increased substantially, and she seemed content to laze about watching television and sipping vodka between shopping trips. I leased her a new Chrysler. The kids, now ages twelve, ten, nine, and seven, were taking care of themselves with little input from their mom. The novelty wore off after several months, however, and Barbara reverted back to the shrew, drinking too much, subjecting the kids to endless cleaning projects. The abuse returned, all the kids bearing the pain, but again Cynthia suffered the most. Barbara's moods varied between Jekyll and Hyde, exhibiting each persona about half the time. I could walk in the door, encounter Mr. Hyde, and execute an abrupt U-turn back to the BOQ, which was often the case. The kids could not run or hide; they were trapped.

It had been our practice to have our mothers visit during the summers, alternating between each. Over time, we stopped inviting Barbara's mother since Barbara and she got along so poorly. My mother became the standard summer visitor for a week each summer, her only real opportunity to travel outside Scranton. It was my mother who first noticed Barbara's water glasses of vodka, but she kept it to herself, as was her nature. Barbara normally maintained a sweet Dr. Jekyll guise during such visits, but finally Mom would observe an incident of child abuse that would shake her to the core.

I was on a twenty-four-hour shift. Always an excellent cook, Barbara had prepared a lavish dinner for Mom and the kids, but as was normally the case, every pot, pan, and serving dish was used. The cleanup was always mammoth, and Barbara had abandoned dish washing to the kids years earlier. Cynthia, our ten-year-old, was one of the two assigned, and since the job was too big, the two kids fought, dragging the cleanup on for hours. Barbara drank too much, lost control, and went screaming into the kitchen at intervals to punish the kids. Cynthia was eventually deemed the most offensive, as usual, and was left alone to finish the job, beaten and sobbing. Fully enraged as the time neared 11 p.m., Barbara finally stormed into the kitchen and plunged Cynthia's head into the filthy dishwater, screaming at the child. Turned loose before drowning, Cynthia was chased stumbling to her room, soaked, spitting up the foul water, eyes burning from the detergent.

Cynthia's sisters and brother were horrified, and my mom was too stunned to speak about it. Mom remained visibly shaken, as though she had walked through the aftermath of a plane crash, but would not say anything specific for years. She did bemoan Barbara's treatment of Cynthia, but Cynthia bore no more than the usual bruises of childhood. Not visible were the psychological wounds, the scars of which that poor child carries today. But at the time and as usual, I would be the last to know.

It slowly became evident that Barbara either never heard me or just forgot the earlier conversations about our marriage. She expected a reconciliation and, frustrated by failure, her attitude and behavior became progressively worse. I stayed busy, following the old submariner's adage of "work hard, play hard," with reconciliation the last thing on my mind. Even with my extra spy income, I still drove taxis, worked on my commercial pilot license, and played with my sailboat summer and winter. The signal came when Barbara began acting as if we were truly married, nagging about my "staying out" and even "seeing other women." Confused, I wondered if I had missed something. We had to talk, again.

It was a rainy afternoon, and since the kids were at school, we had the apartment to ourselves. Barbara was sober and lucid as I politely explained again that the marriage was over. I would continue to support her and the kids in a pseudomarriage arrangement and stressed that she could do worse in divorce court where alimony might not be awarded. Further, she and the kids would lose medical coverage and all the other military-dependent benefits after a divorce. The leased car would go back. If she objected to the arrangement, I would gladly move my small office and few clothes back to the BOQ and pick up the kids on weekends for visitation.

It was not a pleasant meeting, explaining again to my wife that it was over, again upsetting the woman I had once loved. Hadn't I been through all this two years earlier? Go to school, I suggested, pass your GED, get a small job, ease up on the kids. We could afford to hire someone to clean a couple days a week.

Barbara seemed to rally. She began exploring schools and searching for a job; she hired one of the building's many cleaning women for one day a week. The kids stayed on kitchen KP duty, but conditions improved. Barbara started her affair with the guy down the hall during this period, but there was no long-term possibility in her arrangement. He was devoted to his terminally ill wife, so it was an affair for sex only.

My life was so busy that I dropped the Yellow Cab job. I continued to transport cars and trucks when my schedule permitted, enjoying a night in a strange city and airfare back home, which was part of the contract. Our bizarre nonmarriage arrangement would not last, however, as Barbara would confront me, drunk, wanting to know where I was the night before. In an alcoholic haze, she would act like we had a normal marriage and that I still lived at home. She refused to believe I was actually working as a driver and wanted to know what I was really doing. I stuck to my story but spent most nights at the BOQ.

My apartment desk was always locked, but I kept the key hanging from a paper clip taped to the side, out of sight. Every parent knows what kids will do to office supplies if given a chance. Pens gone, pencils scribbled flat, paper clips in chains, and nothing to write a check with but a few broken Crayolas. The key was well known to Barbara, and indeed, she used the desk for household business. It was obvious that someone was foraging through the desk occasionally, but I attributed that to the kids, who probably found the key on the first day (or hour). In one bottom drawer there was a small box of specialized tools used for teletypewriter repair, and it was there that Barbara found the evidence of my nefarious life.

She was loaded for bear, drunk and pissed when I opened the front door. Vodka glass in hand, she started before the door was closed. This was my usual cue to execute an about-face, but before I could move, she screamed, "Explain this, you bastard!" She held up a rather large syringe with clear liquid sloshing within.

I walked in and closed the door, silently admonishing myself, *God, why didn't you leave this drunken idiot in South Carolina?*

The syringe had a simple explanation. In the more innocent 1950s and 1960s, we would pick up the old syringes from the ship's sick bay and use them as oil dispensers. In the maintenance of teletypewriters and mechanical cryptographic machines, the delicate moving parts were difficult to reach and had to be carefully lubricated. A syringe filled with light machine oil was the perfect tool, and we normally just blunted the tip slightly by tapping it on the workbench to avoid painful accidental stabs. That syringe had been in my toolbox for nearly ten years, still containing oil.

Barbara, fully engulfed in rage, had cracked the crime of the century: I was a drug smuggler. My vehicle transport trips were really a cover to move illegal drugs into the northern cities, but worse yet, I was mainlining the drugs myself. When she finally paused in her ravings, I calmly explained that the syringe was filled with oil, it was just an unusual oilcan. That possibility stopped her for a moment, but she held onto her smuggler argument and continued to rail on that point. *"That's"* why you're getting your commercial pilot's license," she raved, "so you can pick up the drugs in Mexico, blah, blah, blah . . ." As she went on, spinning her theory, I wondered which was worse, drug smuggling or espionage? I made a weak denial, explaining that I worked hard to provide for my family, including the part-time driving job. Besides, how could I know what may be hidden in the vehicles. They paid me well and I did not ask questions. As intended, Barbara did not believe my lame excuse and gloated at her investigative ability. Why not make her happy? I reasoned, and, more important, if she thought I was transporting drugs, she would be less apt to snoop further.

Following the syringe incident, Barbara's attitude did improve to the point of enrolling in a travel agent course a couple days a week. Our earlier tour around Europe was her inspiration, and she envisioned herself planning elaborate cruises and tours around the world for her clients. It would probably be necessary for her to work as an intern at no pay, but I assured her that we could afford it.

Returning from class one day, she experienced a minor fender-bender, bumping the bridge of her nose on the steering wheel. That night she greeted me wearing an oversized pair of dark sunglasses and only reluctantly showed me her embarrassing double black eyes. The bump was small but had freakishly ruptured just the right blood vessel. The car was easily fixed and her eyes healed, but Barbara dropped out of the course. Before I could register my ire, she happily announced that she had found a job as a secretary. Thinking it was a joke, I reminded her that she could not type and had no office management skills. She would learn on the job, I was informed, and when I discovered her new employer, it finally made sense. Her boyfriend down the hall had hired her. Christ, I thought, why not? If the fool wanted to hire his nontyping lover for a secretarial position, it was all right with me. Anything that would add some sense of purpose to her life could only be an improvement. The man owned a large utility-service company, and Barbara could perhaps find a useful role.

My grocery bag of secrets, growing almost daily, presented a serious dilemma. Keeping the material at the BOQ and the apartment was a clear danger. Building a hiding place in the BOQ or a rented apartment was impractical. Rental storage sheds had not yet been invented, so what was left? The only solution was to rent a separate apartment with the sole purpose of storing a single bag. Like all military towns, there were countless small furnished rentals available, but just as I prepared to pay the deposit, I was caught again.

The Algonquin apartment seemed empty as I stepped in and flicked on the foyer light. Either Barbara and the kids had gone to bed early or they were out somewhere. I started to leave when Barbara called my name from the darkened living room. Ice tinkled in a cocktail glass in the direction of the ruby cigarette glow across the room. I turned on a single lamp and sat. She was fully blitzed on vodka, slurring and bleary-eyed, in what I came to recognize as her "endless lecture mode." Barbara could pontificate for hours when so inclined, putting to shame the incessant diatribes of the world's greatest dictators. The children were forced to sit through her harangues, eyes glazed over, comalike, often for two hours or more. It was my signal to leave, and I started for the door as I plopped on my cap and pulled up my tie. She had me this time, however, as she flew from the chair saying, "Before you go, I want you to explain something to me." She breezed past me and toward the master bedroom, as I obediently followed the wind-chime of her cocktail glass and trail of Marlboro smoke. Hooking a left into the master bath, she opened a cabinet and tapped on the grocery bag. "What the hell is this?" she demanded with smug satisfaction, thoroughly enjoying the moment.

In training new case officers, the intelligence agencies of the world must include hundreds of examples describing the stupid conduct of their new spies. I felt worse than a rank amateur, having rejected the one piece of rational advice the Soviets had given me. I had moved the weak link back into my life, right into the center of my operation, and created a problem that could not be solved. If the Soviets ever hear of my blunder, I thought, it will become part of the KGB Spy School curriculum, probably under Stupidity 101.

But, while I was justifiably mortified and ashamed, I was also angered by Barbara's conduct. By snooping through my personal papers, she showed no respect for me or my privacy. I had not and would never pry into her personal effects, even after learning of her affairs. At that moment, I realized that my reconciliation with this woman was utterly impossible, but even worse, that I could never be rid of her. I would be forced to drag her through my life like an anchor around my neck, thanks to my own numskull lack of judgment.

In my bedroom office, I tossed my uniform hat and jacket on the bed, kicked off my shoes, and pulled my tie down—it was going to be a long session. I swiveled my desk chair toward the bed some ten feet away where Barbara sat perched in the cat-bird seat. She should have been satisfied thinking I was a drug runner, at least long enough for me to have moved the material. Now I wondered if it was worth the attempt to even argue. "It's just background material for a report I'm preparing," I explained. They were secret and confidential messages, she countered correctly, and were not supposed to be taken home. "They've been declassified," I pressed, but that argument failed since she knew the secret markings would be lined out and the messages stamped "unclassified." No, she knew what the material meant and said so: "You're selling secrets to the Russians." In the final analysis, it was senseless to argue. What she thought she knew, that I was a drug runner *and* a spy, was worse than the truth. In later years, she would say that I flew into a rage and blackened both her eyes, but in reality, I was quietly resigned. Her reaction to my confirmation that I was indeed a spy was entirely unexpected—she wanted to participate, share in my secret agent life. Barbara saw this as a vehicle to reconciliation. As she bubbled over, demanding to know the details, I could only stare back in pity and amazement. I felt even less for her at that moment than at our initial split two years earlier. At least twice I had explained in detail that the marriage was over and why, but she seemed to have heard none of it. She insisted on accompanying me on my next dead drop a week or two hence, acting as if it were a honeymoon adventure. She was displaying self-deception and denial, the characteristics of mania. But what was worse, I wondered, taking her along and facing arrest with me, or forcing her to stay at home? In a bizarre sense, taking her along was best, for if we were caught, the kids would be better off in foster homes than living with their mom and without my support.

While that may sound unusually cruel, it is important to note that the preceding meetings and dead drops had clearly established that I had not been detected and would remain undetected indefinitely.

I made but one short speech, pointing out that my primary job as a husband and father was to support my family, and at that I had never failed. Her primary job was to manage the home and act as the main care provider for the children, and at that she was failing. She agreed that I was indeed a great provider and promised to do better herself. It was senseless to explain our broken marriage yet again, for in her irrational excitement, she would not understand.

It was actually nice to have some help on the drop. With a second driver, we planned to drive up and back in a single day. Babysitter on the scene, we left for Washington at midmorning on a Sunday. Barbara was a good driver, more heavy-footed than I, so she focused on driving, leaving me to watch for tails while directing her to make evasive moves. My mood was rotten, however, brought on by her prying herself into my secret life, her assumption that our criminal bond was also a marital bond. I was also troubled that she had forced herself into so dangerous a situation. But we arrived in the Washington suburbs free of surveillance and went immediately to the procedure. Barbara drove the entire route backward and in small segments as I navigated through the complex maps and instructions. In one sense, it was a pleasure having a driver since I normally spent more time fumbling through a dozen photographs and tiny map sections than watching the road. But once finally convinced I could find the four signal spots and two drop points in the dark, we took our first rest over a long dinner. There was always the chance that our drop point had disappeared. After six months, a tree off the road might have been replaced by a lawn and new house, forcing me into a more complex backup procedure.

The drop was routine and uneventful. I carried no guns, knowing that to do so would be more dangerous than the spy activity itself. Even though firearm laws were much more liberal in the 1960s, the possession of a pistol could result in police inspection and lead to the discovery of a real crime. My amateurish and melodramatic habit of bounding out of the car waving a gun about like a Hollywood heavy had given way to more professional behavior. In fact, the real spies in the field have no formal training in spy-craft and are forced to learn the necessary skills on their own or through rare contact with their case officers. The case officers are extensively trained, however, but their duties are only to pick up deliveries from the field agents and transport them back to their headquarters. They typically enjoy diplomatic immunity and are insulated from arrest anyway. The field agents like me, the ones in real need of spy-craft training, are left to their own devices. But I was learning.

Exhausted after a long day, we nonetheless drove straight back, taking turns at the wheel while the other dozed. As I sat behind the wheel following that endless broken white line to Norfolk, my anger at the situation turned to the Soviets. Why was I making deliveries at six-month intervals? While less-frequent spy drops might offer fewer occasions to be caught and thus might seem safer, they also caused me to build up large caches of documents and film. These mounds of material made my life more dangerous and indeed had caused my exposure by Barbara.

Back at the Algonquin House and after some much-needed sleep, I finally dug into the trash bag dropped by the KGB. They were good at realism, topping the bag with disgusting items designed to ward off all but the most curious. At the bottom of the garbage was a single soda can and a package heavily wrapped in waterproof plastic and tape. The package contained scores of Minox film cartridges, all removed from their boxes and interlocked to save space. The money, about twenty-five thousand in fifty-dollar bills, was somehow rolled tight enough to fit into the can. Barbara gleefully pulled out the wad of bills, which were so tightly rolled that they were impossible to count. Barbara thought to iron them flat, joyfully pressing them into normal shape with a steam iron.

Barbara's attempt to rebuild our marriage left me feeling like a perfect cad. This woman had gone so far as to participate in a major felony, facing a long prison term, just to win back her man. But while I felt the much-deserved humiliation, we had both gone entirely too far to erase all the bad times. An anchor around my neck and the weak link in my secret life she might be, but it was irrationally delusional on her part to believe there was even a chance. I quickly excluded her from my activities, relocated the spy material to a small rental apartment, and tried to lead my weird life without going crazy. Barbara slowly reverted back to the sullen drunk but continued to work at her secretary job. Her horrendous abuse of the children returned to its normal level, a level that would put her in prison today. I could easily reduce her level of violence toward the kids or stop it entirely by positioning myself between her and the latest offender. Foolishly, I began to view my presence as a safety valve, a way to save the kids from severe beatings. In talking with the kids over time, I eventually realized that the opposite was true. If I was absent for days, Barbara would reach an equilibrium that the children could better deal with. My sporadic presence to visit the kids or take them somewhere would result in her increased drinking and a fury that she directed toward the kids. They became my surrogates, receiving the blows that she could not inflict upon me. My divorced shipmates informed me that I was experiencing a tactic often encountered by divorced dads. Conscientiously or unconscientiously, women may frustrate visitation by punishing the children, driving a wedge between them and their dads. The kids eventually associate visits from dad with physical pain and learn to avoid it.

My moving the family from South Carolina began to seem more and more stupid. Children are less aware of substandard living conditions than adults and are better able to adapt. My moving them to a luxury apartment improved their lives not at all. This unexpected turn of events drove me farther from the family and kept me in the BOQ room more often. Spending any time alone with the kids was totally abandoned, forcing me to take Barbara along whenever I took the kids anywhere. I was enrolled in a psychology school of my own making and discovering that most of what I thought I knew about human behavior was wrong.

The "play hard" part of my life continued unabated. I struggled with my commercial pilot course, flying being a skill that I now consider the most challenging of my many activities. The private pilot license course consisted of forty flying hours, not including ground school. The commercial course was one hundred and twenty hours of flying and at a precision level far surpassing private proficiency. I crammed for the formidable written test and worried about the instrument-rating course to follow.

Although I loved that Lightning sailboat, I moved up to a beautiful Yankee Dolphin, a boat-show demo offered at a bargain price. A Sparkman-Stephens design, the twenty-four-foot sloop had two bunks forward, a marine head, main cabin with a four-seat dinette convertible to double berth, a kitchen, and a small inboard engine. The twenty-year-old enlisted WAVES often referred to me as a "dirty old man," regardless of my youthful age of thirty-two, and it was her nickname that prompted the boat's name. For me, the boat was my ultimate toy and probably an unwise investment since I was facing transfer in about a year. She came with a large tandem trailer, however, and unless I was transferred overseas, I planned to tow her to my next duty station.

As I look back to early 1969, it is difficult to imagine how I kept up the pace. My job at COMSUBLANT was as grueling as ever with interspersed submarine cruises. I still transported an occasional car or truck. The commercial pilot course was difficult enough to warrant my exclusive attention, but I somehow found the time. My dysfunctional family life kept me forever on edge, waiting for the next crisis. Three or four women were shuffled. Meanwhile, I spent every spare moment on my boat, often taking her out all weekend plus three or four nights during the week. Then there was the matter of smuggling an illegal camera and film into the top-secret crypto-center, copying material, smuggling everything back out, and stowing the contraband for the next delivery. I may have personified the work hard/play hard maxim, but the pace was driving me nuts.

Chapter 13

A CIA MOLE

I t was a small oversight on my part, the result of no spy training and even less guidance by my case officer, that led to exposing a KGB mole within the CIA.

My tour of duty with the COMSUBLANT staff was for three years, a year longer than expected and the result of a new concept by the navy to reduce the number of personnel transfers. COMSUBLANT was an "afloat" command, classified as sea duty regardless of its location in several land-based buildings. Our frequent submarine cruises for weeks at a time left no doubt regarding our sea duty status, however. If I completed the three-year tour, I would conclude fourteen continuous years of sea duty, and while not a record, I had never personally met anyone who exceeded it. Determined to reduce my tour to two years, I drove to Washington in early 1969 to discuss an early transfer to shore duty.

Our officer community of operations and communications specialists was very small, and our detailer was probably on a first-name basis with most. He was not happy by my altering his long-range assignment plans but promised to help. Much depended upon the officer selection board's decision in advancing new warrant officers, but he did pencil in my prospective relief. As for me, he had need of a chief warrant officer at the San Diego Radioman School later in the year, a plum job indeed. In the interests of espionage and access to material, I should have refused the job. Assignment to one of many shore-based communications stations would ensure my continued access to cryptographic material, but I was more than ready for a rest from the operational navy's war footing, afloat or ashore.

During my meeting with my detailer, I could not resist asking about Vietnam for my following assignment and specifically if he felt the war

143

would last that long. He pointed out that there were very few billets in-country for communications warrants and that Nixon might well end the war before my shore duty tour was completed three or four years hence. My access to classified material regarding Vietnam was far better than my detailer's access, and with Nixon's war-hawk reputation, I did not foresee an early end. Still, I wondered if my much-deserved shore duty tour would cancel my prospects of ever experiencing the war zone.

My mistake with the KGB was in the manner of informing them of my transfer to shore duty. Rather than explaining my decision and reasons in detail, I merely mentioned that I would be transferred and probably to a school command. I did not wish to panic them by suggesting that I may never again have important access, so I sought to assuage their fear by assuring them of better jobs in my future. In fact, one of our chiefs was nearing retirement age at thirty-eight and planned a second career in the CIA's Communication Center at Langley, Virginia. We had all read his job application and recruitment brochure and envied his plan to retire twice—or double dip—from both the US Navy and the CIA. It was with that CIA brochure in mind that I mentioned in my drop that if my future navy assignments were unsatisfactory sources of secrets, I would apply for a communications job in the CIA. Realistically, it would have been most unusual that my future jobs would lack secret access, but in that unlikely event, I wanted the Soviets to know that I was prepared to leave the navy for the CIA, if necessary. This information was included in a drop to the KGB that winter with the knowledge that I would wait six months before receiving a response. My life continued at its breakneck pace, and I was blissfully unaware that I had created panic with my case officer and controllers.

In my spy activity, a standard drop exchange was made that summer; it was both uneventful and routine. My package from the KGB included a carefully written response assuring me that I would remain on a retainer during the school tour and that I would not "apply for that job until receiving further information." The note also expressed some alarm concerning security around me or any signs of surveillance. They asked several questions and requested detailed answers on my next drop. It was only then that I realized the obvious: if the US government was even slightly suspicious of an individual's security reliability, that person is always transferred to a job with less access. It is one signal that the government has launched an espionage investigation and is closing in for the kill. The new assignment always has *some* secrets for the suspect to steal, but usually fake bait that is placed in a spot covered by hidden TV cameras, all designed to catch the spy in the act.

I should have anticipated the Soviets' anxiety surrounding my transfer to a school command—the perfect place to spring such a trap. It was all the result of my lack of spy training, but it also illustrated the KGB's lack of understanding of the US Navy. They acted as if I was a low-ranking enlisted man with no say in my assignment, like some private sent off to battle someplace. Officers, and even senior enlisted men, sit down with their detailers to discuss job preference and review the projected vacancies around the world. We may know the person scheduled to leave the spot we want and the person scheduled to relieve us long before any orders are issued. Since I selected my shore duty station from a wide list of those available, it was certainly not an FBI trick transfer in preparation for my arrest. It would all be explained in my next drop note some months later, but I had inadvertently set into motion the anxiety that I would apply for the CIA, and probably be caught as a result. A polygraph test was part of the application process, and without training to beat the test, a disastrous failure was likely.

My official orders were received in early summer for the Naval Schools Command, San Diego, to report in September. While I would stay at COMSUBLANT for five months beyond two years, I was at least compensated by having the entire summer to ply the waters of Chesapeake Bay in my new boat. The drills and submarine cruises were taxing, however, and I would not complete my commercial flying course before leaving for California. The boat was too large for trailer launching on a ramp, so she rested in a rental slip at Cobb's Marina in Little Creek. It was a sad day when Cobb's crane lifted the *Dirty Old Man* from the water, lowering her to the big trailer for the long trip west. It was a heavy load, but the big leased Chrysler seemed up to the job. The MG was shipped to San Diego, driven by the same transport company that I had driven for so often in the past.

It is shameful that I can count on two hands the truly pleasurable moments we would spend as a family over the next several years. Although a trip across country with a heavy tow and four small children would normally be difficult, this trip was more like a pleasant vacation. I planned the southern route, selecting Holiday Inn motels a mere four hundred miles apart, all with adjoining rooms and swimming pools. Barbara and I alternated on driving one hundred miles each, and by starting very early, we reached our lodging by midafternoon. We ate a late brunch on the road, and the kids were in the pool long before a relaxed dinner. Our time on the road was so short during those years of sixty-five- and seventy-mile-per-hour speed limits and less traffic that there was ample time for casual stops at tourist attractions as a result of my extra spy money. I thought of the old saw "Money can't buy happiness." *Who came up with that stupid saying?* I wondered. We are constantly bombarded by that concept, from Hollywood to funny papers. The original "Dagwood" comic strip character was born to wealth, which he abandoned for the "happy" life as a working stiff living in the suburbs. Hollywood fed us the same theme of the unhappy "poor little rich girl" (or boy) who only finds happiness with the common folks and life. The concept is a myth, foisted upon the working-class and poverty-level public by someone very rich. If the general public actually believed that happiness could be attained only by struggling through the simple life, they would be less apt to threaten the wealth of the rich. The myth dismissed, I could appreciate the pleasure of this leisurely trip as opposed to those all-night-driving marathons when we could not afford a motel. It was enjoyable to linger over a good bottle of wine at dinner. It was nice to let the kids telephone room service and order ice cream.

An old submarine shipmate had offered lodging at his San Diego apartment, which we accepted. The small apartment could not accommodate six people, so we stuck the four kids in the guest room while Barbara and I slept in the boat. Parked directly out front on the street, the boat could serve as a travel trailer. We set up the large main cabin bunks, used the stove for coffee, and enjoyed the small portable television.

Returning to San Diego was like coming home, for in my travels around the country and the world, San Diego was my favorite city. Overshadowed by Los Angeles and San Francisco to the north, San Diego maintained a charming small-town nature. Thankfully, it was off the beaten path and considered little more than a "navy town" by those unfamiliar with the area. Although the city had all the glamour and sophistication anyone would want, I particularly loved the easygoing California style, beautiful harbor, and perfect weather. Our hosts lived just off the causeway to Shelter Island, a man-made oasis of fancy restaurants and marinas ensconced in palm trees. Shore duty at last, and I planned to enjoy this paradise.

We quickly found a perfect four-bedroom house in La Mesa, and since we drove so slowly across country, our furniture had arrived ahead of us. For the first time, we would not sleep on the floor of an empty house without utilities, waiting for our household effects to be delivered. Within four or five days of our arrival, we were ready to move in and start the kids in school.

An unusual incident occurred on the last night we slept on the boat. With the weather warm and balmy, the forward hatch cocked open, and the main hatch slats removed, a mild breeze skimmed through the cabin. Just as the first peaceful burst of sunlight filled the cabin, I felt a gentle nudge on the boat, jerking me awake. It was followed by a couple more soft thumps—someone was touching the boat, perhaps boarding her. I had a special lock around the trailer tongue to prevent a tow-away theft, but theft is always a prospect. Grabbing the big capstan wrench, I crept up the stairs to the cockpit to confront the startled face of Carl Ackerman. He stood on the trailer fender on tiptoes peeking over the gunwale. This elderly and distinguished gentleman was clearly not a thief, and soon Barbara and I were dressed and on the ground to say hello. Carl and Teddy Ackerman were local boating enthusiasts who had earlier seen the boat with Virginia registration and were driven by curiosity. For a twenty-four-foot sloop, she was a well appointed, handsome, and uncommon vessel. Every sailing yachtsperson would be moved to identify her designer and manufacturer. They also wondered if it had actually been trailered all the way from Virginia.

Carl and Teddy would become our closest friends during my San Diego tour of duty, more like our adopted grandparents, in fact. Retired, they were active members of the San Diego Yacht Club where their sloop, the *Thistledown*, was moored. They were en route to the club for an early morning sail when they stopped to look at our boat. After exchanging phone numbers, they went on their way but insisted we join them at the club as their guests once we were settled.

The moving trauma completed, I reported for duty at my new radio school job. The Naval Schools Command is part of a larger complex containing both the Naval and Marine Recruit Training Commands. The school command offers specialized training for recruit graduates and advanced training for fleet sailors. The buildings were strangely attractive for a government complex, done in a Spanish motif, sand colored with red-tiled roofs and breezy, arch-covered walkways. The streets were wide, lawns manicured, and of course, palm trees were in abundance. My building housed Radio "A" School, which taught the basics for the rating, and "B" School, where fleet sailors learned electronics for equipment maintenance. I was quickly assigned to lead the "A" school, where the previous officer in charge had been transferred a few days before my arrival. It was a large command for me, consisting of twelve hundred students and an enlisted staff of instructors numbering about ninety, from first-class petty officers to master chiefs. A chief and three civilian secretaries manned my administrative office. With prime parking, a huge private office, and competent staff, I ruled over more personnel than I would ever again experience.

I also obtained a room at the nearest BOQ at the Fleet Training Center on Harbor Drive. There were no delusions that my fictitious marriage would ever change.

For one accustomed to a hyperactive environment, however, it is difficult to change. The reduction in the "work hard" side of the equation was simply transferred to the "play hard" side. *Dirty Old Man*'s mat was quickly stepped, and she was soon in the water at a rental slip on Shelter Island. I had an entire bay to explore, as well as whales to follow on their migration south, visits to be made to Los Angeles and Catalina Island. My commercial pilot training was transferred to a school at nearby Gillespie Field, and I had much to explore from the air. There were deserts, mountains, islands, Las Vegas, Mexico, and beyond.

Carl and Teddy had us at the yacht club as guests several times and suggested we consider joining. Military officers' clubs can be quite elegant; some even entertained dinner guests with tuxedo-clad violinists or women in long evening gowns strumming harps. The more tasteful officers' clubs were usually too stuffy for my liking, but I found the yacht club offered the perfect balance. It was elegant to be sure, but one felt comfortable in a tuxedo or sailing shorts. I thoroughly loved the place, and after Carl and Teddy provided a few friends to assist in our sponsorship, we were official members. The dues were a bit high, but the club offered a perfect setting, even for the children. At the first opportunity, I moved the boat to the club and signed up for all the harbor and ocean races possible. I had a genoa jib made and a large, distinctive spinnaker of light blue with a huge silhouette of a leaping dolphin in dark blue. To my knowledge, my Yankee Dolphin was the only boat of her type in the area.

Sailboat racing was a new experience for me and it presented a problem as well: I needed an experienced racing crew. My large school staff offered the best source of interested sailors, so I casually requested my master chiefs to ask around for me. Several of the staff responded, and I sorted through the ones most interested in weekend training cruises. One of my instructors, Jerry Whitworth, a first-class radioman, would become my most important crewman and eventually my closest friend. Jerry participated in nearly every race and pleasure cruise during the next two years.

Impressive and likable, Jerry showed a high level of control and competence in handling himself. His maturity and sensible nature was beyond that usually found in young men of his rank. Tall and athletic, Jerry shared my zest for life and level of daring. Our four-man racing crew finally developed into Jerry as tactician and a few others who rotated as foredeck and jib operators. As captain, I manned the tiller and ordered the sail configurations, while Jerry, the tactician, plotted the best plan for rounding buoys and maneuvering to the best advantage against the competitors. Of course, Jerry was all over the boat, trimming and adjusting. On long ocean races, Jerry was captain of a crew as we split into two sections to allow relief, two hours on, two hours off. Racing crews were composed exclusively of men, all serious and very competitive. Pleasure cruises were much more relaxed and always included women.

One of my regulars was from my coed BOQ, a woman marine captain who lived a few doors away. A typical marine, zero body fat and athletic, she later confided that she was a lesbian. I thought that was great, and we became very close buddies without the sexual encumbrances. She was always ready to sail or fly anywhere. My closest relationship was through Jerry, who introduced me to two young enlisted WAVES, Myra Barns and Marilyn McClung, both dental technicians. Jerry had invited me to lunch at his club, the Acey-Ducey Club for first- and second-class petty officers where we were joined by the two WAVES. Myra was a china-skinned beauty with a mop of blond hair. Marilyn was a cheerleader type with vivid red hair and good looks. They were at least ten years my junior and thoroughly enjoying the male attention that two beauties will find in a world of plentiful men. Marilyn was a California girl from Fremont. Myra came from Kentucky wealth. She had her trust fund frozen by her family as a result of her unrestrained lifestyle.

Jerry had been dating Marilyn, and it was obvious that they wanted me to meet her roommate, Myra. I took to that wild girl immediately, and we would become a foursome over the next two years; both girls would remain friends for years later. Myra was a wonderfully extravagant woman with an unabashed passion for excess: she drank too much, smoked too much, dined with relish, and partied too long. And when she flashed her oblique half-haunted smile, I knew to be prepared for her excesses in the bedroom.

My commercial flying course was over, and after my check ride with the FAA examiner, my new license was issued. As a commercial pilot, I was licensed to carry passengers for hire and quickly signed up with a couple flying service operators to fly charter jobs. This service was often called "air taxi," and I was amused by the similarity of driving part-time for Yellow Cab. A flying service would telephone to ask if I could take gamblers to Las Vegas or hunters to Wyoming or tourists to the Grand Canyon. These flights had high priority for me, and if I was available, I accepted. I flew light single-engine planes, four- or six-seaters, usually to remote airports not served by the major carriers. Every flight was an adventure. If my charges did well at the gambling tables, the tip was always great. I didn't do this for money, however; I would have flown the charters for expenses only. Charter flying would open up a new world for me. But more of that later.

The KGB had earlier instructed me that certain instructions and answers to questions would be transmitted by a simple, innocuous greeting card.

The written message would be innocent and normal, but if it was prepared for the card, it would carry a special message. I knew that I had unnecessarily alarmed the KGB with my idle remark about seeking a CIA job in their communication center, but I expected them to relax until I could explain fully on my winter drop. So, it was surprising and embarrassing to receive a card while my winter drop was still months away, a card that made no sense unless it came from the KGB. It was a simple congratulations card with a handwritten note that read roughly as follows:

> Congratulations on your new assignment. If you do plan a job change, contact Echlotes first.

It was signed with scrawled initials, which I didn't recognize. Aside from the KGB, the sender was a complete mystery. The card was mailed from northern Virginia, as best as I recall, and to my work address. I had given the KGB that address on my last drop, and they had no idea of my family address at that time. The name Echlotes, which is as close as I remember the spelling, meant nothing to me; the first name is totally forgotten. It could only be from the KGB, I decided, giving me a CIA contact who would handle my application and perhaps help avoid the polygraph examination. It seemed that the KGB was so worried about the prospect of my exposure through a CIA security check that they took the extreme risk of giving me the name of a mole at the CIA. The card was quickly disposed of, and although duly humiliated, I soon forgot about it. Indeed, the entire incident was forgotten for years, even after my arrest and FBI debriefing. Even when the receipt of the card was remembered, the contact name was lost, no longer in focus. It would be years later while lying in bed at the Marion penitentiary that I suddenly remembered in a flash. I was in that halfway state where the subconscious comes to the surface. My radio was tuned to a soft station when a commercial broke through the haze, some babble about Eckerd Drugs, and there was the forgotten name with a slightly similar sound. The spelling is probably not correct, but there it was, the mole within the CIA who could help me gain employment. As a communications operator or supervisor in the Langley, Virginia, CIA complex, it would have exposed me to the inside track of their despicable conduct around the world. I probably should have taken the job.

Chapter 14

SEEING THE LIGHT

One recognizes the coming of winter in Southern California when the brown and parched grass comes alive in green lawns and hillsides. Some boaters curtail their cruise schedules in winter, but I changed my schedule not at all except for the greatly reduced racing schedule. The approaching winter solstice would also end the decade of the 1960s, a decade so turbulent that many Christians saw the fulfillment of Revelation prophecies, with the end of the world occurring at any minute. Conditions would not improve in the 1970s.

Winter's arrival brought with it a scheduled drop into Washington, my first during my school tour of duty. I took great pains in reporting the security situation around me, explaining the transfer procedure and hopefully becalming the Soviets' distress that I had been caught. Prospects of employment with the CIA were abandoned, I informed them, and I stressed my intention to remain in the naval service until retirement.

The lack of worthwhile secret material was as expected, but I did not try to explain the sea duty pressure and mental stress behind my much-needed tour of shore duty. My school obviously had the operational classified material necessary for preparing the school curricula, and it was easily copied on my office photocopy machines; it was even assigned to my office staff on occasion. Our students trained on actual cryptographic equipment, and since the keying material consisted of unclassified training editions, the keylists were of no value.

The best secrets were secured at the Administrative Command, a command that provided administrative services for the many schools on the base, including mine. Two of my best friends were assigned there, a commander who lived across the street and a lieutenant commander WAVES. As general classified material was received at the base, it was routed to those with a need to know, then secured in a vault under the

153

watchful eye of the classified material control clerk, a middle-aged civilian. While little of the material was routed to me, I complained that as a "fleet sailor," it was necessary for me to stay current with fleet operations and plans. Most officers assigned to school commands appreciated the relaxed duty and were happy to avoid the burden of reading the normally bland secrets. Everyone agreed with my position, however, and I became a regular visitor to the guardian of the secret vault. I would review her inventory list, mark those of interest, and she would produce the originals. Material in hand, I would carry it to a nearby reading room where I was normally the only occupant. The reading room had no guard and was configured like any drab government conference room with a large wooden table surrounded by about sixteen chairs. Indeed, it probably doubled as a conference room when necessary. I had no safe access to photocopy equipment anywhere in the administrative building and filming the documents was out of the question in a room with two doors and frequent traffic. Making notes was too slow and burdensome, so I had to form a new procedure.

Filming material at the school was also too dangerous, so on a few occasions I carried the material home to the BOQ to casually film in my room. *But I could keep my school secrets overnight without difficulty; could I carry the secrets from the reading room to the BOQ?* I wondered. It was at the opposite end of the base and had to be three miles away or farther. Mentally I took the trip: material into the attaché case, out of the building and into my car; drive to the Rosecrans Avenue gate, drive east to Harbor Drive then south to the Fleet Training Center and another gate; park at the BOQ and rush to the room. It had to be ten minutes each way, minimum. Filming multiple pages of a small package would take at least ten minutes. One routine item was the secret *Intelligence Digest*, a monthly magazine about the size and quality of *Time* magazine that could take well over ten minutes to film. Then the trip back, passing through two separate bases or four gates total, all with marine guards. Thirty minutes minimum, I judged, and dangerous. A routine search by the marines could easily expose my activity since there was no time to disguise the material as a legal courier package. Then there was the clerk who might notice my absence from the reading room. She could be directed to collect and secure all the secrets for any number of reasons, from a simple fire drill to the admiral's need of the conference room. These dangers notwithstanding, I signed for and rushed the best material to the BOQ for filming about once a week. The marine guards never searched my attaché case during my San Diego assignment. I had one close shave with the secret control clerk, however.

On one routine photographic trip of about forty minutes, I calmly returned a stack of secrets to an unusually suspicious clerk, who was eyeing me curiously. "Mr. Walker," she intoned, "I passed through the reading room and noticed you were gone." I had planned only one excuse for such a confrontation and I soothingly explained as convincingly as possible that I needed to use the head (naval jargon for the restroom) and took the material with me rather than burden her with signing it back in for a few minutes. The explanation was perfectly reasonable, and she dropped her suspicion completely. Still, I could never find an easier method of photographing the material or even a new excuse for leaving the reading room. I felt the alibi could work one more time, so I continued with the crazy practice, but thankfully was never again questioned.

My delivery was pitifully small and far below the quality to which the Soviets were accustomed. However, they would be very busy as they worked to decrypt secret messages using the cryptographic keylists I had supplied to them for the previous twenty-two months. They were surely working day and night, sorting through millions of tape-recorded US messages. Searching through miles of tape would likely take years, and there was no guarantee of any value once the message was finally read in the clear. Hundreds of man hours might be expended only to yield a year-old weather message for the eastern Mediterranean Sea. Then again, it could be that rare top-secret message concerning US war plans.

Admittedly, the Soviets' concern that I had been exposed and was being set up by the FBI did affect me to an extent, so I traveled carefully to the drop. Perhaps the FBI counterespionage team was so slick that they *did* engineer my transfer into a trap. So, for my first leg, I sneaked to Gillespie Field where I had quietly arranged a ride in a Cessna 182 with two commercial students under an assumed name to Dulles Airport, where I rented a car. In the unlikely event that the car had an electronic homing device and bug installed in advance by the FBI, I unbolted the seatbelt, complained of the problem to the rental agent, and moved to a different car. The FBI would never prepare two cars in advance, I reasoned, and I lost myself in DC traffic.

The drop was smooth and uneventful, but the intoxicating rush of the spy business did not decline with repetition. Creeping to a stop next to the drop point, the night pressing down, always filled my whole body with a strange, cold excitement. With a hard fist of danger growing in my stomach and a quick intake of breath, like preparing for an icy plunge, I was out the door to drop my package behind some pole or tree.

Adventure is difficult for me to describe, but I believe that the basic core of man's spirit is his passion for adventure. The joy and quality of life comes from one's experiences. The excitement of adventure requires an element of danger, like the Sword of Damocles hanging by a thread over one's head. True excitement comes from scoffing at that sword, playing out one's drama below the blade—not from watching the sword hang above the head of Arnold Schwarzenegger in some movie. It is for that reason that I dislike all the psychologists and psychiatrists I have ever met. All were weenies and academic dweeb-types who experienced nothing on their own and tried to gain excitement by living vicariously through their patients. "What is it *like* to parachute from an airplane?" they asked or, "How does it *feel* to be depth charged in a submarine?" They just love to hear our sex lives described in graphic detail, probably because they have none of their own. To all those who experience nothing on their own, my response was the same: "If you want to know how it feels, go do it yourself."

But there is much, much more to the euphoria associated with the veiled drama of espionage, and this is even more difficult for me to articulate. Since entering the prison system, many criminals have described the supercharged tension and nearly explosive thrill of committing a crime, but that is only a small factor in my experience. The real exhilaration came from the knowledge that I was *changing* things on a worldwide level, creating events that would affect thousands of people, perhaps entire countries. It is hard for me to describe the emotion, but a CIA gun-money-drug-runner pilot came close when describing his overwhelming excitement after transshipping twenty tons of illegal arms through an obscure Israeli airstrip in the Negev Desert. "I looked at all those guns knowing they would soon be in the hands of some group that would change governments, defeat nations, redraw maps of the world—and I made it happen," he said. Although that gun-runner's passion was based upon the violence he had created, I could at least associate with the thought of creating international change. I was *doing* something, I was part of the equation, a player in the world drama that most people only sit and watch. And while I knew my actions to be criminal in nature, I thought back to an old army field manual addressing military leadership. It said in part: "If you believe you are right after sober and considered judgment, hold your position . . . even if your action may not be in your best interest." My actions were illegal, but the fraudulent cold war was wrong to a much greater degree—it was killing thousands and squandering America's national treasure. Working toward its end was indeed an exciting adventure.

My bizarre family life with Barbara continued with me spending evenings in our La Mesa home somewhat less than half the time. It was made more bizarre by Barbara hanging onto the idea that one day I could come back to her, and nothing I said could change this delusion. She foolishly believed that happiness could be worked out when even the contemplation of it was anathema to me. The marriage had been over long ago, but she could not get past this reality. And as someone once said, optimism is based on false logic.

Barbara continued to frustrate my attempt to visit privately with the children. At best, I could take one or two on a short grocery shopping trip, but there was never any opportunity to speak with them one-on-one, to ever get to really know them. Slowly I learned to distance myself from the pain of becoming a stranger to my kids. But this arrangement did not prevent us from enjoying quality "family" time. We sailed every inch of San Diego harbor together and flew or drove to every attraction in Southern California and beyond, from Disneyland to Tijuana.

The kids all became adept at steering the boat and flying small aircraft from the right seat. A highlight was the two-week rental of a large motor home and a family tour of four states. We explored the sights of Death Valley, Hoover Dam, the Grand Canyon, Lake Powell, the Rockies, the Petrified Forest, Bryce Canyon, Painted Desert, the Great Basin of Utah, Zion National Park, and more. At night the motor home served as our "motel"; we usually just pulled off some back road where we prepared lavish dinners, lounged around the TV, or explored the area. We even spent a night in Las Vegas where Barbara and I wandered the casinos while the kids enjoyed the motor home by themselves in the casino parking lot. It was a legendary vacation, and one that would never again be repeated.

Outside of my family activities, however, Barbara remained nearly comatose. The children, the eldest of which was thirteen, carried out all of the household duties, leaving Barbara to drink, chain-smoke, brood, and grumble. I had stopped taking her to official military functions when she became an embarrassment during my previous duty at COMSUB-LANT. The admiral would arrange two or three events a year, and while his staff was "cordially invited" to RSVP, attendance was considered mandatory. The wives of the senior officers could be annoying as they assumed the rank and power of their husbands, and Barbara took offense with this concept. These women had no *rank*, they were no better than any wife, she would argue. But every junior officer knows that these women do influence their husbands, and pissing off your boss's wife or the wife of an admiral can have disastrous consequences on one's career, rightly or wrongly. After a couple of dangerous confrontations, I elected to go alone or even take a date. Showing up with a woman other than one's wife was a social felony as well, but my fellow officers and their wives were aware of Barbara's moodiness and seemed to forgive me.

Again I urged Barbara to get that GED. The campus of the University of California, San Diego, was a few blocks away. If she didn't choose college, real estate sales were booming in California with courses cropping up everywhere to train the needed agents. It was evident that school of any type frightened her, so I even suggested volunteer work: hospital, charity, preschool, the elderly. Cost was not a factor. I felt it necessary that she move out of her comfort zone, have a reason to get out of bed in the mornings. She rallied, enrolled in a GED course and real estate agent school, but completed neither. She was going nowhere. But worse, her behavior was becoming deadly.

My commander friend from across the street, Jim Whiteman, was the administrative officer for the school command. Like all shipmates, we occasionally met for a drink at the officers' club before driving home and would carpool when necessary. These two-beer stops usually delayed us an hour, though never more than two. Jim had a strong marriage, his wife was a former navy petty officer, and Jim let her know if he was to be a little late. Barbara always knew of my plans to be home for the evening, but I was less apt to be precise in my arrival time or to inform her if I was to be late. My reasoning was that I did not actually live there, and as a casual visitor for the evening or for dinner, I was admittedly remiss in keeping Barbara informed.

We had a busy afternoon as participants in a special court-martial and left the base later than normal. Three officers and one enlisted man made up the panel that would seal the fate of a young enlisted WAVES accused of improper sexual advances upon another WAVES. The city police were the accusers, and the young woman simply hung on for survival amid the demeaning and sardonic testimony. The four of us finally retired to determine the verdict, and after an hour, unanimously found her not guilty.

The base traffic was long gone when we started for home, our emotions spent, a pounding ache starting behind my eyes. We agreed to stop for a beer, and I pulled into a tacky bar, one of those frayed and crummy businesses one would avoid in the light of day. It turned out to be a semi-strip joint, dark and with air that had been breathed too many times. We drank two very expensive beers and left, our spirits greatly lifted. It was dark but still within the dinner time frame when I parked the MG in my driveway, and halfway through a joke, I walked with Jim across the street to his sidewalk. We both noticed Barbara open the front door behind us, silhouetted in a splash of light sixty or seventy feet away. Jim turned for home and I started to cross the street when I heard the sharp crack of a pistol shot and a keening whine past my right ear. My four kids now bobbed in the doorway, frightened and confused as Barbara scurried back into the house. I stormed across the street after snapping a quick glance at Jim, but he was halfway in his door and obviously not shot. Inside my home, the kids were stunned with fright, a couple crying, not knowing what to do with their hands. Drunk and befuddled, Barbara babbled some explanation that she had "dropped" the pistol and it had gone off. Furiously, I grabbed the revolver, a cheap .22-caliber Saturday night special we bought years earlier in our poor days; one round had been fired, the brass still hot.

Her story made no sense. My car was visible in the driveway, Jim and I were talking and laughing outside in plain sight. It was not a burglar lurking out front, so why had she dug up that old pistol and carried it outside at all? Further, all revolvers have built-in safeties that prevent accidental discharge when dropped, unless it is already cocked. But why in the hell would she cock it except to fire it? No, that crazy drunk had consciously taken a shot at me, endangering Jim in the process and causing ever more psychological damage to our sobbing children, now numb in terror. Barbara stood there as though fastened to the wall, shifting uneasily but at least seeming to be frightened by what she had done. I calmed the kids as much as possible and quickly realized that they were recovering much faster than I was. My nightmare had reached a new level, for Barbara very much wanted to kill me, even if just for a fleeting moment. Now what? Were the kids safe with her? Would she snap again and kill me in my sleep?

My eldest daughter, Margaret, was not present at the door when I barged in, but she showed up a few minutes later, curiously out of breath and pale, a look of disbelief and frustration on her face. Decades later she told me what had happened. Barbara's irritation had grown as I was later and later, and when I finally pulled in the driveway, she flew into a rage. My lingering outside with Jim inflamed her further. She ran to the bedroom for the pistol, stormed outside, and fired the gun. Afraid that Barbara would kill me, Margaret dashed to her room, jumped out the window, and ran to the home of a deputy sheriff who lived several houses away. She stopped short, however, realizing the police would do more harm than good, so she raced back and through the window to "save her father." Fortunately, Barbara was emotionally good for only one shot, as I made an easy target in front of the house.

I spent that night at the BOQ and cut back even further on visits to the children. The kids were safe from serious harm, I believed, since they were under her tight control, on her side. I avoided Jim for a while, uneasy and anxious at having to explain Barbara's conduct, but thankfully, he never mentioned the incident. Perhaps he failed to recognize the small pistol's sound, not unusual for those lacking small-arms experience;

the volume of movie gunfire is woefully exaggerated. Years later, Jim continued to deny hearing the shot, a gentleman to the end, considering how close that round came to hitting him in the back.

Admittedly, my work output at the school's command was far below my normal dynamic and vigorous level of 100 percent plus. Working at only 30 to 40 percent efficiency, I was transferring my unused energy to recreational pursuits.

During this period, my brother Arthur was promoted to lieutenant commander and transferred to Anti-Submarine Warfare School in Norfolk, Virginia.

My access to classified material had changed dramatically, and I missed the operations plans and orders, material that kept me abreast of fleet activities. But of more importance to me was the progress of the cold war, signs for any improvement to US-Soviet relations. Was there any evidence that the Soviets were moderating their stance, initiating peace or disarmament initiatives? My twenty-two months' worth of material had surely convinced them that, while surrounded by menacing US forces poised to attack, an invasion of Russia would not happen. Moreover, the Soviets had to deduce without question the superiority of the US war machine and the futility of ever achieving parity, much less dominance, over the United States. This realization alone should have prodded them to abandon the arms race and seek safety behind peace treaties and agreements. The school's command did receive excellent analytical secrets, and I carefully reviewed everything, looking for any sign that I was doing some good.

I wish every citizen had the opportunity to leaf through the secret *Intelligence Digest* magazine. Most people imagine secret documents to be stapled sheets of poorly printed material. While that is often the case, the *Intelligence Digest* was professionally printed on magazine-quality glossy paper, multicolored, well illustrated, and with many photographs.

From a distance, the periodical could easily pass for a *Time* or *Newsweek*. It was while carefully studying the *Intelligence Digest* that I came upon a secret article concerning arms control. To my surprise, hard intelligence reported that Soviet premier Brezhnev had proposed strategic arms limitation talks with the United States back in 1967. The Politburo, the principle policy-making committee of the government, seriously debated the proposal in light of the aggressive nature of US imperialism and their fear of impending war with the United States. Brezhnev vowed to maintain a strong strategic force to defend the Soviet Union, but feelers were secretly transmitted to the United States to discuss limits on the size of their arsenals. There was no reply to the Soviet proposal. Brezhnev's initiative was eventually referred to as SALT, for Strategic Arms Limitation Treaty.

My spirits soared, for 1967 was the very year I had begun delivering documents to the Soviet Union. Did I influence Brezhnev's proposal? I privately wondered. Perhaps it was wishful thinking, but while the Soviets did not need me to convince them of the aggressive posture of the United States, my material surely showed that they could safely consider the reduction of their weapons without being destroyed. They could relax and slow the arms race that they could never win anyway—the Americans were not coming. I believe that with my help, the Soviet Union began to see the light.

Disarmament had actually been the subject of the United Nations since 1952 and some progress had been made, albeit unremarkable. Antarctica was made free of weapons in 1959, and 1963, the big year under Kennedy, saw the Washington-Moscow Hot Line, the Limited Test Ban Treaty, and a US-USSR treaty not to place weapons of mass destruction in space.

Progress chilled under Johnson, although the United Nations did adopt a lukewarm treaty in 1966 barring orbiting nuclear weapons and the use of the moon for military activity. The Glassboro State College conference between Johnson and Alexei Kosygin had great potential for progress in 1967 but achieved little more than a promise that third world invasions by the United States or the USSR would not lead to World War III. Brezhnev again proposed SALT with no results but began pressing for an all-European conference to reduce tensions between East Germany and West Germany and nearby countries.

One important agreement was the 1968 Nonproliferation Treaty, which kept nuclear weapons out of the hands of over one hundred countries, but the United States seemed to lag while the Soviet Union pressed on for peace initiatives. Through the Conference on Security and Cooperation, between East European and West European countries, over fifty countries worked to increase cooperation. The conference resulted in a nonaggression pact between West Germany and the Soviet Union, acceptance of East German and West German borders, and a declaration that all frontiers were inviolable.

It was at this point in my life that I was struck with the awful realization that nothing would ever change. The Soviet Union had reluctantly accepted that she could never win a hot or cold war against the United States—hopefully aided in that decision by my small contribution—but if the Soviets simply quit, would the CIA end its make-war policy? No. I saw the US government run by a secret fraternity, a fraternity not restricted to the CIA but including moguls from academia, politics, news media, banking, business, and industry, the secret aristocracy of America. International communism was their convenient whipping boy, a dangerous enemy to be stopped at any cost.

Chapter 15

THE BOMB

In the summer of 1971, I blew up the city of San Diego, the Naval Station, Submarine Base, Naval Air Station, Marine Air Station, Amphibious Base, Security Group, and SEAL team using a smuggled nuclear bomb. While the nuclear device was relatively small, the surface detonation was particularly "dirty," lifting a huge cloud of water and debris that killed hundreds of thousands in a vast area downwind and contaminated the land for hundreds of years.

It all started with a formal officers' cocktail party that had degenerated to the women gathering to discuss diapers and brownies while the men assembled to decide a more weighty issue: national defense. The men congregated around the most senior officer, an experienced captain on the fast track for rear admiral, politely allowing him to officiate. Vietnam and the Soviet threat were the usual topics at such gatherings, with everyone expressing their frustration at being denied victory in Vietnam by the White House and Pentagon leadership. Every military professional knew exactly what should be done to defeat North Vietnam. The young, less experienced junior officers wanted to bomb the port of Haiphong to rubble or bomb the Hanoi area dikes and flood the land or just nuke the entire country. We older officers understood that the purpose of the armed forces is more than just the defense of the United States. Just like the Soviet Army, the use of military power is also a means of communicating one's interests to the world, building prestige, and reassuring allies. A secondary mission of our military is to assure pro-Western nations that the United States will come to their aid in time of need. The United States also had its policy of containment against the spread of communism. But the *real* reason we were in Indochina—the make-war policy of the CIA—was not understood by most.

The Soviet threat was a deeper, more arcane problem. Would they chance a preemptive strike, all but guaranteeing an overwhelming retaliatory strike? Could the United States strike first against the USSR and prevent even a single retaliatory missile launch against us from land or submarine? These conversations never went anywhere as those with the warrior mentality tried to compare missile size, throw-weight, multiple warheads, emergency launch message delivery, bomb shelters, and so on. When the conversation finally bogged down, I decided to shake up everyone's preconceived notions with an unorthodox question. Addressing the captain, I asked why we were so overly concerned with missiles and submarines. If the Soviet Union or any nuclear-armed enemy wished to destroy the United States with nuclear weapons, why not just smuggle the weapons across our open borders and preposition them at every major city? A determined enemy need not waste resources in developing and building intercontinental rockets when drug smugglers carry tons of drugs across our borders yearly. All eyes stared at me with a curious surprise as I spoke, then turned to the captain for his answer. There were several seconds of strained silence. I had him, I thought, for there is no way to stop such a smuggled preemptive strike without sealing our borders behind an iron curtain. I tried not to smile.

As officers become more and more senior, they actually become less military and more political. A naval captain, equal to an army full colonel, is at the point of transition, ready to become a fully political rear admiral. The captain stared back, undefeated. "What you describe, Mr. Walker, is a terrorist act, not a military act. Matters of terrorism are the responsibility of civil authorities, the FBI." I had to smile with admiration as the captain successfully evaded the question, passing the buck without diminishing the mission of the military. This guy was ready for promotion.

My question seemed to break up the group, and a young lieutenant junior grade followed me to the bar, anxious to speak. He and I had recently attended a short leadership course together, and once we were out of earshot, he gushed that I had really stumped the captain for a moment. But more important, he felt that it would not be that easy to smuggle nuclear weapons across the Mexican border. "Bullshit, Chris, I'll smuggle an H-bomb across the border on my next trip to Mexico," I challenged. Chris was an experienced sailor and had been on my boat previously.

While he stared back with curious suspicion, I continued, "We have a slot on the upcoming San Diego to Ensenada race. Make the race with me and I'll smuggle a thermonuclear bomb to San Diego on the return trip."

Chris never considered that I was serious as he howled and shook my hand. "You're on," he said, grinning.

To make a long story short, I actually made that trip, proving how easy it would be to pick up a bomb in Mexico and bring it into San Diego without any US government interference or customs check. Chris was forced to eat some crow when he saw that, theoretically, I could have blown up San Diego.

When we got in, we enjoyed a celebration lunch while the owner of the new spinnaker ran the colorful sail up the mast on his pierside yacht to inspect the beauty. We celebrated with my friend Judy, whose excitement was electric as we toasted her good fortune at landing a job in country and the likelihood of her improved prospects of promotion to major. I hid my envy and did not tell her that I had blown up San Diego the night before.

Chapter 16

BACK TO SEA

My spy delivery lately was small at ten or twelve rolls of Minox film, thirty-six shots each, but I followed a pattern of strict security regardless. A cross-country flight to San Diego would be most convenient but was deemed far too dangerous. The terminal was always full of traveling sailors, and since I was known by scores of shipmates and hundreds of students, my travel east could be noticed. So I took a PSA commuter flight to LAX under the pretext of visiting a girlfriend. I had met the woman a year earlier and after riding a navy cruiser from San Diego to Long Beach, she was well known to my friends. Once lost in the endless crowded caverns of LAX, however, it was simple to safely board a cross-country carrier under an assumed name.

I continued renting cars without a reservation, a practice still possible then, and switched cars after disabling some system, usually removing a fuse to the wipers or flashers. While this practice seemed unnecessarily cautious, I nonetheless decided to extend the switching practice to my motel room. Renting a room under an assumed name is simple when using cash, and it was highly unlikely that such a room would be bugged. Guaranteeing advance reservations with a credit card was obviously not done since the FBI could then rig a room with bugs and cameras in advance. But it was possible. If I were being tailed by a large counter-espionage team, they could rush into the motel ahead of me, arrange for my room assignment, and rig the room while I registered. They could even creep into the room after I registered, planting a bug or two, in the few seconds necessary, while I parked and grabbed my luggage. Years later I would bug rooms the same way as a private investigator.

The methods of disabling a hotel or motel room are limited only by one's imagination. My normal practice was to carry the snipped-off corner of a kitchen sponge and, once in the room, stuff the sponge deep into the sink drain. Room air conditioners or television sets could also be disabled without causing any real damage. A blocked sink drain or any inoperative room equipment would guarantee a room shift and possibly frustrate a "black bag" team. It would at least panic the bug crew as they tried to beat me to my new room.

The dead drop was exhilarating but otherwise routine, and I remained in the District until Monday for part two of my trip. My motel was just a couple of blocks from the navy building in Alexandria, and I sat at my detailer's desk as previously scheduled. It was clearly the first time in his career that anyone ever asked for early transfer from such a coveted position. Most personnel visits were by whiney nonseamen begging for early release from sea duty. But finding my replacement was not the problem—it was my request for a Vietnam billet that presented the difficulty.

But back at my detailer's desk, my prospect diminished as he explained how some applicants had attempted special schools in preparation, become qualified in specialized equipment, and had even learned the Vietnamese language on their own. My assignment to the Beach Jumpers was the closest to a covert war assignment, so I described that experience of radio jamming, deception, and imitative deception operations as they would apply to Vietnam, but it was a weak sales pitch. That assignment was over ten years earlier and with a structure designed for war against the Soviet Union. This was a different war and the Beach Jumper mission had changed along with its name. I would not be one of the lucky twenty.

My detailer was at least sympathetic as we sought out a fleet unit that would make me happy. I was not interested in impersonal heavies, like aircraft carriers, but something smaller and with an interesting mission. He finally hit on a combat stores ship, a unit that made frequent port calls, including Vietnam ports. One of its missions was to provide armed forces courier services, a position normally carried out by the communications department. It seemed perfect, so he penciled me in as the communications officer of the USS *Niagara Falls* (AFS-3), home port San Francisco.

Since family life had declined to something less than a farce, I decided to move the family to the Bay Area. My two-year transfer date was for September, so moving a few months early would have everyone settled a couple months before the kids started school. The La Mesa house was immediately put up for sale, and I began the research for buying a house near my next duty station. My ship was normally berthed at the Navy Supply Center piers at Oakland or at the Navy Air Station Alameda facilities.

What was out of the question was living in Oakland, the Bay Area's center for disfigured urbanization. In my usual overorganized way, I studied the real estate ads and street maps of the area to select our home site. My East Bay area street map was carefully marked in color code by first, second, and third choice of neighborhoods. At the top of the list was Alameda, an island snuggled up against Oakland, one half owned by the Naval Air Station, and the remainder an older but cultured town with real identity. Careful shopping would be necessary to find a home for my large family, but Barbara was anxious to start the search. She had always been a frustrated real estate agent, and since she showed some rare enthusiasm, I decided to let her make the purchase alone. I would enjoy some time alone with my children, a most unusual event, while Barbara flew to San Francisco and spent a week shopping, staying in a motel, and driving around in a rental car. She was equipped with a map showing the second choice of San Leandro to the south, and Berkeley or Richmond to the north as third choices. I genuinely expected to end up in San Leandro, where ample houses were available, but since I planned to moor my boat at Jack London Square, San Leandro was fine.

Barbara telephoned several days later to announce she had found the ideal house, a large four-bedroom with central air and attached two-car garage in a new neighborhood. New neighborhood? Yes, it was located in Union City. She assured me it was close to Alameda and I would love it. Consulting the map, Union City turned out to be a dot on the East Bay at least thirty miles from Alameda and halfway to San Jose. The commute would be a bitch, an hour or more each way during drive times. It was an awful location, and I had to believe she did it with the intention of keeping me farther from the kids. But what did it matter? My ship would be my real home at sea or in port and the travel time would be a minor inconvenience.

Spending a few days alone with the kids was a bittersweet experience. I probably overdid it in recreational activities, but we also were able to talk candidly without Barbara hovering near. It was then that I realized how badly Barbara had talked about me, leaving the kids afraid, slowly alienating me. My youngest daughter, Laura, was the coldest, and I grew hopeless that our relationship would ever deepen.

With the family settled in the Bay Area, I focused my spare time on commercial flying. Jerry had obtained his commercial license and was flying an old Luscum tail-dragger on swordfish-spotting flights out of Mitchell Field. These huge and expensive fish are surface feeders and easily seen from the air. Fliers spotted the fish from the air and vectored small fishing boats to move in and spear them. I had to try it, and with Jerry's help, I flew several spotting flights and made a few kills. We collected a bonus based on the size of the fish, but the flights were very boring and the planes were a mess.

At work, secret material crossed my desk referring indirectly to high-level meetings in progress between the United States and the CPC (Communist Party of China), a situation that I saw as very dangerous. The Soviet Union had long worried that the United States would create a major armed conflict between the USSR and China, then attack the exhausted victor of the war, eliminating both communist enemies in one sweep. Whatever they were discussing in China, it could not be peace, I reasoned, since the United States was in the process of bombing China's client state of North Vietnam. I could not have been more wrong. The world would learn the following year that Henry Kissinger, secretary of state, had personally visited Chairman Mao Zedong in order to launch a peace process that continues to this very day.

My official orders arrived in early fall to report to the USS *Niagara Falls*, shortly after her return from Vietnam in December. My good friend Lieutenant Commander John Cabana received orders for a carrier, which was also scheduled for return to the combat zone. John was director of Radio "B" School, where more-senior radiomen received basic electronic training. We sat at the FTC officers' bar over lunch, our new orders still warm in our pockets, and discussed our return to the fleet. John was as anxious as I was to again experience the adventure of the sea, visiting those old familiar Pacific ports, doing the jobs we were really trained to do. Eating sandwiches and sipping beer at the bar, we noticed the usual crowd of officers, all of whom seemed to be staff officers. John was a line officer, identified by a star on his sleeve, which signified that he was in line to command a ship. Staff officers wear insignia, designating their profession, such as doctor, dentist, lawyer, or supply corps member. These officers are not in line for command and cannot drive or fight the ship. Thus if the commanding officer is disabled in combat, the next-senior line officer assumes command of the ship. If he becomes injured, command keeps shifting down the line, even including warrant officers like myself. It has happened that a junior line lieutenant has assumed command of a ship while a supply corps commander was onboard.

John and I searched the lunch crowd in vain for just one other line officer, but there were none. How typical of shore duty, we mused, all staff officers. Then in a joke that we would laugh about for years later, I muttered with disgust, "Christ, John, two hundred staff pukes and only two killers." At that we howled, both ready for sea and Vietnam.

Myra telephoned me at work a few days later, upset and asking me to join her for lunch. I picked her up at the dental clinic where she worked, and we drove to the basement bar at Rooms. With Myra's flair for melo-drama, I could never gauge the level of her problems at first glance, but she was distraught. Over a stiff drink, she revealed her problem—she had orders for sea duty. I struggled to conceal my amusement; her depression in the face of sea duty was the exact opposite of my elation. She was ordered to the new hospital ship USS *Sanctuary*, which was undergoing final outfitting at a San Francisco shipyard. The ship's operating schedule called for the permanent stationing of a hospital ship off the Vietnam coast with two or three ships rotating on station in the combat zone.

I was comforting and sympathetic, since it was most unusual for WAVES to experience sea assignments. Myra was more of a country club girl, a little too independent and rebellious for the navy, but while profes-sionally competent, she was always in trouble with her bosses. She was probably the only WAVES assigned to the *Sanctuary* who had not volun-teered. Life for a young third-class petty officer WAVES would be diffi-cult aboardship, living in a small compartment of thirty girls, stacked tight in tiny bunks, three high. But I reminded her that my ship would also be in the Bay Area, and after a couple double bourbons and a few of my sea stories, she seemed more resigned to joining the fleet.

We had a haul-out party for *Dirty Old Man* in the fall. My friends and crewmen unstepped the mast and watched silently as the crane lifted her dripping from the water and plopped her on the big trailer. Now it was my turn to be depressed and Myra's job to cheer me up, for the San Diego party was over. Bon voyage parties were held with friends at the Yacht Club, at the airport, and at the BOQ. The usual "hail and farewell" party at the school involved a hail to my incoming relief from the fleet and farewell to me upon my return to sea. I received the usual trinket gifts and the obligatory command plaque; Barbara received a silver serving tray in absentia from the officers' wives she had barely met and never knew. Then, sooner than expected, I was behind the wheel heading north on I-5, boat in tow, rolling toward the East Bay and my pseudo home.

Chapter 17

THE NAM

Her bow was visible in the distance, moored to one of the big Naval Supply Center piers, the big white "PS-3" standing out on her gray hull. That wonderful feeling of excitement was rising inside, and I had to control the urge to increase my pace. It was a sunny and brisk weekend morning in mid-December, so the supply center was quiet and closed for business; the buzz of traffic could be heard from the nearby double levels of the Oakland Bay Bridge. As I approached the gangway, the quarterdeck watch turned their attention to this stranger, a chief warrant officer in dress blues carrying that well-known brown envelope in his left hand—his official orders.

The ship and crew would be beat up and tired after a long deployment to Vietnam, the half year cruise extended by months. A little rust scarred her hull, but the ship looked surprisingly good for a lady that was worked so hard. No smoke or gas rose from her stack, indicating that her three Babcock & Wilcox boilers were shut down, so she would not be moving soon.

The USS *Niagara Falls*, a combat stores ship, was part of the fleet's service force, those ships that provided ammunition, fuel, repair parts, and food to the combat units. But under a new concept in the 1960s, these service ships were made bigger and faster so they could operate with a battle group and were even armed so they could also fight. The *Niagara Falls* was one of six ships of the class designated as a mobile supply center, providing battle repair parts for ships and aircraft, plus a full range of food including dry, fresh, and frozen. She lacked the glamour of a cruiser or destroyer, but I found her sleek and beautiful at 501 feet in length, 80-foot beam and with a main deck 26 feet from the water line. Installed on the fantail was a helicopter pad, hangar, and control tower for two CH-46 Sea Knight helos, big twin-engine, twin-blade machines con-

175

figured for cargo. Fully loaded, the ship displaced almost ten thousand tons and could cruise at twenty knots for almost ten thousand miles. Four three-inch guns gave her teeth.

Snapping a smart salute to the fantail colors, then a salute to the officer on watch, I announced, "Chief Warrant Officer Walker, reporting aboard as ordered, sir." The three-man quarterdeck crew looked over their new guy—submarine dolphins on my chest, a couple rows of ribbons, a submarine Polaris patrol pin beneath—and wondered what they had. My arrival was entered in the quarterdeck log, and as the messenger escorted me to the Command Duty Officer (CDO), I experienced a satisfying sense of place: I knew that I was home.

Myra had taken an apartment up in the hills above the waterfront area in the Bayview district, which was understandable in light of her shipboard living conditions. My shipboard work routine normally included a hustling twelve-hour day, then without breaking my pace, I jumped into the shower, into civilian clothes, and into my car. Myra's apartment was so high up that often the streets and houses were hidden by the fog, which always slowed me down, but since Myra was never ready on time, it didn't matter.

She shared an apartment with two gay men who were also never ready for whatever they planned at night. While I sipped scotch in the living room, they crowded around the bathroom mirror in a cloud of marijuana smoke and bitched like three women, fighting over makeup, combs, and hairspray. The show was hilarious. Eventually Myra would take charge, issue a few drill instructor commands, and the trio would finally be ready. Occasionally we would join the men for a drink at one of the gay bars, which always had better music and better atmosphere. The presence of a straight male and an honest-to-god female was far too disruptive, however, and we never stayed long. Fisherman's Wharf and the Canary area was our usual target for dinner, shows, shops, and general entertainment.

There was a surreal sense of living a Hollywood romantic drama as our Asian cruises grew near. Like in some old movie script, the young woman in the medical corps and the older, experienced veteran were driven to eke out as much living as possible before sailing into a war thousands of miles away. The passion was deep; we could not get enough of each other. Yet strangely, there was no talk of a commitment, as though there was no future once our ships sailed; only this moment existed. Our evenings always included walking through Ghirardelli Square, the old converted chocolate factory overlooking Aquatic Park. We would snuggle at an outside table with steaming Irish coffee, mesmerized by the panoramic view of the bay that possessed the greatest natural beauty in the world. The romantic ambience is unparalleled with a billion lights, boats plying through the black water, mournful foghorns echoing, lights twinkling across the Golden Gate Bridge, the arcing light of Alcatraz Island. Then, as if on cue, as though ordered by the San Francisco Tourist Bureau, the cold, white, ghostly fog would float from offshore. Slowly the bridge would fade to gray, and eventually the swirls of mist would reach us. This *had* to be a movie set.

Myra's temperament did not permit her to sit still for long; that girl exuded reckless passion and she knew how to party. She drank too much, was the life of the party, and could be depended upon to create classical comedy. One night she went to the bathroom naked and returned to the wrong room. That one was unforgettable.

My life was back to normal, busy at work and busy at play, the vacation of San Diego long behind me. I was at my peak, thriving on three or four hours of sleep, running three miles a day, and hitting the books hard to learn my new job of operating an eighteen-thousand-ton ship. Somewhere along the way, CWOs had to take the brutally difficult examination for master chief radioman as part of some crazy plan that allowed us to progress in our old enlisted ranks. If some crew members still harbored a hope that peace would come before our June sailing date, it disappeared on March 30. The North Vietnamese would not make it easy for President Nixon to extricate himself from the war by launching the biggest attack across the DMZ in four years. In fact, the decrease in US ground forces caused an increase in naval and air activity. The news brought a groan from those not wishing to sail—which was the majority—then another groan two weeks later when US bombing commenced again on Hanoi and Haiphong. Hope was abandoned; we would sail on schedule.

Barbara was nearing a state of vegetation at this point. The children did the cleaning, laundry, and most of the cooking. They got themselves up for school, made breakfast, chose their clothes, and supervised homework themselves. Needless to say, they went to school in some strange outfits and did not perform well academically. I had almost totally taken over the household administration and financial responsibilities, and that now presented a serious dilemma as I faced a long cruise. Since San Diego, Barbara had taken to ignoring the mail and sometimes even lost the routine monthly bills. Since I would occasionally retrieve the mail, however, I would discover "final notices" threatening to discontinue telephone or electrical services. While feeling under the bed one day for a dropped item, I discovered a mound of mail, some opened and scattered, some still sealed, a pile that could fill two bushel baskets. There were unpaid bills of every description, from utilities to lapsed insurance policies. Barbara seemed to have abandoned the last vestige of home and family management, but since I lived in the relaxed atmosphere of radio school, it was simple for me to perform that task at work. A careful check-off list allowed me to quickly identify missing bills and to keep from falling into arrears on some long-lost bill. But now I faced a long cruise, and as simple as the job was, it could not be done from sea. Barbara was certainly capable, and in view of my illegal source of extra income, I was forced to pass the project back to her. But at least I could make the process as easy as possible for her.

Sea duty would complicate my spy activity in selecting the dates for my Washington dead drops. My very slim summer delivery was made before leaving San Diego, and since I had the ship's schedule, a drop was scheduled for within a couple weeks of our June sailing. My wild guess at a date met with luck, since I was duty free on the weekend I had selected six months earlier. But even without the duty, my shipboard obligations were important enough to have kept me aboard. It is impossible for a shipboard officer to ever "catch up" on his duties, but with no ongoing crisis, I turned the division over to my very capable chief.

My poor access to classified material came to an end with my transfer. As communications officer, my office consisted of a walk-in vault within the radio room, which, in itself, was a vaultlike security area. All of the communication cryptographic materials were stored in my vault in addition to the storage of all top-secret operations orders, plans, documents, and messages aboard the ship. The secret intelligence library filled a five-drawer filing cabinet located in the radio room; the intelligence officer and I had the lock combination. One of my duties was to issue the monthly crypto-material to the watch supervisors, so it was a simple matter to film the material a day or two before issuing it to the watch. I was the only crew member who was permanently issued a .45 pistol, normal hardware in the crypto-vault.

The trip to Washington would be quick, the luxury of elaborate anti-surveillance procedures was not possible. My drop material included most of the crypto-systems for the past six months and a few top-secret messages, operation orders, and operation plans relating to the eastern Pacific and First Fleet. I had only Saturday and Sunday to complete the spy exchange and I flew out on the earliest flight on Saturday from Oakland International. No special precautions were taken except to use an assumed name. So much time is lost in normal airport delays—three lost time-zone hours in the air, car rental and motel registrations—it was growing dark by the time I could start the drop procedure.

The motel I selected was just outside the Beltway and near the drop site, and I immediately drove the drop route in reverse. The two drop sites were identified—not plowed under to build a new subdivision—as were the four signal spots. The timing was so close that I barely had time to buy two 7-UP signal cans, eat a hasty dinner, and start the long procedure. Practically no security precautions were taken, which increased my tension greatly. Traffic was mercifully sparse, but I knew that if I'd been followed, it would not be one or two cars tailing behind, Hollywood-style.

The drop and pickup went smoothly, no goblins leaping from the shadows, but with the very incriminating Soviet package on the floor behind me, it was much too early to exhale. If an arrest were to be made, it would be while I carried a bag of money and a pound of Soviet instructions for my next dead drop. How would they make the arrest? I wondered, while gnawing on my lip. Probably a stationary roadblock ahead and a "moving roadblock" behind would be best, trapping me in the middle. It was a black night with no moon, stars, or even a lighted farmhouse. My headlights stabbing into the night was the only sign of life. The narrow blacktop road wound lazily along the Virginia countryside, and with each tenth-of-a-mile click of the odometer, my safety seemed more assured and my anxiety decreased ever so slightly.

I was in a slow left turn when a faint red glow swept the trees ahead. Then again, but brighter. *Fuck . . . was this it?* A police car was hidden ahead just beyond the turn. Instinctively, I slowed and quickly recalled the absence of intersections, driveways, and even dirt logging roads behind me. The blackness in the rearview mirror was solid, no moving roadblock. I could go in reverse, turn around, and run like hell, but that could result in an arrest. One of my first axioms was that when "dirty," do nothing stupid that would create suspicion, cause a stop, search, or arrest when otherwise I could continue as normal. That is why I had long before stopped carrying a gun, since a chance arrest for possession of a weapon could lead to a much larger discovery. So I relaxed and continued around the curve to two police cars off to the side, standing around a third car, the flashing and rotating lights practically blinding in the gloom. They ignored me as I drifted past at twenty miles an hour. A couple more miles down the road, I finally exhaled.

That little fright with the nonexistent roadblocks prompted a reevaluation of the spy business, the real dangers involved. After the first year or so, my Hollywood-inspired concept of FBI invincibility had faded along with my fear of pending arrest. Since they had failed to identify me entering the Soviet embassy in 1967, and failed to track me when I left, the real danger for future capture rested not with the FBI but with me—doing something stupid. My first and only stupid mistake was not divorcing Barbara and living my secret life in the shadows. But beyond that single error, I handled my extra money carefully and did nothing to create any suspicion. Barbara was the problem, not imaginary cops lurking in the bushes. The nature of my job did not allow the time for complex security measures on these drops, so I drastically cut back on the crazy sneaking and creeping on my trips to Washington. From then on, I usually slipped in and out on a short weekend without anyone realizing I was out of town. Flights and motels were paid in cash and under assumed names. Official navy leave was never used, so there was never any trail or record of my quick trips to Washington.

Myra's ship sailed, bringing to a close our torrid movielike romance. In a strange role reversal, I drove to Hunter's Point to bid her farewell as her ship went to war. The officer of the deck gave me permission to board during the final minutes before the gangway was pulled away and the lines cast off. Myra stood on the main deck, her mouth in a rosette pout, that dusting of freckles across her nose unhidden by makeup. She exuded sexiness regardless of her ill-fitting men's work uniform of black leather shoes, dungarees, blue chambray shirt, and a cap squashing her blond hair. Our attempt to look casual was unsuccessful, the busy deck crew sensed the electricity between us, my impulse to reach out and touch her. I led her to a nearby doorway for a moment of privacy; I could feel the heat of her body, the unintended excitement. Our lips touched slightly, then became full of passion. She shuddered with a sigh as I hurried away and down the gangway even as they prepared to hoist it away. I watched until the ship backed into the channel, Myra at the starboard rail, looking back with her sensuous sleepy-cat smile, determined not to let me see her cry. As I drove over the bridge back to Oakland, her ship sailed beneath. That marvelous girl left a hole in my heart.

The time was nearing when I would be shipping out. When Barbara was in a mellow mood and free from alcohol, I chose that moment to discuss the household bills. My three-ring binder contained check-off sheets with each bill listed and a space for the check number. Our two payment books were in pockets on the inside cover, payment envelopes in their pockets. One hundred postage stamp rolls were loaded and ready in the desk drawer. The checkbook was balanced to the penny. She and I drove to our bank located at Southland Shopping Center and into a private booth with our safe deposit box where the final phase was covered. Our monthly bills were about $800 a month in those days, and I stacked eight envelopes in the box, each marked by month for the next eight months. They contained enough cash for the monthly bills plus $1,000 extra for spending money. Write the checks at home and seal them for mailing, I explained, then come to the bank and remove the envelope for the month. Keep $1,000 and deposit the rest to cover the bills. At worst, the ship's cruise would be extended by two months, making it eight months total, so she had close to $15,000 to get comfortably through the period. The checking account had a couple thousand in backup. The system was well organized, and she seemed impressed.

Still I worried about emergencies, even the unlikely prospect that I would not return from Nam. I had a lot more cash, most of which came from my last dead drop exchange earlier that month. Some I stored aboardship, and the remainder I hid in the house, where Barbara could retrieve it in an emergency. In a corner of the garage, the builder had constructed a footing that resembled a short step about eight inches in length. I built a wooden mold on the step, extending the step along the wall by about ten inches, and made it ready to pour in concrete. With about $20,000 in cash wrapped in plastic, I called Barbara to the garage after the kids were in bed for the night.

The package of cash was placed in the bottom of the mold, and a fresh batch of concrete was poured on the top. This is your emergency money, I explained, and it would survive a fire or major earthquake. It dried a couple hours later, and with the mold removed, matched the wall perfectly. If you need it, just take a hammer from the peg-board and break it out, I instructed. I could then relax; my family would at least be financially stable during my trip.

Things were going so well between Barbara and I that I decided to push for a favor. News reports at sea are always difficult and spotty, and the lack of information was torturous for a news enthusiast like me. In fact, my radio shack usually provided the only news source for the crew, since some news was transmitted over our communications channels. We also tuned into the one-hundred-word-per-minute international teletype radio channels of AP and UP, but that was only possible on a not-to-interfere basis with our hectic workload. The radiomen would at least cut and paste a few pages of news, photocopying a dozen copies and spreading them around the ship. In port, we would consider ourselves lucky to find an old copy of *Stars and Stripes*. My *Time* magazine went to Union City, and rather than change the address to my ship, I decided to ask Barbara to mail it when she finished reading it. She agreed, so I made up thirty-two large envelopes with proper postage affixed and addressed to my ship. The envelopes were placed in a convenient place in a desk drawer and with Barbara's good mood, I expected the plan would work.

The children were old enough at ages fifteen to nine to grasp the length of time Dad would be gone. We talked about it collectively, that I would be gone beyond Christmas, but individual conversations with any of them was nearly impossible. They all seemed anxious to ask questions, to talk to me privately, but Barbara would have none of it. Cynthia looked absolutely forlorn, like her protector was leaving her to the tortures of some insane foster home. I had the strange feeling that I was leaving the dog in charge.

Every sailor could recognize the distinctive bump of tugboats as they were nudging their noses against the hull, trying up to drag us from the pier and turn the ship toward the channel. It was my cue to amble topside to the bridge and take a last look at the bay. A hard wind blew from the northwest, gray scud hung low, soaking everything in that invisible chilling mist. The pilothouse was crowded and busy, but my target was the starboard wing where a wet lookout watch and the junior officer of the deck (JOOD) stared into the hazy dawn. As we passed under the Oakland Bay Bridge, I scanned Treasure Island with binoculars for a look at my boat. The recreation pier sat exposed to the bay, almost facing the Pacific weather without protection. I spotted her bobbing hull, her mooring lines taut against the rain-chilled wind; I should have hauled her out for this cruise.

Pounding the channel to the west, we passed Alcatraz Island, and thankfully the channel buoys were visible below the scud. The Golden Gate Bridge was beclouded, only her upright supports visible. I stood there, foul-weather jacket zipped to my neck, until we steamed past the sea buoy far beyond the bay, the last buoy of the channel. The emotion of most crew members as they faced the long cruise was dejected acceptance; I was thrilled.

When we reached the coast of Vietnam, our job consisted of supplying the ships off the coast. My memory of our swing through the fleet has long ago blurred to a nonspecific montage, but not so with my first swing through the "gun line." A string of destroyers and cruisers hugged the North Vietnamese coast in the Gulf of Tonkin and down past the DMZ to Hue in the south.

Chapter 18

THE 25,000-MILE DEAD DROP

Our first line swing came to an end after about two weeks when we rendezvoused with the amphibious task force of at least eight ships. Several battalions of combat-ready marines stood prepared for an amphibious assault on a moment's notice. We set a slow course as the guide—each ship coming alongside in turn, matching our course and speed—and took our supplies by helo and suspended-line transfer. This impressive collection of ships centered around an LPH, a carrierlike ship designed for the "vertical assault" of thousands of combat-ready troops by CH-53 Sea Stallion helos carrying thirty-five troops each and CH-46 Sea Knights like ours but rigged to lift twenty-four troops. Next came the LSDs—landing ship docks—huge ships for seaborne assault by landing craft and tanks. The landing craft and tanks were loaded with troops in a large internal well deck. The ship's stern was then submerged several feet to float the small craft, which then swam ashore through a large rear door. The final ships were LSTs—landing ship tanks—that drove their noses on the beach and disgorged tanks and troops directly on dry land.

Fighting along the gun line was intense, and although the US fleet presence was massive, the line was stretched along three hundred miles, from Quang Tri to the Haiphong area. The destroyers were hardly lined up shoulder-to-shoulder or even in sight of each other, so we steamed in lonely separation along the coast from one customer to another. But everybody aboard was looking forward to our coming shore leave in Hong Kong.

Victoria Peak came into view first as the *Niagara Falls* steamed into the West Lamma channel. But as we turned to starboard and toward Hong Kong, everyone's attention was to the port side where the sunken hulk of the British luxury liner *Queen Elizabeth* rested. Beyond that lay the allure of Hong Kong.

The next two months were spent in our usual routine of running up and down the Tonkin Gulf, interspersed by port calls in Taiwan, Singapore, and the Philippines. As our time in the western Pacific neared five months, the supposed end of our deployment a few weeks away, we all knew that we had entered the usual undefined "extension." Crew morale sank sharply, so to spur their spirits, the CO obtained approval for another R&R. He tried for the exotic port of Surabaya, Indonesia, which generated considerable excitement.

Leave was also authorized at the six-month point, allowing 10 percent of the crew to see their families in the United States. None of the officers and few of the enlisted men applied for leave, mostly due to the travel expense, which was naturally paid by the service member. I had pushed thoughts of Barbara to the back of my mind, but I could tell that she had sunk into her comatose management style. Our strained marriage did not generate much personal mail, and she had sent only two terse letters in five months. Only one *Time* magazine was received, and that in the first month. My worst fear was that the cruise would last longer than her money envelopes. So, I reluctantly asked the CO for leave over the span of our R&R. He agreed, but I could tell that he did not want to lose any of his officers, even while the ship stood down from our war commitment.

My trip to the United States was not for the purpose of a spy exchange, but I did carry about six months' worth of photographed cryptographic material.

The spy film was not concealed in some spy novel device, just stuffed into empty Kodak 35-millimeter film boxes, which held about eight Minox rolls each. They were glued closed to look like new film rolls and tossed in my camera bag along with new and exposed film. My Canon F-1 hung around my neck, so my film stash looked reasonably normal. It was totally spooky, however, carrying these film rolls around the base and into Danang City (the spy film taped to my leg). The rolls sat in a pants pocket hanging on a hook during my mosquito-filled night.

My flight was ready to go by midmorning the next day, a C-130 rigged for troop transport. I was the first aboard and took a seat all the way forward on a piece of fabric stretched between aluminum poles, back against the windowless outer wall. Moments later, a troop of Republic of Korea (ROK) soldiers ambled up the rear ramp, filling the aircraft to capacity; their feet touched ours in the cramped space. These guys obviously came from the bush—their uniforms were filthy and stinking of sweat, jungle rot, and kimchi, that dreadful-smelling cabbage dish. The trip to Saigon was a short four hundred miles, and I wondered if I could breathe through my mouth for the entire trip. The smell was suddenly forgotten, however, as a loud bang sounded below my feet. The plane rolled into a steep left bank. Jesus, I thought, we've been hit; I'm gonna die in Danang with a bunch of ROK troops. The North Vietnamese had recently begun using Soviet SA-7 shoulder-launched antiaircraft missiles similar to the United States Redeye heat-seeking missile. The ROK troops were yelling in Korean at a crewman, and he did not even try to answer. But we banked left again, and I concluded we were turning on a base leg to land, which was the case. An embarrassed crewman ran out the side door and right back in a moment later, and we were soon airborne again. He had neglected to remove a safety pin from the nose wheel during preflight inspection. The bang was simply the nose wheel trying to rise against the pin. The only harm was to my nose, which was subjected to fifteen extra minutes of jungle stink.

As the big jet started her descent into Oakland International Airport, we smelly zombies came to life, necks straining for a glimpse of "the world," or any place that was not Vietnam. My leave was only for seven days, but faced with the problems of moving off a ship at sea, then having to find the ship again somewhere in the Pacific, our leave actually started when we boarded the plane and ended when we touched the ground in Saigon. Still, it was ridiculously short for the difficulty and cost involved, to say nothing of the danger.

The children could have stepped out of a specialty catalog; they were dressed to the nines, faces glowing in anticipation. They huddled around me, ignoring my apologies for smelling so bad, all talking at once. Barbara and I exchanged our perfunctory peck without actually touching. Our dog, Sailor, waited in the car, nose pressed on the window, but became agitated as we neared, wondering who the hell I was. It took all four kids to hold the dog back from attacking since he failed to recognize me, unable to smell through the aroma of Vietnam. Eventually he got the scent right and went nuts with happiness—his buddy was home after nearly six months.

The house looked okay on the surface, but the bill organizer had a couple of early entries, then nothing. The payment books were missing, and as I seethed in the knowledge that the household finances were probably a disaster, I growled to Barbara that I should be grateful that the damn lights were on and the telephone worked. She babbled about how rough it was; I hoped it was possible to repair our finances in the short time available.

We were buying four pieces of property: two prime waterfront lots in Florida, one in the Bahamas, and the bar in Charleston. I burned up the phone lines the next day and discovered that all of the real estate payments were in arrears, even the bar where our lease payments far exceeded the mortgage payment. The Florida property was near foreclosure. It took two days and cost a couple thousand dollars to catch up on all the bills, as most of the creditors demanded cashier's checks. Barbara was nearly broke, and before we visited the bank, she admitted that she had taken all of the cash envelopes home and that the safe deposit box was empty. I was so disgusted that I decided to travel to Washington regardless of the meager amount of time left on my leave.

My oldest daughter was fifteen, and I seriously thought of taking her along for company and to become reacquainted. But it was a school week, Barbara objected, and it was far too dangerous anyway. So, physically and mentally exhausted, and suffering from acute jet lag, I climbed aboard another jet for Washington, the spy film still in my camera bag.

A thought germinated as I shuffled to a car rental counter and prepared to start the procedure: this business was too difficult for one man. I followed absolutely no security precautions and was too exhausted to safely carry out the exchange. How valuable was I and my material to the Soviets if I had to travel to *them* for the exchange? With the thousands of agents working for the KGB, why didn't they come to *me*? In fact, why didn't they pick up my material every month wherever I might be in the world instead of sifting through material as much as six months old? I now saw this as a two-man operation, one to obtain the secrets and a second to make the pickup and deliveries, and if the Soviets would not do the courier work, I would develop my own two-man team. But I was less than three years away from my twenty-year minimum retirement date. My plan was to do thirty years, but perhaps it would be best to retire on twenty and become the courier between an agent of my choice and the KGB. I flipped through my mental Rolodex for a recruit, and one name kept coming up, Jerry Whitworth.

I checked into a motel around sunset, but since I was still biologically on Saigon time, I was fully awake and ready for work. We had not set a date for the drop exchange due to my long cruise, so I would use a backup plan to alert the KGB that I was in town and ready. The procedure called for me to draw or leave a signal at a specific place and the KGB would check that spot every morning. If my signal appeared, the drop exchange would occur that night using the written procedure I had picked up six months earlier. The signal was of a strip of black tape wrapped around a five-foot metal pipe, probably the remains of an old chain-link fence, located near a city park. Since I was wide awake, I decided to start then.

With a new roll of extra-wide electrical tape, I marked the spot in the cold darkness. The drive between the signal can and the drop points was long and uneventful. A housing complex was under construction in an area that had been solid woods six months earlier, but the tree that marked my drop point somehow survived. It stood off a dirt road but now had cleared land directly behind it and the skeletons of new houses stood a hundred feet away. I killed some time in a small bar and somehow missed the blaring of country music, the tropical scent, the aggressive and beautiful bar girls, the entertainment. This was boring. Around dawn, I checked the post just in case some nut had removed my tape, then crawled into bed for a solid eight hours of sleep.

The drop went smoothly, even though my drop bag was hardly well concealed behind the now naked tree. Back at the motel, I dug through the long notes that were always included for the next procedure and discovered that I had been given a raise from $1,000 a week to $1,500. My package consisted mostly of money, about $30,000, almost entirely in $50 bills, which was preferred by my handlers. The $100 bills were still too obvious in those days while the $50s took up less weight and space. My problem was airport security, so I taped most of the bills around my waist in a makeshift money belt and taped a few bundles into the lining of my coat. With that done, I turned in my rental car and hung out at the airport until my early flight back to San Francisco.

There was just a small touch of apprehension as I approached airport security, maybe just one extra heartbeat. I realized at that point just how pathetically safeguarded our national security secrets were. In the twelve thousand–plus miles that I had traveled to this point, my greatest and only threat would come from an overweight, barely literate, minimum-wage security guard who was more interested in her next coffee break than inspecting my waistline. Why bother following all those extraordinary security precautions when no one was even trying to find me? I just could not shake the thought: If those secrets were so important to the United States, why did they not protect them? If the material was so important to the Soviets, why did they not pick them up every month (or week or day)?

After passing through security with not so much as a glance, I decided to discontinue all those elaborate security procedures in the future. I would handle my extra money prudently and avoid leaving financial and travel paper trails, and drop all the rest.

Once aloft and in the privacy of the restroom, I ripped the packets of money from my waist and stuffed them into my camera bag. Looking at the neatly wrapped stacks of cash, I knew that this extra money provided the means for keeping my family together, even in its simulated form. But maybe this extra money just made things worse. Everyone might be better off, I mused, if Barbara and the kids had moved to Maine while I stayed in the navy for thirty years and supported them by working extra jobs. Hell, I worked part-time jobs regardless of the spy money. It was always possible to stop this spy business and get that divorce, but the crime was done on that first day in 1967, and quitting now would help me in no way if I were ever caught.

I should have insisted on bringing Margaret with me, not only for the company but because she was an assertive young lady with no reservations about speaking her mind, so I would hear her point of view of my train-wreck marriage and our dysfunctional family. There were only two days remaining on my leave when I returned from Washington, but I managed a little time alone with her when I wasn't otherwise frolicking with the kids and the dog. Margaret knew about the money envelopes, and apparently Barbara had removed them all from the safe deposit box right after I sailed and simply carried them around in her purse. The kids still got themselves fed and ready for school without supervision most of the time and were allowed to rummage through her purse for lunch money. Great sums of cash disappeared. She also revealed that Sailor was out of control and had jumped through a window screen to attack a mailman; he had only been released from animal control a few days before I arrived. Cynthia still received most of the abuse, and while she was wonderful company, she remained neutral to stay out of trouble with Mom. She had again been beat up and stuffed into a half-full garbage bag. My youngest daughter was cold, the main recipient of anti-Dad propaganda. Michael, my youngest, was the least affected by his strange family and just plugged along, enjoying himself regardless of the ongoing crises.

The sad faces of my kids were still etched in my mind when I landed in Saigon. They all wanted to talk, to question me, to make some sense of their abnormal family. Barbara had enough cash for food, utility bills, and normal expenses for the next four months. The cash sealed in concrete remained as a backup. If it had been possible, I would have left the money with Margaret to dole out to her mother, but that would never have worked. I would pay the important bills from sea, including the house mortgage payments. The utility companies would provide enough incentive for Barbara to pay those bills.

Anxious to find my ship and concerned that the war had plunged her into an emergency with me on the opposite side of the world, I rushed to the navy liaison office. All was well, however; she was lingering offshore between Danang and Hue. I grabbed a quick flight north on an old C-123 and had a message sent from Danang for my ship to pick me up. The excitement of seeing the USS *Niagara Falls* in the hazy distance was tempered by guilt as I recognized that that gray lady was more of a home to me than my house in California. When my feet hit the deck after about ten days, my strange trip had taken me over twenty-five thousand miles.

Chapter 19

LOOKING FOR A NEW ENEMY

I took some good-natured ribbing in the wardroom by the envious officers: the Surabaya port call was not approved, so they had to suffer another Hong Kong R&R while I enjoyed the world. Little did they know how miserable my trip was: two days correcting my finances, two days with my children, and two days with the KGB, the latter done mostly to get away from Barbara. Many officers remained faithful to their wives, and I played along with their sexually related jokes about how nice it must have been to end the long sexual dry spell. Little did they know that I could not even remember my last sexual encounter with Barbara. A few of my closer friends grinned, aware that I had hardly been celibate on this cruise or even before the cruise. But now we were on our way home, experiencing a lump in our throats as we passed under the Golden Gate. The war was winding down, and our country and the CIA had to search frantically for a new war.

I received word the dog had committed another felony and, as a two-time loser, was now on death row at the pound.

The ship had received her secret update to our operating schedule just days before entering port. We were to return to Vietnam in just eight months, the shortest turnaround time between deployments that I had ever experienced—perhaps the shortest ever. We would enjoy a couple weeks of R&R, then start our brutal preparations for our return to Southeast Asia and our box seat to the end of a ten-year misadventure. We would enter one of those small, private shipyards in San Francisco for minor repairs, which would again prevent me from making it home most nights due to my long hours on the job and the impossible commute. Worse, those eight months would include a shakedown cruise, endless training cruises, and finally the required readiness examination by the Fleet Training Center in San Diego. Far from relaxing, it would be a grueling eight months.

On the surface, the house seemed in good order. That would prove to be a terrible misconception.

Chapter 20

THE TURBULENT SEVENTIES

It starts with a nagging feeling that something is wrong, but you cannot put your finger on it. The house was reasonably clean and orderly, but small things were out of place or missing. Our huge master bedroom doubled as an office, and as I changed out of uniform, I noticed my paperweight was missing. One of those gag gifts, it was a stack of one-dollar bills with a hundred-dollar label, all encased in a block of clear plastic. Only the top and bottom bills were real, naturally, with ninety-eight blank bills sandwiched between. Surely no one would steal it; even the real bills would be destroyed by cracking it open. In the top drawer of the desk, I kept four silver dollars that the Ackermans had given us, one for each of our children, minted in the year of their births. Gone.

I bolted to the closet and experienced that sickening feeling of having been robbed. My three accurized match pistols and all the accessories were missing, along with a rifle. The box containing our photography equipment—8-millimeter movie camera, projector, 35-millimeter camera, and various lenses—was empty. It was then that I noticed signs of vandalism, broken items, missing property. We had been burglarized.

Back in the living room, Barbara lounged in her usual posture, cocktail in one hand, cigarette in the other, her face a combination of defiance and amusement. She was enjoying this, I realized. Then I noticed the absence of the kids and the roar of the silence. They were all waiting for me to explode, the kids, hiding in horror, and Barbara, waiting with glee.

I went to the garage to look at the delicate parts of my partially constructed homebuilt BD-5 single-seater aircraft. There was obvious damage; some parts were beyond repair. The molded Plexiglas canopy, similar to that of a jet fighter, had dozens of burn marks from butted cigarettes. It had been rendered useless and was probably irreplaceable.

Then I realized that the cache of cash hidden in the concrete molding had been smashed open.

Strangely calm, I strolled past Barbara and onto our back porch, which had been converted to a windowed family room. The kids' half-size pool table was wrecked. The kids and I had built a mounting frame for the pachinko machine, and it was now a blackened skeleton, having been set afire. The mindless vandalism of children, I realized.

Back to the living room. Barbara was absolutely squirming with uncontrolled excitement, primed for my explosion of fury. Lord only knows what speech she had prepared, how this disaster would somehow be blamed on the navy or me. I would not give her the satisfaction. More important, I wanted to spare the children, who were hiding quietly upstairs, yet another argument.

Barbara patiently waited for me to finally speak and start a wonderfully long tirade. I calmly asked: "The money in the garage?"

She answered with a sneer. "I needed it." Showing no agitation, I answered, "Well, that's what it was for," as I turned to the front door. She seethed in fury as I walked out. *Fuck her*, I thought, *I'm gonna get my dog.*

Californians tend to be liberal and laid-back, and those who work for the pound are often reluctant to kill an animal. Still, I did not know what to expect when I walked up to the counter and asked if I could have my dog. They seemed genuinely relieved and took me back to the rows of cages, mostly filled with dogs and cats, all staring through their bars in despair. Sailor sensed freedom as I signed some papers, and soon we were heading home. He was naturally excited to be in the family car and with his pal, but he also seemed sobered by the experience. I learned from the pound manager that Sailor had not done anything wrong; there was no complaint on file. Instead, Barbara had called to have him picked up, saying she was unable to care for him. That part was at least true—she was incapable of taking care of anything. So I had merely gained a small eight-month reprieve for the poor mutt. There was little chance that he would survive my next deployment.

Back at the house, I hollered for the kids and we frolicked in the small park across the street, the dog in canine ecstasy as he chased balls and Frisbees. Later we strolled into the woods, but since the kids all seemed a bit shell-shocked, I resisted asking a lot of questions. I got typical "I don't know" answers about the burglary and just let it drop.

I did learn that Barbara had taken a job as manager of a small restaurant in Hayward. Later, they directed me to her job site, a small, ugly kiosk of a building about the size of a large van. It had two service windows with a hand-painted menu on the weathered outside wall consisting of a dozen or so fast-food items. Customers did not enter but huddled at the windows. There was one woman on the grill, another working one of the windows. There were no customers. If the thing was on wheels, it would resemble one of those lunch vans that service construction site workers.

I stared at the ugly little shack in disbelief. Located in a mostly business area, it abutted a ratty neighborhood. There could not be more than six people working there, maybe even four, including Barbara, the "manager." Wages must be minimum, profit scarce.

A few careful questions to the kids revealed that Barbara was either asleep or gone most of the time, so they were still raising themselves. Her "business" was monopolizing most of her time. My God, I thought, like a junkie, she was returning to the same crazy business addiction that buried the family in South Carolina six years earlier. Then it hit me. She had *bought* that wretched hovel with the money from the garage. And worse, this miserable mess could not be generating any profit. She always knew she could work anywhere she wished so long as she hired someone to manage the kids. Instead, the kids were abandoned and she invested in what must be a business that probably generated a negative profit and loss statement each month. Her employees seemed happy, but then, they actually drew a paycheck.

Just let it go, I reminded myself, it's her crazy life and I can do nothing about it. Maximize my "visitation" time with the kids, I resolved, and hope that they do not grow up as crazy as she is.

The kids were silent with fright regarding the burglary, so I arranged a meeting with the investigating officer at the Union City police. The detective was former navy himself, and since I was in uniform and sporting my Vietnam decorations, he took the time to enlighten this naive citizen.

The burglary business had changed considerably in the twenty years he had been on the force, he explained. In the old days, there was a mom in every house, Dad took the only car to work, and nothing could happen in the neighborhood without the housewives knowing. Burglars had to sneak about very carefully at night and target the houses where people were out for the evening or on vacation. Cat burglars actually entered the homes of their sleeping victims. Today, neighborhoods are like deserted ghost towns, everyone off to work or at school. The cop explained that anyone could back a moving van into any driveway on any street and clean the place out in broad daylight. I had to agree with this old policeman, I had observed the social change myself.

The neighborhood kids were the first to notice and exploit this new situation, the cop continued. When we were kids skipping school, which was quite rare, we might go to a movie or go play in the woods. Today, the kids just hang out on the corner until the moms go to work, then go back to their own houses to party with their school chums.

The cop paused several beats, probably wondered whether he should go on, and finally judged that I could take it: "Mr. Walker, your own kids robbed your house." My face went hot with hurt and embarrassment, but he signaled a traffic cop's "halt" before I could respond with a roaring "What!?"

"I made a couple calls to the local schools, got their absentee lists, and found out exactly who was in your house." The light of understanding finally penetrated my brain as my anger was replaced by shame. My house had become party central for the neighborhood low-lifes while Barbara rushed to see how fast she could lose $30,000 in a business venture.

"Your wife has a drinking problem, Mr. Walker, and I counted at least twenty bottles of hard liquor in your well-stocked bar, enough to keep every truant in the neighborhood drunk for the school year," he pointed out. "You also have three beautiful teenage daughters that every dirt bag in the subdivision would just love to take to bed. The boys probably trashed your house when your girls refused them sex or booze. Your situation is out of control." I asked if my property was recoverable, especially the handguns, since he knew who had been in the house. He admitted that the pistols worried him, but he explained that they were "probably sold at ten cents on the dollar. That Colt .45 worth a couple hundred was most likely swapped for a $15 bag of cheap Mexican grass.

I just hope the Black Panthers in Oakland don't have 'em and they end up getting used in a homicide."

"I guess you won't give me the names of the kids who were in my home?" I asked, knowing the answer. The cop smiled in a controlled and mirthless way: "Hell no, I don't want any homicides in Union City either. You don't look like a violent kind of guy, Mr. Walker, but you do have a little of that Vietnam chaos in your eyes."

The next evening, I exacted a small measure of satisfaction. I suspected, and my kids confirmed, that the two boys living next door were involved, probably in a major way. My first target pistol had survived, a .22-caliber High Standard semiautomatic, hidden away as a self-defense weapon. Sliding an eight-round magazine of long rifle into place, I jammed the pistol into my waistband and strode next door. It was early evening and everyone was at home; a light windbreaker covered the pistol.

One of the boys answered my knock, but he scurried away as though the devil just touched him before I barked a single word. The father shortly appeared, body rigid with tension, licking his lips in a paroxysm of apprehension. His obvious fear made me feel better already, but I also realized that his reaction meant that he *knew* what his kids had done and why I was there. That made me angry, but I was strangely calm and controlled and, using my best marine drill instructor voice, I delivered my diatribe through clenched teeth.

I have long forgotten my exact words, but I do remember that I used the "F" word as an adjective far too much. In essence, I told him that if his kids stepped foot on my property or in my house again, I would take it out on him and personally kick his ass. He answered in a few incomprehensible mumbles, and with my message delivered, I turned for home. Walking back, I realized how dumb it was to carry that pistol. Would I have shot him? Lord knows I wanted to send him crashing on his butt with a fat lip. That old cop was right: Vietnam was still rattling in my brain. I really did want to shoot that bastard.

Somehow I managed to intermingle my overextended life of working too hard, playing too hard, and maximizing my "visitation" rights. I made myself available for charter flights at the local airport and actually found time to fly charters, mostly to the Lake Tahoe and Las Vegas resort areas.

The condition of my boat at the recreation pier on the Treasure Island Naval Base was of great concern. As we entered port, I carefully scanned the pier with some uneasiness from the bridge wing, but I could not spot her with the big naval binoculars. I quietly admonished myself for the stupidity of leaving her in the water unattended for nearly a year. Any number of problems could have occurred: her bilge pump could fail and sink her from accumulated water; her mooring lines could chafe and part, sending her free to crash and sink in a storm. So it was with great anticipation that I drove to Treasure Island Naval Station, only to find the sloop pert and jaunty, riding high and looking no different than the day I left her. A freshly charged battery in hand, I climbed aboard, cracked the hatches, and aired out the musty interior. Everything looked shipshape, and I celebrated my good fortune with a fresh cup of coffee from the galley.

The engine exterior seemed fine, so I hooked up the battery and climbed to the cockpit to turn it over. To my delight, she started immediately and ran smoothly. I then engaged the forward drive, and the engine strained correctly against the mooring lines, leaving a satisfying wake astern. Then a clunk! The engine continued to run, but there was no drive. I guessed what had happened: the screw had fallen off.

There are several ways to create electrical current, the simplest being to place two dissimilar metals together. The metal with the greatest number of electrons will slowly lose its electrons to the other metal. As the metal loses electrons, it decays in a process called reduction. To protect against this hazard, a special zinc attachment is screwed to the propeller nut. The zinc will decay first, protecting the brass propeller. So I had been gone too long. The stainless steel shaft had eaten first the zinc, then the brass propeller.

Warrant officers and chiefs are able to get anything on a naval base, and I was soon back at the boat with a wet suit, scuba tank, and all the accessories. I recovered the screw to find that it was severely pitted and the shaft threads were totally gone. The stainless steel shaft looked in good health after its ten-month lunch on my propeller. Within an hour, I was back in the water, attaching my replacement screw. I returned the scuba gear before the end of the day.

I rented a far-too-expensive slip at the Jack London Square marina, one of the few exciting spots in the otherwise dreary Oakland, a city with an utterly charmless personality. Jack London Square was on the tourist map; however, it included an oasis of gracious waterfront shops and restaurants on a wide estuary. Tiny boathouses were clustered on both sides of the estuary, romantic villages bobbing in the quiet water. The kids helped me transport the boat to her new berth and the primary haunt of my R&R period.

The ship soon moved across the bay to one of those small shipyards in that grimy waterfront section of San Francisco. The work pace was grueling, even in the radio room, where we installed new satellite antennas, which would soon replace the high-frequency systems forever. I visited the kids when possible but spent many nights aboard ship or on the boat at Jack London Square.

Parking was a problem in the crime-ridden area, so we sailors were forced to park on the street. In the evenings, when the shipyard workers went home, we would dash for our cars and move them to the safety of the shipyard for the night. We could move them back to the street after sunrise when the criminals—like vampires—returned to their beds. After one particularly long and hectic day, I moved my car inside the fence at about 9 p.m. but was attracted to the distant shimmering neon light of one of those grimy waterfront bars. A beer seemed perfect. My uniform was filthy and I needed a shower, but that little sign lured me on.

As expected, the joint was grubby and catered to a half dozen ship-yard workers silently stooped over their drinks; they should have been home four hours ago. A TV flickered at low volume, no one watching. The vapid bartender drew me a draft, and I gulped down a large swallow, that first quaff being the only enjoyable moment for me.

I did not notice her at first, a woman sitting in the shadows at the short end of the L-shaped bar. By my second sip, she was sitting next to me. She was trim and attractive with sun-washed blondish hair and a shiny smile. Her opening line was, believe it or not, "Hi, sailor." She took me for an officer from one of the many merchant ships nearby, and I prob-ably looked the part. "Out of uniform" was an understatement: I was wearing dirty work khakis, no tie, steel-toed boots, and a hardhat. She could not be a hooker, I reflected, she would starve in this neighborhood. In reality, we were kindred spirits, experiencing wrecked marriages and sharing sexual attraction. After my second beer, we were climbing up the hills of the Bayview district to her duplex—weirdly, not far from Myra's old apartment.

Next morning, I moved the car back to the street and climbed aboard the ship, sleepless but happy. I had not planned a life of celibacy and I saw that young woman frequently during those eight months. You know the old cliché: two ships passing in the night, never to meet again, but never forgotten.

Our eight months in the United States meant that I would make two dead drops in the DC area, my thirteenth and fourteenth since becoming a spy. Both trips blended into one as I arranged my duty rotation for a full weekend off. The drops were scheduled for Saturday nights, so I flew out early Saturday morning. Once on the ground in DC, it was a high-tension hustle of renting a car, renting a motel room, and reviewing the complex driving procedure. There was little time for food or relaxation.

All too soon, it was time to start the process and signal that I was ready: the usual dropped 7-UP can on a dirt road. The dark anxiety starts and slowly builds as I speed to the KGB signal site and confirm that the game is on. Now to my drop site, nerves at full stretch as, contrary to any sense of self-preservation, I drive into a possible ambush.

Package dropped, it is on to my pickup spot and the more likely site for an ambush. Tension at full flash point, filled with anticipatory adrenaline, I grab the KGB package and dash away as quickly as possible. Success. Exhale.

Slowly, that weird electric hum between the ears starts to fade away, and I come back to life. Back at the motel, I showered and fell atop the bed, totally exhausted, staring up at the cracked ceiling. These cheap rooms never smell right; the only sounds are the groans and gurgles of an old window air conditioner. My depressed state and the seedy room had all the facets of a film noir. All that was missing was a creaky ceiling fan to complete the picture. My day had started at dawn, three thousand miles away, and my wake-up call was four hours away. Still too wound-up to sleep, I pondered the whole strange, dreamlike lunacy of it all. My mind wandered to junior high school and the good nuns instructing the class on

Ecclesiastes, in which Solomon reflects on his life, his good deeds, and his evil acts. I recalled a line of Solomon's wisdom:

A righteous man perishing in his righteousness,
and a wicked man living
long in his wickedness
Do not be over righteous,
neither be overwise—
why destroy yourself?

—Eccles. 7:15

The import period ended all too soon. Like Alice in Wonderland, our cruising schedule was reversed in this surreal world still dominated by Vietnam. Where once we had experienced one major deployment every two years, our import periods at home were now as long as the old deployments and we were *deployed* for most of the two years.

I spent maximum time with the children, enjoying plenty of sailing trips on the nice days. They were still too young to crew in the races, but the bay offered endless attractions, and we all enjoyed stopping at Zak's pier in Sausalito for hamburgers. The dog enjoyed the boat, odd for a shepherd, but that's why he was named Sailor.

My Honda was an excellent off-road vehicle and provided great opportunities for adventure in exploring the hinterlands. The kids enjoyed riding with me, so I bought two small Hondas for them, a 70cc and a 50cc. Any reservations I had about them learning to ride was greatly dispelled in the first lessons.

Anyone who can ride a bicycle can easily keep a motorcycle upright. The problem for new riders is coordinating the throttle, clutch, and gearshift. The 70cc had four gears and a manual clutch. The 50cc, with three gears, was easier to drive with an automatic centrifugal clutch.

The kids learned to kick-start the bikes and in less than thirty minutes they were riding slowly around the van on test rides. Margaret and Cynthia were on the 70cc, Laura and Michael on the 50cc; I soon cut them loose to explore the simple dirt track. Michael, at ten years old, carefully puttered away on his own. Margaret, however, roared off at full power, snapping through the four gears and flying out of sight in boiling dust, waist-length hair blowing straight back in the wind. My first thought was that she had panicked and jammed the throttle on full. Then I remembered—we had passed a house on the otherwise deserted road about a half mile back, and there was a boy in the yard about her age. She returned a half hour later, sporting a little toothpaste grin, and I knew what she had been up to. She had driven back and forth in front of that house, tantalizing that poor boy. Such are the games that fifteen-year-olds play.

We had many of these memorable family events, including summer tailgate parties in different areas of the East Bay. The kids never spilled, and even Sailor enjoyed running around doing dog things.

My charter flights were averaging about three or four a month, and I took one of the kids as copilot whenever possible. All of the kids became quite proficient at flying straight and level from the right seat. In fact, on one dead-head flight to Lake Tahoe in the big six-seat U-206, Michael flew the entire flight on his knees so he could see over the instrument panel. I would simply point out a distant landmark, and he would fly to each point with ease. On the return trip, our four passengers in the rear, I would subtly signal him to take the controls while I consulted charts and handled radio clearances.

Most of my evenings after work were spent at Jack London Square for dinner at one of the many restaurants, then to the boat for a sunset cruise and cocktails. At least one crew member was necessary to sail safely, and I could usually find someone from the ship to tag along. If not, it was far too easy to lure a couple of adventurous female tourists aboard who were interested in an evening cruise. I must have logged a thousand miles sailing up and down that long and wide estuary, its calm waters protected from the choppy bay by a long breakwater. Even a girl from Kansas can learn to handle the jib sheets and mooring lines in less than ten minutes.

A landmark on the square is a lavish restaurant hanging over the water on large pilings. I would cruise back and forth in front of the diners, adding to the romantic flavor of the San Francisco Bay along with other boaters. Since I occasionally ate at the waterside restaurant, my running joke with the maître d' was that I should be compensated for adding to the nautical ambiance of the setting. He agreed that the boat looked splendid, red sails aglow in the setting sun, running lights reflecting across the water. I was responsible for hundreds of extra cocktails by entranced lovers, and several proposals of marriage surely resulted. Still, he would not cut me a check, but he did provide a bottle of fine wine on occasion.

Chapter 21

VIETNAM AND A SECRET MISSION

I smiled with remembered pleasure as I greeted the Pacific Ocean like an old friend. We sliced smoothly through gentle swells on my first bridge watch, the Golden Gate far astern. My mind flipped through a mental atlas of faraway and exotic ports, our first port-of-call, Subic Bay, Philippines, nearly halfway around the world.

After the mistakes I made during the last deployment, my personal affairs were in better order. The boat was hauled out at one of the many boatyards and set ashore on a cradle. My motorcycle was aboard, lashed to a pallet, ready to offload ashore. The major family bills would be paid from sea, the payment books safely in my stateroom. Barbara had her monthly envelopes with more than sufficient cash for the family's requirements. She needed only to pay the utility bills. There was no emergency cache of money for her to squander this time. Mostly, I could relax in knowing that the house payments would be made and I would not return to find the family living in a shelter.

There was nothing I could do for Sailor. His big brown eyes clouded with hazy sadness as I left the family to climb aboard the ship. I knew I would never see him again—perhaps he knew it too.

The troubling thoughts about my family were always present, that nagging feeling that I should do more. They had a better-than-average home, cars, clothes, and money—I was certainly fulfilling my economic requirements as a husband and father—but we did not function as a family. The acrimony between Barbara and me prevented any love or warmth within the family. I doubted that I had the ability to become more amicable with Barbara or if I even desired to do so. So, with a heavy heart, I was off to the Orient.

Olongapo City in the Philippines still set the standard for debauchery in the Pacific region; it was still the boomtown of the military's advanced base for the war. There was no sign that the waning war was tempering the frantic activity of shops, bars, restaurants, moneychangers, and hookers. Taxis and jeepneys were thick as flies, but my motorcycle gave me the freedom to escape the perversion of the main drag for the quieter outlying areas.

We had been gone for such a short time that my membership in the Cubi Point Flying Club was still current and my check-rides were up to date. I managed a few charters to Manila and Baguio during our one week in port. Many of my friends on and off base did not realize we had returned to the United States, our absence seemed so short.

The crew looked battered as we left port to earn our pay; the festive week of liberty left them broke, hungry for real food, and starved for sleep. An amphibious task group, our first customers, lurked in the Philippine Sea to the north, stuffed with battle-ready marines. Then we headed west into the Tonkin Gulf, and the familiar string of ships stretched along the Vietnam coast. The entire Seventh Fleet seemed to be waiting for us, anxious for overdue supplies, food, and mail. I made several courier deliveries, riding the helo wench to the smaller ships, wondering how much the general public would *pay* for a round-trip ride between helo and ship.

The Vietnam coast looked deceptively deserted and forlorn, for the North Vietnamese were pressing ever south, a storm surge that could not be stopped. I remembered talking to a young South Vietnamese soldier months earlier and taking in his blind confidence that the United States, the most powerful country in the world, could never allow the South to be defeated. Was he already dead, captured?

Diego Garcia lay below the equator at seven degrees south. Part of the Chagos Archipelago, it was discovered by the Portuguese during the era of their fifteenth-century maritime discoveries. I could learn little of its history, but the library informed me that the islands were part of Mauritius, a British island colony. In the 1960s, Mauritius sought independence, and Britain offered its citizens freedom if they would give up their claim to the tiny island of Chagos (which included Diego Garcia). Britain sweetened the offer with a payment of £3 million. Mauritius accepted, and the British established a new Chagos colony called the British Indian Ocean Territory, or BIOT.

My research led me to believe that something was very wrong. Secret messages discussed Diego Garcia's US communications station but described the island as having no civilian population. If that was so, what had happened to all those happy islanders of the BIOT? With my usual cynicism, I suspected that the "disappeared" civilian population had something to do with the high level of secrecy surrounding this mission. There was also no question that our secret cargo was involved.

My first jolting thought was of Bimini Island and the nuclear tests. That island was totally remote and the population relocated: the exact description of Diego Garcia. Perhaps this *was* a weapons test, perhaps we were carrying something more fiendish than the H-bomb that would kill all the Commies in Southeast Asia.

The island hung so low in the water that only the radio station antennas were visible. We came sneaking into the sleeping island at dawn, a flaming orange sunrise at our backs. We dropped the anchor far from shore.

The chart showed the island as a narrow horseshoe-shaped atoll, about thirty-five miles from end to end. It seemed to be no more than two feet above sea level. The tip of India was one thousand miles north by northeast. The Horn of Africa was sixteen hundred miles to the southwest. Sumatra was seventeen hundred miles to the east. This was the middle of nowhere, to be sure, not a single ship illuminated the radar screen at its maximum range. The encyclopedia said there were goats on the island, perfect test subjects for a secret weapon?

By a strange coincidence, my good friend Jerry Whitworth was stationed on the island. We had stayed in touch, and I was sure he would know of our arrival and meet me. With his top-secret clearance, I hoped he would settle the mystery once and for all.

The cargo transfer was a major evolution with me in the limelight. I assigned my alternate to the helo tower and prepared to escort the pallets ashore. I assigned a radioman with a PRC radio to ride with me, and we lifted off on the first aircraft. Once aloft, we attached a pallet to the belly hook and flew to the small island airstrip, the pallet dangling below.

A contingent of trucks, a forklift, and a couple dozen people huddled in a knot just off the runway, awaiting our arrival. The pilot touched the pallet to the ground with the gentleness of a baby carriage, the crewman unhooked the tether, and we quickly circled to land.

Helicopters are infernally hateful machines: slow in flight, torturously loud, and with an ungainly vibrating ride. It was made worse by the heat; at somewhere over 100 degrees my flight helmet popped off like a wet dishrag. Several passengers scrambled down the rear ramp and into the worst part of any helicopter: the whirlpooling hurricane of dirt, debris, and gravel. We jogged under the blades in the futile effort to escape, all covered with a patina of grime, particularly on the large wet spots of our shirts. Coral sand crunched in my teeth. The humidity seemed like it was at about 900 percent; breathing was like inhaling hot syrup.

My radio operator stayed with me, for among my other duties, I was the "control tower" on the ground for this operation. Their loads and passengers off, the helos flew back to fetch more cargo, the visit of a supply ship, even in secret, being a bonanza. Orders of every type were packaged for delivery, from ballpoint pens to vital repair parts.

A guy in civilian clothes spotted my courier sidearm and rushed to identify himself. He reminded me of the CIA-types one sees in Vietnam. He would never reveal the contents of the cargo, but all spies learn that if you act as though you already know a secret, the unwary will often consider it safe to speak freely. All I really knew was the secret project code name, "Jibstay," so using it could make me seem informed. He had to be CIA or National Security Agency (NSA). As he checked the boxes, I tried a question: "You got the jibstay antennas up yet?" He gave me a quick glance on hearing the code word, calmed down, and fell right into my trap. "Almost finished," he replied. I explained that I was a communication specialist retiring soon and was considering NSA. I held my breath, but I had guessed correctly. He answered that I might enjoy it, but some of the postings (he waved a hand across the dismal island) can challenge your sex life.

So there it was, the answer to all my wild fantasies about secret weapons. Diego Garcia was just another NSA ELINT/SIGINT (Electronic Intelligence/Signals Intelligence) spy listening post. Exactly what electronic intelligence they could glean from the middle of the Indian Ocean was beyond me, but it did illustrate the extent of America's electronic spy network. If they were in the middle of nowhere, then they were everywhere.

Perhaps Jibstay was part of the spy satellite system. Since such satellites travel on polar orbits, those passing over the Soviet Union would fly south over the Indian Ocean and Diego Garcia. It could be possible to download the gathered photos and electronic data to the island, where it would be relayed to the United States. I never learned for certain.

Once the cargo was ashore, the aircraft shut down to allow several officers and crew to tour the island. I hitched a ride to the communications station where Jerry waited. First we had a cold beer in his hooch, then we took a tour of the wonderfully air-conditioned radio facility.

My main interest was in the fate of the civilian population of about two thousand. Jerry scrounged a jeep and gave me a tour of the former town and villages, now deserted. The houses, shops, buildings, and small factories were quaint and somewhat primitive, to be sure, but the citizens had lived and prospered there for centuries. Small piers extended into the lagoon where their fishing boats once rested, probably their main enterprise. A couple goats wandered in the brush.

I caught the last flight back to the ship, and we sneaked away before dawn as quietly as we slunk in. With our treasure trove of supplies, we would not steam directly to our station in Southeast Asia, however. In fact, we had sailed so far west that we officially became part of the Sixth Fleet, the fleet of the Atlantic Ocean. Unable to refuse, we were ordered to steam northwest a thousand miles or more toward the Arabian Sea where Atlantic fleet units were on duty to protect our Persian Gulf oil. They raided our store of supplies with glee, and with no one left to service, we at last turned east to rejoin the Pacific Fleet.

I mailed the family's monthly bills from the Arabian Sea to a ship that was en route to the Gulf of Oman. In my idiosyncratic family life, my mail would travel the wrong way around the world to the Fleet Post Office in New York, but it somehow made the trip to San Francisco on time.

The cruise back was uneventful until the challenge of the Strait of Malacca. I came across a newsletter from one of the seafarers' unions that discussed piracy in the region. The figures are long forgotten, but hundreds of acts of piracy still occur; victims include even large merchant ships. Using fast powerboats, the pirates grapple their way aboard and rob the captain and crew, pillage what they can carry, and motor away. In fact, "boogiemen" is not just a term used to frighten young children into behaving. Boogiemen are members of a tribal group from the Indonesian waters and are among the fiercest pirates. To this day, one does not want to be caught by a boogieman. Small ships and private yachts are particularly vulnerable.

We spent an idyllic week of R&R in Singapore, my favorite city. Since departing a month earlier with a full load of fuel, we had steamed about seven thousand miles. With a range of ten thousand miles, we had consumed nearly 70 percent of our fuel. Since we had been picked clean of perishable food, we spent the week resupplying as well. We were pierside, so my motorcycle went ashore, and I was able to roam that beautiful city. Our secret mission had given us a pleasant reprieve from the war zone, but we would return all too soon.

Chapter 22

NEW THOUGHTS ON WAR

Following the Diego Garcia secret mission, we fell into the old pattern of our last deployment: port calls in Subic Bay, Kaohsiung, Hong Kong, Singapore, and line swings up and down the Tonkin Gulf. It all became routine, even for the new crewmen, until a surprising message arrived. As a result of the Paris peace talks, the United States had agreed to *remove* the mines from Haiphong, and the USS *Niagara Falls* would be part of the mine removal task force.

The remainder of the cruise blurred into the same stations in the Tonkin Gulf and the same liberty ports. We did change the pattern with a port call to Yokosuka, Japan, and Chi-lung, Taiwan. Chi-lung is the port city for the capital, Taipei, and my friend in Kaohsiung was so excited about my visit that she insisted upon taking the train north to show me the sights. She knew my tastes, so we toured the more Chinese parts of the city where American tourists rarely if ever travel. For example, one small restaurant featured caged snakes displayed on the street, each in an individual wooden cage. Customers selected their meal, which was carried inside to their table and slaughtered by the smiling cook. That part I could have done without, as well as the soup made from the fresh blood, but otherwise, the meal was superb.

Somewhere during the seventh month of our six-month deployment, we turned our bow toward a rising sun and started for home. We had logged in a colossal amount of sea time, and I had become an adept ship handler. Our captain was an experienced merchant shipmaster and had taught the bridge officers the fine points of maneuvering in impossible situations.

We all became quite proficient, surprising even ourselves at handling a huge, unmaneuverable hulk. Single-screw ships do not handle well and can only back in one direction, whereas twin-screw ships can back in either direction and "twist" in place, if necessary. A merchant ship trick is to use the anchor liberally to assist upon arrival but mostly at departure to pull the ship from the berth.

The test not only involved departing from and arriving in port but included every imaginable drill from combat emergencies to man overboard. I studied the contest booklet with interest but really perked up at the winner's prize. Along with the usual certificate and maybe a low-level medal, the winner received his choice of duty! I immediately knew what I wanted and started an extensive study and practice program to prepare. My choice for my next duty station would have surprised the chief of naval personnel, for I would have asked for another three-year tour on the *Niagara Falls*. If I won, they could not refuse. Indeed, I wanted to stay at sea forever.

Chapter 23

FORGE A CLEARANCE, RECRUIT A SPY

The dog was dead. I accepted it calmly, having suspected it would happen. I discreetly quizzed the kids, but they were evasive and clearly did not want to discuss it. I could never understand Barbara's animosity toward the dog. The children handled the burden of Sailor's minimal upkeep (along with all of the housework), so the dog did not challenge her comfort level. Perhaps she disliked the dog because he was my pal. Decades later, Cynthia would finally explain Barbara's problem with the dog, and it was more horrible than I could imagine.

Barbara's beating of the kids was much more frequent and brutal than I had believed. While Cynthia still received the brunt of her fury, all the kids felt the lash of belts and other convenient weapons. Wire coat hangers were a favorite. Sailor was outraged by her attacks and, like a good shepherd, he instinctively tried to protect his small flock. He was becoming more successful and finally turned to snarling attacks against Barbara.

Barbara defused that problem by ordering the children to lock the dog in the bedroom. This ceremonial arrangement meant that one or more of the kids were about to be assaulted and battered. Once Sailor was locked in the bedroom, Barbara was free to thrash the object of her scorn without interference. Sailor, however, hearing the screams and wailing of his flock, would go insane. Growling, barking, and clawing at the door, he would try in vain to protect the children. The dog eventually became a physical threat to Barbara, but rather than recognize the loathsomeness of her own conduct—behavior that even a dog's brain could recognize and understand—she simply returned Sailor to the pound for execution. That beautiful dog tried to save my kids.

There was one small hint that could have alerted me to this dire situation. The inside of the bedroom door was severely clawed by Sailor, deep gauges over half its depth. I asked Barbara why the dog would have damaged the door, but she was ambiguous and nonresponsive, her normal attitude.

The crew earned and enjoyed a thirty-day R&R, maximum leave encouraged. It was August, so I wasted little time in renting a slip at Jack London Square and dropping the boat back into the water. The ship was moored at Oakland Supply Center, a few blocks away.

Home was neither comfortable nor relaxing; the tension between Barbara and I vibrated in the air. The kids were a joy, tagging along with Dad everywhere during the last month of their vacation. House and vehicle repairs kept me busy, and the kids were anxious to help.

It was easy to ignore my part-time spy job; the trip to Washington was low on my priority list. I had set up a drop and exchange date for September, but we always had a signal procedure if the cruise was extended and I couldn't make it. The infrequency of our exchanges still bewildered me—how information so seemingly important could be delayed for months. By September, I would have data that was as much as nine months old.

My major concern was the forthcoming ship-handling competition. After R&R, we were scheduled for two short movements: one to off-load ammunition in the port of Richmond, and the other to off-load supplies at Mare Island. By October, we would enter the Bethlehem Steel Shipyard in San Francisco for an extended overhaul of about six months. The skipper worked out a plan for my test and asked for an observer on the Mare Island trip. I was ready and even overconfident of success. Then disaster struck in the form of a yeoman from the ship's office. He casually walked into my office and dropped a letter on my desk, announcing: "Hey, Mr. Walker, you've got orders."

I read the orders in disbelief. My three-year tour cut short, I was ordered to the staff of Commander Amphibious Atlantic in Norfolk, Virginia. My reporting date was in about thirty days, forcing me to depart before the ship-handling competition. My entire plan for a second three-year tour on *Niagara Falls* was shattered.

I begged the executive officer to intercede with Washington to try for a cancellation. My detailer was surprised to hear me pleading by phone to stay at sea when the entire fleet usually begged for shore duty. Between the XO and my detailer, I accepted what I already knew—warrant officers were too valuable and scarce to waste on a ship undergoing overhaul. Worse, warrant officers were at the peak of technical expertise in their fields, so I should be in charge of a major communications center and not wasting my time conning a ship and running a modest radio shack. My skills were critical at the Amphibious Base to replace the departing staff communications officer. My orders were firm and without delay. Even my R&R was cut short.

Surprise orders are nothing new to a career serviceman and his family. This would be my twelfth transfer in nineteen years—actually a routine event for us all. The family functioned on automatic, packing, arranging for a mover, selling the house. The second car, the MG that had been in the family for over ten years, would be left behind, sold. The family car, a big four-door sedan, could carry us back to Virginia, the boat in tow.

The thought of leaving the sea to be grounded behind a desk for the next three years was a profound blow. I had never considered early retirement—had always planned a thirty-year career—but the misery of prolonged shore tours for the next eleven years was completely distasteful. That I was to be cast about upon the rocky shoals of shore duty was bad enough, but combined with my wretched family life and disappointment with my spy activities, I began to entertain the thought of putting an end to all three and retiring the following year.

My mind rattled with disconnected thoughts. I needed to be alone, away from noise and people, to work out a plan for my next twenty years. I worked late that night, ate in the wardroom with the duty officer, and ambled over to Jack London Square around nine p.m. With a fresh pot of hot coffee on the alcohol stove, I found the square much too distracting for contemplation. The boat was too large for one person under sail, so I tossed the lines off and lit off the inboard engine. Down the estuary and into the bay, I put the ceaseless hum of the Oakland Bay Bridge astern and powered south to the quietest part of the bay. Clear of all boats and shipping, I shut down the ending and allowed the silence to wrap around me, drifting in the light breeze. The south bay was moon-washed in silver and blue, the mellifluous ripples against the hull the only sound.

Mug of black coffee in hand, a drop of Courvoisier for flavor, I was surrounded by a billion scintillating harbor lights reflected across the water. I lounged on floatation cushions in the cockpit under the stars, nearly hypnotized by the eerie lines of descending lights from the south, two threads of flickering orbs on a string. They were passenger jet landing lights strung four or five in line, two miles apart, inbound for landing at SFO and OAK airports. The growl of their engines was mercifully beyond my hearing. The perfect environment for serious thought is the peace and quiet of a slowly drifting boat.

First, the marriage issue. I was convinced that my presence in the house always irritated Barbara, drove her to excessive drinking and growing anger. This made conditions worse for my kids, for once I was driven off, they became the object of her torment. I resolved then to move the family, buy a house in Norfolk for them, and end the sham marriage. Since interaction with the kids was impossible in Barbara's house, I would find a nearby apartment for myself where the kids could come to me. Walking distance to a refuge. There was no need for a divorce, but I would discontinue the illusion of a marriage. The children were old enough, at twelve through seventeen, that they could choose which parent they wished to live with if the courts became involved.

Second, my spy activity and its frustration. I always knew from my dad's Hollywood experience that all spy films were inaccurate, all James Bond movies sophomoric and ridiculous, and even the better spy-genre novels had some inaccuracies. The reality of my seven years of spying matched nearly nothing that I ever read. I received only scant advice, little spy-craft instruction, no gadgets, and absolutely no training.

Further, even though the deliveries were conducted but twice a year, I had to drop everything and travel to Washington, regardless of my location. Shouldn't my handler travel to *me* on the other side of the world? Couldn't they afford a courier?

Even the compensation was poor: about $50,000 a year. Experienced steelworkers and teamsters made more for a much less dangerous occupation.

Worse, there was no hint of any progress. Was the Soviet Union even reading this material? I wondered. They knew they could not win the cold war, they knew the United States would never invade the motherland, so why did they continue their mad spending and impoverishment of their people?

I could not and would not continue in my roles as serviceman, spy, and courier for the next eleven years. It was then that the thought struck me: I did not need a courier, since I already performed that job. I needed to recruit a spy.

Spy recruitment is not the domain of a successful field operative. Even after the most careful appraisal, a certain number of potential recruits will refuse to spy upon their own country and will report the recruiter to the authorities. An active spy is the *source* of intelligence, and the source is too valuable to hazard in recruitment. Recruitment is performed by specialists called "case officers," who are highly trained in the process of spotting possible spies, assessing their potential for cooperating, and finally offering some reward for transferring secrets to a foreign government. Case officers often have the enormous protection of diplomatic immunity for those occasions, just in case their recruitment attempts go wrong. A case officer would be sent home in disgrace for his failure—I would be sent to prison forever.

I had absolutely no training in spy recruitment, knowing only the case officer's mantra: spot, access, and recruit. By recruiting someone, I would be laying my head on the guillotine block and placing the blade-release rope in the hands of the recruit.

There was only one person I would consider for recruitment: Jerry Whitworth. Jerry was one of my instructors at radio school five years earlier, college educated, politically astute, my sailboat racing partner, my best friend. We had maintained communication since we last met at Diego Garcia, and I knew that he had separated from the navy three months earlier. Jerry was taking advantage of a little-used provision that allowed discharged enlisted men to reenlist within ninety days without losing their rank. While he was a civilian by definition and received no pay, he planned to reenlist before the ninety-day deadline.

Jerry had used his vacation to sail from Los Angeles to La Paz, Mexico. Jerry and his lifelong friend, Roger Olson, would sail Roger's twenty-two-foot sloop down the coast past San Diego and along the entire length of Baja California. Around Cape San Lucas and up into the Gulf of California to La Paz, the thousand-mile cruise was a true adventure for so small a craft.

Jerry was back in San Diego, the sailing trip completed, and I resolved to telephone him the next day. I was within a couple weeks of departing for the East Coast, and I had to make this very dangerous recruitment offer before we were separated by three thousand miles.

My course of action was thus set. First, I would move out of the house after the family was settled in Norfolk. Second, I would recruit Jerry as part of a two-man spy team, with Jerry collecting secret material and me acting as courier between him and the Soviets. Third, assuming Jerry agreed, I would leave the service as quickly as possible.

The hazard of recruiting Jerry created a flutter of fear in my chest that even the cognac could not settle. It would indeed be a test of our friendship. There was another issue equally as frightening, however. My top-secret clearance was due for renewal.

My initial top-secret clearance was granted about fifteen years earlier. Clearances do not last forever, however, and must be updated every five years. A complete "national agency check" was performed by the FBI, and while not as strict as one's initial background investigation, it would involve agents questioning relatives and friends and reviewing my finances. My only concern, as usual, was Barbara.

With every message I received from the Soviets, they always quizzed me in detail about Barbara: her attitude, spending habits, drinking problem. What they really wanted to know, of course, was if I had her under control. Obviously I did not, but I would not admit it to my handlers. From my observations, the Soviets had little regard for the reliability of women in general and their effectiveness in the spy business in particular. That Barbara was maligning me to her female relatives and friends was obvious by their demeanor toward me. They formed a sisterhood that glared resentment at the evil male who had wronged one of their own. While I felt confident that she would not reveal my spy activity, I could not be sure of any treacherous hints she may have expressed. Many of these women would be questioned in depth about me, and they would savor the opportunity to repeat Barbara's complaints. Individually, such disclosures would be ignored, but an astute investigator might see a disturbing pattern, a reason to dig deeper for the source of Barbara's hostility.

I was more familiar with the clearance process, having initiated and received the clearances of dozens of my men over the years. The process was unsophisticated and lacked effective oversight. I reached a new decision, added a new item to my mental memorandum: I would forge my clearance. That perilous act seemed safer than the consequences of agents speaking to Barbara and her friends.

Relieved that I had an established plan, I started the engine, running lights on, anchor lights off, and headed for my slip. It would be quiet at the square, well past midnight. The forward berth would offer a good night's sleep.

Time was short, so I started on the forgery process the very next day. I drew the proper form from the ship's office and had my division yeoman deliver my service record. In the privacy of my office, I reviewed my last clearance update, a single sheet bearing a red stamp from the FBI certifying that no derogatory information was uncovered that would preclude granting my clearance.

The quadruplicate request form was a typical government document, with attached carbon paper between the pages. I filled out the form properly, backdating it about one year and listing our previous captain as the requesting officer.

Under normal circumstances, the last carbon copy is placed in the serviceman's record to show that the investigation had been initiated. For a new clearance, the CO would grant an interim top-secret clearance, issuing a final clearance when the FBI report was returned. I would follow none of these steps, however, and was interested in only one carbon—the salmon-colored sheet that the FBI returned with their magic stamp. I held onto that sheet and shredded the remainder. All I lacked to complete the forgery was that stamp.

I studied the stamp on my last update, a rather large 2¼ × 2¼-inch square that looked approximately as follows:

FBI NATIONAL AGENCY INVESTIGATION
CLEARANCE LEVEL
☐ Secret
☐ Top Secret
☐ Top Secret—SI
☐ No Derogatory Info Encl
Investigator   Date

Once the FBI completed the background investigation, some functionary affixed the stamp in red, checked the appropriate boxes, signed and dated the stamp. That salmon-colored carbon copy was returned to the ship where a yeoman would insert it into the service record, replacing the unstamped pink copy.

The Oakland phone book listed several rubber stamp outlets, any of which were capable of manufacturing the FBI stamp. I carefully sketched a stamp of exact dimensions on a simple index card. To make it look official, I typed a military requisition, form 1148, for an "open purchase," adding a half dozen other stamps to help disguise the stamp of interest. The requisition bore the name of the USS *Constellation* (CVA-64), moored nearby at Alameda, and the fictitious name of a supply officer.

After lunch the next day, I drove to the main shopping district of Oakland to a business that manufactured custom stamps. In uniform and carrying the fake requisition, the clerk was happy for the business. He assured me that the big stamp would conform to my sketch. I watched carefully as he studied the FBI stamp, but he showed no suspicion. He waved off his copy of the requisition. The stamp would be ready in twenty-four hours.

The pickup would be the difficult part, so I employed a little spy-craft the next day. If the clerk grew suspicious and called the FBI, I knew they would have the shop under surveillance. I also knew that I would never see them, but perhaps I could force them to reveal themselves.

I parked around the corner of the shop and walked completely around the block to approach it from the side opposite my car. The same man was on duty; no extra employees were lurking about pretending to work. The stamps were produced and I paid in cash, explaining that such small purchases were handled by the ship's petty cash fund. (Ships have no such fund.) The clerk again did not collect his copy of the requisition, a clear sign that I was not compromised. If the clerk had notified the FBI, they surely would have instructed him to collect the requisition for evidence.

Out the door, I turned the opposite way to confuse any trackers, then turned again at the corner. The street was one-way against the traffic, which would prevent vehicle tracking and force them to follow on foot. I saw nothing, especially on the opposite side of the street where potential stalkers were more apt to be. Still clear. At my car, my cap off, windbreaker covering my uniform and blue Cessna cap pulled low, I zipped across traffic and into an alley. Still seemingly clean, I drove back to the ship.

The stamp was a near-perfect match, a credit to that small shop. After a couple of practice tries with the red ink pad, I used the bogus stamp on the counterfeit form and forged the invented name of some FBI employee. With the flawless form inserted into my service jacket, my top-secret clearance was renewed for five more years. When I reported to my new command, the security officer would be so pleased that I possessed a current clearance update.

One must wonder if I was out of my mind to risk such an insane stunt. The only real hazard, however, was from a suspicious store clerk, and I considered that risk to be very low. The average person would perceive the greatest danger from a simple cross-check of all recorded clearances against the FBI's database. How hard could it be for each command to send a list of top-secret, cleared personnel to the FBI for confirmation, even annually? Or for the FBI to send a list to each ship and station from their database requesting confirmation of clearances and upgrade dates?

Somehow, in my heart and soul, I knew that there had been no cross-check. First, I could not envision the bloated and essentially lazy civil service bureaucracy mounting such a vast project. Second, the keepers of the secrets knew very well that the threat of World War III was an artificially created fantasy and the secret data flying about were mostly in support of that illusion. Once the minor risk of the print-stamp shop was behind me, I never worried again about the forged document.

I would discover a decade later that my flippant disregard for any risk to my clearance forgery was not only well founded, but the government was more inept than I thought. The FBI and other agencies performing clearance updates were so overwhelmed with requests that they had *ceased performing them entirely.* So, weirdly, I had the *only* clearance update to be issued during those years, an event so unusual that the presence of a red-stamped completion form alone should have generated suspicion. But then, no one cared and no one was looking.

Jerry had completed his sailing adventure, was met by a friend with a car and boat trailer, and they towed the boat back north to San Diego. I took advantage of an air-taxi charter to some obscure backwater in Southern California, discharged my passengers, and diverted to San Diego for an overnight.

Pilots love the spectacular view when landing at San Diego International, day or night. Assigned the south runway, the striking panorama of the towering cityscape to my right and the deep-blue bay with ships and yachts to my left presented a serious distraction to safe flying. On the ground, I taxied to Jim's Air, tied down the aircraft for the night, and strolled to a nearby restaurant where Jerry and I arranged to meet. It was a splendid early afternoon; summer would hang on for a couple more months in Southern California. I was thoroughly enjoying the ambiance and felt oddly relaxed, even as I prepared to take the most dangerous step in my life. I should have suffered that sickening sensation of rushing in lunatic flight to destruction, but somehow I trusted Jerry enough to induce calm.

We met at Boom Trenchard's Flare Path, an aviation-themed restaurant located just off the airport. Named for a British aviation pioneer, the nickname "Boom" probably resulted from his bombing raids against rebellious colonialists somewhere. A flare path is a runway, probably referring to the flares used to illuminate the runway before electricity was widespread.

I sat at the bar, indulged in a cocktail since I was not flying until the morning, and watched for Jerry. Boom Trenchard's was the perfect pilots' watering hole. The basement was a replica of a World War I aerodrome pub, complete with 1917 music, a plank bar across oil drums, and walls covered with aviation mementos.

The main lounge and dining area were dedicated to World War II aviation; appropriate photos and paraphernalia were in profusion. Behind the bar, instead of a televised sports channel was a radar screen displaying local aircraft traffic. The small third level was devoted to modern space travel and included photos of intrepid astronauts and their spaceships.

Jerry appeared at the door, his walk spry and confident. A tall, rangy-rugged guy, he was rakishly good looking. Amusement always lurked in his eyes, and he grinned as I waved from the bar. We retreated to a quiet table, Jerry anxious to relate the details of his cruise and to learn the reason for our mysterious meeting. The huge window overlooked the busy airport, scores of boats rested at anchor in a nearby cove. One was homebuilt to resemble a water-borne flying saucer. Only in California!

We discussed every detail of his daring trip, reliving every problem and event in a way that only ocean-going sailing men could enjoy. The story wound down, and Jerry finally leaned back and asked what was so important that I would fly five hundred miles to talk about in person.

Many people have asked me how I could trust Jerry not to report our meeting, what characteristics he possessed to warrant that faith. It was mostly a gut feeling on my part, but I had also developed a good understanding of his politics. First, Jerry had always run against the current of political conformity and seemed primarily a libertarian with liberal leanings. He had the sensitivity of a scholar, was politically shrewd, and I sensed that he shared my view of a superior US military power in a world of weak, harmless enemies. Finally, Jerry had a unique trait of devotion to his friends, almost obsessively so. He maintained contact with a wide range of friends, often traveling great distances just to talk. I counted myself in that category and felt that his dedication to his friends was so strong that to betray them would be in direct contrast to his nature.

There was an incident in Jerry's life that was exaggerated by the media as a defining moment that led to my trust in him. It involved Jerry's first and very short marriage. He was on active duty and had applied for the basic allowance for quarters to which married servicemen were entitled, then a mere $77 per month. After his divorce, he neglected to remind the disbursing office to cancel the allowance. He continued to draw this overpayment until his discharge. He should have corrected the oversight and returned the money, but instead he took advantage of the error.

Jerry had told me about the unreturned overpayment, which showed his high level of trust in me, the officer in charge of his division. I was impressed by the strength of faith that he had in me, how highly he regarded his friends. The media, however, emphasized the inaccurate view of this event—that I recognized the "larceny of Jerry's heart." Believe me, it was not his small act of theft that made him a target for recruitment but the absolute certainty of the trustworthiness he had in his friends.

Jerry leaned forward anxiously, brows lifted in question. This was no time for complicated explanations or justification, just direct and simple language. "Jerry," I said, "I've been a spy for the past several years and I want you to join me as part of a two-man team." Jerry took a quick breath of utter astonishment, sat back, and seemed to hold that breath. I unconsciously held my breath as well. Finally, his half grin burst into a smile of amazement, then a bark of laughter.

Still shaking his head in disbelief, he asked the expected questions: You were a spy when we were at radio school together? Yes. How long have you done this? Ten years or so. *What* are you trading? Everything, including crypto. *Who* are you trading with? On that question I became evasive and claimed to be working with an ally, Israel, in an attempt to lessen the impact. Jerry was skeptical and asked how contact was made in *my* recruitment. I explained that they approached me, which was my second lie.

I had trapped myself by lying, and Jerry wasted no time in asking the checkmate question: "If they approached you, how do you know the recruiters don't represent Russia, China, or anyone else?"

Servicemen generally assume the political posture of conservatives, the expected stance of the warrior class. Given the choice between guns and butter, the warrior will always choose guns, the liberal opts for butter. I had always displayed the attitude of the conservative, particularly after entering the world of espionage, as a way of concealing my otherwise suspicious left-wing beliefs. Jerry listened, grinning with amusement, shaking his head in wonder, as he heard my true beliefs for the first time. Jerry agreed with my basic premise: first, that the Soviet Union possessed a seriously inferior military that would decline in power over time. Second, that there was no creditable threat to the United States anywhere in the world. Finally, I appealed to Jerry, the career serviceman, by pointing out that we were sworn to *protect* the country against its enemies. Since World War II, however, the function of the US government seemed disposed toward *creating* enemies by taking sides in civil wars (itself an act of war) and overthrowing regimes we dislike, such as Chile and Iran. Making enemies around the world contradicts our pledge to protect the land.

Many countries in the world live in dread of the United States, fearful of economic sanctions, regime overthrow, and even military attack. The role of espionage for these countries, I explained, is to provide "transparency," revealing to their leadership the plans (or lack of plans) the United States may be contemplating. The Soviet Union, if indeed they are my employers, are genuinely fearful of US invasion. Since you and I know that there is no such plan, how can it hurt to allow three hundred million Soviet citizens to relax in the knowledge of that fact? This logic conformed with Jerry's views, and he nodded in thoughtful agreement.

The fact that I had succeeded in this activity for so many years was a major selling point for Jerry. There was no reason for either of us to be detected, and though it screamed of danger, the plan had the promise of excitement that appealed to Jerry. He was in.

To his credit, Jerry did not broach the issue of money until later in the conversation. I explained the inaccurate Hollywood portrayal, in which a one-sheet secret plan or a simple micro-dot was worth a million dollars. In actuality, I was compensated about a thousand a week, sometimes a little more, sometimes less, depending on quality and quantity. Cryptographic earned the highest. The problem, I explained, was that my sponsor was unaware of my recruitment and would be told only after Jerry produced the first usable product. I would then negotiate similar compensation for him, but I stressed that I would actually be asking for double their payment—half for each of us—and I could not know how they would react. Jerry was surprised by the low payment, even disappointed, but his sense of adventure prevailed as he agreed to the uncertain terms.

Only the details remained, and we hammered them out quickly. Jerry had already planned to volunteer again for Diego Garcia for a one-year tour. My lack of spy training shocked him, but I explained again that this was not the movies. The few techniques I had developed were reviewed—covert use of the copy machine, camera techniques, and so on. I was on my third Minox spy camera, having worn out two, and offered to buy Jerry's Minox. An avid and experienced photographer, Jerry elected to buy his own camera and film.

The secret presence of the United States in Diego Garcia presented a problem, since I could not travel there to recover his film. He would thus be on his own for a year, and I needed only to know if he had started assembling material. Jerry had planned to learn scuba diving during this tour of duty, and we agreed to use "scuba reference" as a code for spying activity. Successful dives would mean success in photographing material. Good or bad dives would indicate the quality of the material obtained.

Once I received his "first dive" letter, I would inform the KGB of our new spy team. My actions would surely cause an apoplectic reaction in the Kremlin.

The arrangement was made with the shake of hands, and I slept that night serenely at an Embarcadero motel across the street. I never had any doubts about Jerry's loyalty.

Chapter 24

MY LAST TOUR OF DUTY

The movement of one's household effects on military order is not as stressful as one may think. All is paid for by the government, including the protective wrapping, boxing, inventory, and transportation. Family members are required to do little more than pack their own suitcases. There are really just two requirements: first, stay out of the movers' way and, second, watch your suitcases carefully so they will not be wrapped, boxed, and loaded on the truck.

I went to the ship on moving day and officially checked out. The yeoman handed me the distinctive brown envelope containing my service record, pay record, and official orders. The moving company is obligated to pick up the family property from two locations, so I arranged for them to pack and carry my mini-refrigerator, TV, recliner chair, and uniforms from my stateroom. I said my good-byes from the CO down, promised to be at the club later for my farewell party, and walked to the gangway. After a snappy salute to the quarter-deck watch and the ensign astern, I stepped ashore and away from my last ship.

Was it only two years and eight months ago that I walked toward this ship on the same quay, the electric sparkle of excitement filling my chest as I spotted her sleek gray form? I looked back once at the same proud lady, and my heart sank. Part of me was still aboard, still in the South China Sea, still in harm's way, still going somewhere in a hurry.

The boat rested on her trailer in the parking lot, the mast lashed across the bow pulpit and stern rail. I rigged a brace for the motorcycle where it rode securely on the trailer next to the bow. The car, a large Chrysler from the last days of the muscle cars, was ready for the three-thousand-mile effort of towing her load east.

The navy had instituted a new concept for transferring families called the Navy Lodge. These were inexpensive on-base motels where families under orders could stay during the transport of their household effects. We would spend the night at one of these lodges, which was about a block away from the club and three blocks from the piers. The days of spending our last night on the floor of the old house and more nights on the floor of the new house awaiting furniture were over.

The movers were pulling away as I arrived home to find Barbara as surly as ever and the kids showing the anguish of a long day with their ill-tempered mom. The kids and I did the final cleanup—vacuum, sweep, and swab—and I loaded the cleaning equipment and luggage into the car. It was then I noticed the movers had grabbed some vital items from under Barbara's nose, the trailer's spare tire, heavy-duty jack, and a box of tools. I looked at her in disbelief and recognized that she was in that controlled stupor of an experienced alcoholic. I have always been a believer in Murphy's Law—whatever can go wrong, will go wrong—so I knew we were guaranteed a trailer flat. Replacing that big truck tire and wheel would be difficult.

Settled in adjoining rooms at the Navy Lodge, Barbara and I left the kids to two TVs and walked to the service club. I gave the obligatory smile to disguise my deep gloom, my spirits on the bottom like a lost anchor. The wives of the officers gave Barbara the usual sterling silver farewell gift, I believe it was a candy dish. I received an excellent plaque and several sexual gag gifts from the junior officers, back-alley trinkets from Hong Kong.

My drinking had declined over the years to the point of light to moderate social drinking. I was always able to pass a roadside sobriety test (which I never received). But I drank to excess that night, enjoying the alcoholic-induced false sense of happiness that buoyed my spirits; I was drunk for the first time in many years. Back at the lodge, unable to find the bathroom and confused by switching rooms with the kids, I embarrassed myself by throwing up on the floor.

The trip was uneventful and pleasant, the Chrysler hauling her load over the Sierra Nevadas and Rocky Mountains with no difficulty. We followed our old pattern of five hundred miles a day or less, stopped early for a relaxed family dinner, and retired early at reserved motels. Back on the road at dawn, we took breakfast and lunch at random stops. The big boat and California license tags generated a lot of interest as we rambled farther and farther east.

My attitude toward Barbara, my wife of eighteen years, was hard to explain. I looked at this eccentric woman riding beside me, our relationship far from that of husband and wife. She seemed more like a distant aunt, homeless and cantankerous, living with a family of strangers. The old proverb seemed appropriate. Children keep marriages together, not love. The oldest kids could hardly wait to move out of the house. Margaret had but one year to wait for adulthood. Cynthia could easily be certified as suffering from post-traumatic stress disorder as badly as anyone I had seen in Vietnam; her expression was often pained, troubled. Could she survive the next three years to age eighteen? Could I rescue her then? I worried that her soul was already broken.

Motoring through the flat plains of Kansas, I could only wonder at the insane social system of marriage in our culture. No rational person would enter into a lifetime contract without guarantees. We are taught from childhood that we are lord and master of ourselves; makers, shapers, and authors of our destiny. In actuality, however, the circumstances of a blind choice in a mate ends up as the real shaper in our lives. The philosophers would tell us that while we cannot directly choose our circumstances, we can choose to *shape* our circumstances.

In that I will accept failure, but in all sincerity, I expect there are few who could successfully shape Barbara. There was an escape clause in the insane contract that allowed me a way out, but the wife always gained custody in those days. Were it a decade or so later, I would have sued for child custody and obtained an injunction to prevent Barbara from any physical abuse of our kids during visitation. Barbara was indeed the molder of my life and of the children's lives. But then, any Hindu Brahmin would advise me to relax, explaining that all life is sorrow. Hinduism had that right. Going even further, a neophyte of the ancient mystery schools is taught that those who have trials and troubles in their lives should rejoice because of them. By the reconciliation of these negative forces, man is opened to the Divine Light. While I essentially believe this, I found it difficult to celebrate my marital strife.

Our route was generally across the central states, and as we neared Virginia, I reviewed my next drop procedure. We should reach Norfolk on the day I had scheduled the drop, so I planned to use the alternate date of about a week later. I encountered difficulty with the tow, however, because the boat had slipped to the rear by a few inches. Tied fast in at least six places, it still managed to move, unbalancing the load and rendering the trailer unstable. I could safely travel at only forty-five miles per hour—above that, the trailer fishtailed dangerously. Even slight fishtailing exerted powerful stress on the trailer tires. Eventually Murphy caught us, applied his law, and demolished a tire in a powerful explosion. Shaken, I made it safely to the shoulder, more rattled than I'd been that night when the North Vietnamese missile passed over my head on the bridge.

We lost a half day finding a truck wheel and tire and, still creeping along at slow speed, we entered the DC Beltway the day before my scheduled drop. Our motel was just beyond the Virginia line and only a few miles from the drop site. I decided to take advantage of this coincidence and perform the drop on schedule.

I explained to Barbara that I would be gone on business for several hours after dinner, but she quickly deduced that my absence involved a spy mission. Oddly, she asked to accompany me, begged to go, and finally insisted. Barbara would relate years later (to the FBI) that we serviced the drop together. I recall going alone, following the laborious six- or seven-hour pay exchange procedure, and nodding off behind the wheel. I started late, about 7 p.m., driving the long route backward and adjusting for road changes that had occurred in the year-old procedure. In the long hour wait between the signals and the actual package drop, I actually did doze off, my head resting comfortably on the driver's side window.

Snapping awake in alarm, sure that I had blown the exchange, my nap had lasted only a few minutes. I realized then that I should have waited. I had driven three thousand miles over the past few days and was far too exhausted to maintain the high level of alertness necessary for this job. Indeed, I could not muster the slightest amount of adrenaline for the actual drop and package pickup. I went through the motions by rote. My weariness reinforced the need for a two-man team for this dangerous activity.

Back at the motel by about 1 a.m., I finally realized how utterly irresponsible I'd been to leave my temporarily homeless family in a motel while I risked arrest. Had anything gone wrong, my lack of care would have resulted in a family catastrophe.

After the family was settled in adjoining rooms at the Navy Lodge, my first stop was to meet my new boss and crew. I knew that the Amphibious Force was to be decommissioned under a huge reorganization. The force commanders would consist of Naval Air Force, Surface Force, and Submarine Force. The Air and Submarine Forces would remain unchanged, but the three arms of the Surface Force would be combined. Thus the Amphibious, Cruiser-Destroyer, and Service Forces would be individually decommissioned and the new Surface Force created. I would be assigned as staff communications officer for the Amphibs and then would assume the same post under the new Surface Force. What I did not know was where the new force would be headquartered. Everyone hoped the new command would remain at the Little Creek Amphib Base, the most pleasant and spacious military installation in the area. By my estimation, it was the only base large enough to accommodate the new, massive command.

My new workplace was a wooden World War II building that had probably served as a barracks in earlier years. My office was spacious but consisted of shoddy office dividers. Our stunningly attractive secretary was within reach over the government-green barrier. My chiefs and radiomen were efficient, routing and delivering massive stacks of messages to the staff officers. A central base communications center performed the actual transmissions and receipts of the messages; our status was reduced to that of messengers. The atmosphere was efficient and productive but also laid-back in the style of the "Gator Navy" (the slang term for the Amphib Force).

The outgoing CWO2 I was to replace spent most of the day designing a house on a three-foot-wide pad of graph paper mounted on an easel. It took him ten minutes to explain his job, which caused me to grimace at my "rush" orders and my "critical" need. Even sitting in dry dock in San Francisco, I had left a real job in exchange for a nontechnical, nonchallenging paper-pushing post. Just as I suspected. I thought of exchanging orders with the aspiring architect, but he was one of the few who were anxious for sea duty on a new LHA helicopter assault ship.

The worst news, however, was that the new command would be located at the CINCLANTFLT compound where I had earlier been stationed at the Submarine Force Staff. Already overcrowded, with no spare office space, a scarcity of parking, and no real estate for building within the cramped compound, it seemed the worst choice. The commander in chief of the entire Atlantic Fleet was headquartered there, and he surely wished to have his junior force admirals close at hand.

We found a perfect house with a short commute to my future assignment. On the meandering Old Ocean View road, the four-bedroom, two-story brick house was located among quiet streets in a sleepy, peaceful neighborhood. The purchase was completed in a couple of days, and we moved in within a week.

It is difficult for an energetic fleet sailor to adjust to the boredom of shore duty. The chiefs ran the message center with total efficiency; my input was unnecessary and thus avoided. My workday consisted of a couple of hours reading my copy of every outgoing and incoming message to the force and checking for proper distribution. I also supervised the top-secret control office, which included "Eyes Only," and I maintained a separate safe for that material. The security officer was delighted that I had the foresight to update my top-secret clearance before transfer.

There was no access to cryptographic information, so the value of my material was reduced. I had scheduled an exchange for the winter when the Soviets would see for themselves. If Jerry was "diving" by then, they would also receive the startling news of my unauthorized recruitment.

Jerry reenlisted in the navy in October 1974, but unbeknownst to me, it was for just two years in a reserve-training program. I had expected him to sign up for a standard four-year term, so this shorter enlistment contract showed a certain reluctance on his part. He had volunteered officially for a return to Diego Garcia, however, and was assigned to the Army Communications Electronic School at Fort Monmouth, New Jersey, in December for a satellite communications course. We agreed that he would visit me in Norfolk after graduation.

President Nixon would finally resign in 1974, replaced by Vice President Gerald R. Ford. President Ford would pardon Nixon unconditionally, proving yet again that royalty does not go to prison.

Still bored to death in my "critical" job at the Amphibious Base as we entered 1975, the expected defeat of the South Vietnamese induced sadness nonetheless. President Ford had gone to Congress asking for more financial aid for Saigon, but Congress refused all but $300 million in emergency aid to evacuate US citizens from Saigon.

With my job functioning in automatic and winter heavy upon us, it was time to begin implementing my plan to move out. My guilt was palpable as I thought of leaving the kids in the clutches of the Wicked Witch. There were hundreds of apartments in Ocean View within a mile or two of my house, most shabby and catering to the lowest-ranked enlisted sailors with new wives. I looked at a few; they all reminded me of the inadequate housing Barbara and I suffered through in the first years of our marriage. Nothing satisfied me. It was then that I experienced the reality that every newly separated or divorced man encounters—living conditions will decline significantly.

I decided on something temporary, wishing I qualified for a BOQ room. The sailboat could have worked were it not high and dry on her trailer in the middle of winter. Finally I noticed the signs along the somewhat seedy Ocean View motels offering bargain rates during the winter off-season. I settled for a one-room efficiency at a surprisingly low monthly rent with a plan to move out in the spring. It would never do for the long term, but at least I was ready for my announcement to Barbara.

Jerry graduated from the satellite school in February and traveled to Norfolk before proceeding to California. My intention had always been to keep him separated from Barbara for his own protection; his identity as a spy would be known only to me. As a show of good faith, I paid Jerry a small advance of between four or five thousand dollars. I reiterated that the "buyer" would not be informed of my new partner until I received his "diving" letter. When he touched down in the United States a year hence, or perhaps sooner if leave was granted, I agreed to meet him and settle his account. As I recall, the terms were for four grand per month if cryptographic material was involved, something less without.

Jerry had correctly sensed a possible danger with Barbara, a hazard he had not thought about during our initial meeting. I assured him that she had no knowledge of my activity and I sincerely hated lying to my friend. Regardless, I stressed that he should never contact her or allow her to learn his identity. If anything ever went bad on my end, Jerry's name should always be unknown to her.

Lastly, we made a blood oath (without exchanging blood) that if caught, we would never reveal the identity of the other. Jerry would conceal the origin of his material by covering the identifying routing stamps and other markings that could trace anything to his station. Thus in the event of my capture, the material could not be traced to him. Or if Jerry was somehow caught, nothing he possessed would identify me as the courier. In full agreement, we shook hands warmly, two old friends sharing a mutual confidence.

Conditions at home seemed to improve, and I spent more time there than I had planned. There are always many projects in a new house, and I enjoyed the kids' assistance. The house was not air-conditioned, so I contacted Barbara's old boyfriend from the Algonquin House, the owner of a heating and air conditioning company, and contracted him to install a central system. He and his crew did a superb job, and I was amused by his strange glances as he wondered if I knew of his affair with Barbara.

All of my children were strangely silent, never relating any mistreatment at the hands of their mother. Even when I was alone with them and we were beyond the hearing of their mom, they answered the most subtle questions with monosyllable evasion. When they were very small, Barbara would often admonish them with the threat "Don't make me tell your father what you did." I always found that to be disingenuous, since Barbara was the heavy-handed disciplinarian—I rarely administered punishment and if I did, it was fairly gentle. Did that hollow threat still work now that they were so much older? I wondered.

It was time for Margaret to get her driver's license, and since transferring servicemen frequently sell their vehicles, I bought the kids an inexpensive car to give them some wings. A five-year-old Chevrolet Nova, it was not much to look at, but it was safe transportation and a dent could be ignored. I thoroughly enjoyed taking Margaret through the phases of getting her learner's permit, taking driving lessons, and the achievement of the holy grail coveted by every teen—her driver's license. Still, though we spent hours together, she was as unresponsive as a POW when asked how things were going at home and with Mom.

Spring arrived with no word from Jerry. Waiting for his diving letter, or lack thereof, had placed my life on hold. Whether I would spend the next ten years in the service or retire in the next year was entirely in Jerry's hands. The motel shifted to its summer rates, and with all decisions in abeyance, I chose to pay the modest increase.

At the first hint of warm weather, the boat was hauled into the water, her mast was stepped, and she made her first cruise of the season. Her new berth would be a slip in one of the scruffy marinas in Little Creek. It was a far cry from Jack London Square and the parade of attractive tourists.

The suspense ended in June 1975 when I received Jerry's letter informing me that he had qualified as a scuba diver and had made this first dive. He did indeed become an avid diver, but the letter's true meaning was that he had assembled secret material that would be transferred to me. Jerry had become a spy.

Jerry's letter arrived before my summer drop exchange, and while I had no idea of the quality or quantity of Jerry's material, my drop note would inform the KGB of my most unorthodox recruitment. My complaints concerning the excessive travel requirements were reiterated and my new position as "courier" in the two-man team was explained. I would request retirement, I went on, which would take effect in the summer of 1976. This stunning news, I suspected, would cause the pulse of my handler to kick into tachycardia. Any change in a spy's routine is always viewed as the result of his being caught and turned by the FBI. It would take sustained performance by Jerry and me to prove otherwise.

The summer drop was almost a pleasure after the extensive travel over the past five years. The casual four-hour drive took me to the signal, drop, and pickup sites, and after a couple of hours to review the procedure and timing, I checked into an economy motel until start time. The operation was routine, and were I hooked up to a hospital monitor, only a slight increase in blood pressure would have been recorded at the actual moments of the drop and the pickup.

There was much for the KGB to ponder in my delivery note. Not only was I quitting the business after finding my replacement, but my transfer would come as a surprise. Intelligence agencies *always* transfer spy suspects upon detection, always to jobs with less access to secrets. This delivery from my new assignment lacked cryptographic material entirely, a bad sign, but did include a large quantity of other material. Overall, they would likely conclude that I had been caught. In our weird arrangement of contact only twice a year, they would have six months to craft a reply. They would also worry that their KGB agent would be captured in our next exchange, which would greatly embarrass the Soviet Union.

In July 1975, just short of twenty years of service, I asked the departmental yeoman to prepare my retirement request letter. Pen poised over the signature line, surrounded by a cloud of gloom, I could not bring myself to sign. I loved this crazy navy life, my friends could not believe I would ever retire at twenty years, but the plan was in motion and could not be changed. I signed. One year hence, I would be a civilian.

Chapter 25

OVERDUE DIVORCE

My motel accommodations brought about an unexpected problem. Since all servicemen, and especially officers, need a telephone number on file for emergencies, my radiomen quickly learned that my primary number was an Ocean View motel and my secondary number was that of my wife. Like any motel, the front desk takes the call and announces the motel name. As communications officer, I would receive a couple of after-hours calls every week for various emergencies, some just to keep me informed, others to summon me back to the office. Once my crew figured out my room number (bottom floor facing the beach), I began to have visitors, especially from WAVES. Requests to change clothes, stow beer in my refrigerator, or use the head were only mildly inconvenient. Complications soon developed. Perhaps as their boss, I was viewed as an exciting challenge by these young women. It was most dangerous when a WAVES would show up alone, smiling seductively. My voice of reason would tell me no, but the biological imperative said otherwise. It was time to move.

The paradise of summer in Chesapeake Bay had come to an end before I finally found better living conditions. The depressingly inadequate apartment was located only two blocks from my house. Two postage stamp–sized bedrooms, a one-person kitchen, and a weird living room–dining room combination made up my new home. I never entered the kitchen, and the refrigerator stayed empty. It was definitely temporary, but with a rent that was nearly as high as my house payment. It did have that second bedroom for visiting (or escaping) kids.

With retirement just a year away, I was faced with the difficulty of creating income without stifling my ability to meet with Jerry anywhere in the world and make my twice-yearly trip to Washington. My charter flying in the past had always been more a source of recreation than of profit, and Cavalier would offer only scant income. I needed an additional source of income that also gave me that necessary freedom to travel.

It was while writing a new lease for the South Carolina restaurant-bar that an opportunity presented itself. A lawyer friend was rewriting the business lease when the conversation turned to the lack of effective private detectives in the area. The lawyer lamented about the abysmal success on the part of those he had used. As he cited a few unsuccessful cases, I could not help but relate how I would have done the jobs. The lawyer then surprised me by asking if I was willing to take on his cases. I lacked a license, I pointed out, but he explained that Virginia was among the easiest states for obtaining a PI license. A simple form was executed, and a few days later the license arrived in the mail. My profession at that moment had become that of naval officer, commercial pilot, private detective, and spy.

My first case involved a young woman who had been cheated out of a sum of money.

My work on this case ended with a final call to the dealer, reminding him that he had only twenty-four hours to pay or face the consequences. I slipped the names and other facts about his two accomplices into the conversation as though I knew everything about them. The dealer seemed sobered by that fact as I slammed the phone down in his ear. The subsequent phone calls between this hapless trio of scam artists would have been enjoyable to tape.

Someone returned the money, and my first case as a private investigator was a success. The conduct required for such work was inconsistent with my style, however, and I informed the very pleased lawyer that I would never again collect money or deal with such a criminal element. Unfazed, he kept me busy and referred me to a few other attorneys. Perhaps I had found the perfect profession to keep a spy occupied between jobs.

My life in the presence of Barbara was theatrically depressing but interrupted by odd moments of civility and even pleasure. It was one of those rare periods of friendliness that led to Barbara actually accompanying me on a spy drop. She had obtained tickets to some show, but since it conflicted with my winter drop exchange, I informed her that I would be busy that entire weekend. Barbara was roughly aware of my schedule and quickly deduced that I had spy work to do. She asked to accompany me, even insisted. I tried in vain to dissuade her, but I finally relented simply to avoid an argument. Her motivation, however, did not escape me; it was a pitiful attempt to become involved in a part of my life, even my criminal life, as a way of rekindling our relationship. To expect our marriage to ever rejuvenate was a psychotic concept illustrating her flight from reality. Did she believe families that spy together stay together?

Regardless, it was the height of irresponsibility to leave four children behind while carrying out a major crime. If caught in the act, Barbara and I would surely go to prison forever, leaving our kids to grow up in foster homes. Barbara was insistent on going, however, and in my heart I knew that if we were caught, the kids would actually be better off raised by someone other than Barbara.

So, off we went to Washington to conduct an uneventful exchange, an entirely routine procedure. Barbara was useful in helping with the driving and keeping watch for surveillance. Watching for tails was useless, I knew, since FBI surveillance is entirely invisible. The KGB had informed me of that fact.

During those rare moments of amiability between Barbara and I, we did enjoy occasional family gatherings and outings together, but there were many clues that conditions were very wrong. First, a lot of my clothes and personal files were still at the house, protected by an outside dead bolt lock on my den door, so I was at the house nearly every day. I would always telephone before stopping by and usually found one or all of the children gone. Barbara would brush off my inquiries with a casual remark that they were on sleepovers or at the mall.

Second, while driving past the house one morning, I noticed a pile of clothes behind a shrub at the side of the house. The kids would say nothing, and I assumed they were changing into some item that their mother had forbidden them to wear to school.

Then Bob, the refrigerator and air conditioning friend of Barbara, hired me to perform a PI job for him. During one of our meetings, Bob told me that he had to repair one of my air conditioning units. A Freon pipe ran up the side of the house into the attic where a condenser was located. The insulated pipe had been ripped from the house. Bob was concerned, and while he did not say so, it was obvious that one of my kids had climbed out a second-story bedroom window and climbed down the pipe during an escape. The thin copper tubing, perhaps a quarter-inch in diameter, had broken. Obviously the child had not been killed or injured. Bob handed me the bill. To this day, I do not know who made the daring escape, but there should be no shame in telling me. I, too, had escaped, but I was old enough to just walk out the front door.

Finally, Barbara's money management had declined to a new low. I would give her a substantial amount of cash at the start of each month for food, clothes, and recreation. I still paid the mortgage, utilities, and other bills, plus any major purchases. Barbara could have and should have saved a large portion each month, but instead she began running out of cash early. She would be broke by the third week, then by the second, finally after one week. Where was it going? I wondered. I hoped she was not trying to start a business for a third time, because Barbara lacked the energy or dedication—to say nothing of sobriety—for a small business.

Barbara telephoned me at work with an urgent request for an early payment of "next month's" allowance. I had already planned to seriously reduce her monthly stipend overall and pay it weekly. She was only temporarily bewildered when I handed her two hundred dollars for the week—she had been receiving about one thousand dollars a month. Her only real expense was for groceries, which cost two or three hundred a month in the mid-1970s. But I was not to win. She tipped her head back in the manner of a British duchess of yore, thickened her Boston accent, and forced me to look into her nostrils. "Laura has run away from home," she smugly recounted, enjoying herself immensely as she blamed me with her scorn. "I have to fly to Wisconsin to pick her up," she continued. Airline, rental car, and motel would cost hundreds. Worse, Laura had pilfered Barbara's monthly allowance to make the trip in the first place. I would soon learn that Cynthia and Laura had been running away for years, financed by Barbara's allowance, which was easy to filch from her handbag while she slumbered in a drunken stupor. These kids ran away using public transport, possibly even by air, but at least that was safer than hitchhiking. This was not Laura's first long jaunt either; she had flown to California a few months earlier. Barbara flew cross-country to retrieve her then, also without my knowledge.

Barbara strode out of the house like one going on holiday, smiling, enjoying herself. Although my kids were old enough to manage, I stayed home until Barbara and Laura returned. Where in Wisconsin Laura had traveled was a mystery, but I overheard my children talking about her California trip and that she had stayed with Dorie, an old school friend. They described Dorie as a tramp, hardly good company for my child. Every father thinks of his fifteen-year-old daughter as a virgin, but if she was associating with Dorie, this was probably not the case.

Laura's return was one of the darker moments in my life. A haughty Barbara sauntered in the door, Laura in tow, as defiant as ever. I drew Laura aside for the obligatory quiz, receiving only a cold glare in response. Infuriated, I slugged her several times, hard, before I realized that she had never cracked to the interrogations of her mother. I doubt the Gestapo could have gotten her to talk. But then I suddenly understood that I had sunk to the level of Barbara. Laura had not only survived endless cross-examinations at the hands of Barbara but had also endured savage beatings. I had not inflicted corporal punishment on my kids in years, and after my humiliating conduct with Laura, I would never forgive myself for striking her.

It was late in winter of 1976 that I informed Barbara that I was moving out permanently, ending the charade. She could continue living in the house and I would support her as before—there would be no divorce. My apartment was within walking distance, and the kids could visit at any time. I advised her to seriously consider finding a job. She would hear none of this, refused to respond, and finally fled from the room. Barbara had other ideas, I would learn later.

Jerry's tour of duty in Diego Garcia ended in March, and he wrote that he would visit me in Norfolk, saving me a trip to California. He was taking thirty days' annual leave and traveling to the Virgin Islands to visit a friend, Bruce. Jerry's next duty station would be the USS *Constellation* (CV-64), home port, I believe, of Alameda, California. He had been selected for promotion to chief radioman and would assume the rank in October 1977.

Jerry was expected to deliver classified material covering several months and would expect payment, no doubt to finance his Caribbean vacation. It was inappropriate and bad business practice to pay him in advance—and from my resources—but I felt it necessary to do. If the KGB found his material to be of no value, it would be a personal financial loss to me.

Following my "separation" announcement to Barbara, the kids went from being very scarce to completely absent. Since I continued to pay all of her bills, she agreed that I could keep my locked den for personal effects. Occasional trips to the house would thus continue, always preceded by a phone call. But even when one of my children answered and I told them I would be there shortly, I always found Barbara there alone, reveling in her small conquest. She always somehow managed to hustle the kids out of the house before my arrival. The mall on Tidewater Drive and Little Creek Road was just four short blocks away. A video game center was just behind the K-Mart, in an area called Old Town, and the kids probably wondered why Mom would finance this unexpected entertainment. Meanwhile, I was experiencing full force the life of the noncustodial parent at the hands of a vindictive spouse. From the moment of our separation, I never had a single opportunity to meet with any of my kids and invite them to spend a night or weekend with me.

Jerry had not made travel arrangements when we spoke, but he had my apartment address and phone number and knew I was to pick him up at the airport. Then one evening I decided to stop by the house unannounced in the hope of seeing the kids. The house was only dimly lit, and while I expected no one to be home, Barbara answered the door. Her taunting smile signaled that she had triumphed over me again; at the dining room table sat Jerry, enjoying a romantic repast with wine glasses aglow from shimmering candles. I immediately knew what Jerry was doing; he was playing super-spy with Barbara in a subtle attempt to learn if she was aware of my spy activity. He had seriously erred, however. First, he had agreed never to contact or meet with Barbara, for now he was at the top of the "suspects" list if I were ever arrested. Second, he was no competition in an intelligence-gathering tête-à-tête with Barbara. She was far more cunning and would turn the tables on poor Jerry. He would learn nothing while Barbara would surely figure out Jerry's involvement.

I quickly completed my business in my locked den and departed. The kids were not present, as usual.

Jerry seemed properly embarrassed when we met the next day at my apartment but still did not seem to grasp the likely potential that she would name him as my partner if anything went wrong on my end. And, as I predicted, Barbara had prevailed in their game of wits, although Jerry seemed satisfied that she knew nothing of my activity or of our cooperation.

With Jerry's misstep in the past, we moved on to spy business. I received a couple dozen rolls of Minox spy film and the details of what they contained, none of which I recall. I felt obligated to pay him, even though he should have waited for payment from the buyer. I paid him (as I recall) $18,000 for the handful of film. He seemed more than satisfied and flew off to the Caribbean the next day. (A month vacation in Iceland would seem a better choice after a year on the sweltering equator.) I would deliver his film, along with my own, in about three months. A long nine months would pass before hearing again from the KGB regarding the quality of Jerry's material and if he was accepted as a member of my two-man team. That is when I would receive his payment for the material as well. Of course, if his material was of no value or if the photography was inadequate, I was out the advance and final payment.

When announcing my separation from Barbara, I delivered the household payment books and informed her that she was again responsible for paying the bills. She would receive ample cash to cover all the expenses, but I would no longer rescue her from fiscal problems. If her utilities were turned off, she could live in the dark. If the mortgage company foreclosed on the house for lack of payment, she could find new quarters. I suggested she hide her cash from the children, who had developed some very expensive habits.

I should not have been surprised when I received a call at my office from a Norfolk divorce attorney. Barbara had filed for divorce on the grounds of desertion, and the lawyer had scheduled a settlement meeting. I could attend, with or without my lawyer, or she would have a summons served by the sheriff. I agreed to attend without service and without legal counsel.

Barbara and I sat in the office of her high-priced attorney who read through the three-page divorce decree in the solemn tones of a eulogy. All of our assets were in real estate, and Barbara was entitled to half. As the lawyer droned on, I thought of our plans stretching back to the 1950s of Barbara and me living aboard a large sloop, forty-five feet or more, sailing the Caribbean and beyond. My real estate purchases had always been with that thought in mind, regardless of our imperfect marriage. Our first purchase was that waterfront lot in Cocoa Beach, Florida, just off the Banana River on the Intercoastal Waterway.

After buying that property, we quickly followed up with two bulk-headed waterfront lots at Port Charlotte on the gulf side of Florida. Then two lots on Great Exuma Island, back when the Bahamas were still a British colony, one waterfront, the second, more expensive lot, on the high ground. Our last lot was another bulkheaded waterfront in North Carolina on the Albamoro Sound near Kitty Hawk and also on the inland waterway.

Our plan in those earlier years had been to build inexpensive A-frame rentals on the properties but reserve berthing for our boat at each location. The properties in North Carolina and Cocoa Beach were connected by the inland waterway, and Port Charlotte was connected to the waterway by a canal that ran the width of Florida following the Tamiami Trail. In fact, at the time Barbara began divorce proceedings, I was already looking at waterfront property in Norfolk, also on the inland waterway, as my northern-most port.

The overly grave lawyer finally got to the division of assets portion, which was surprising. Barbara took the house, as expected, but not the South Carolina business that actually generated monthly income with no effort. Instead, she took possession of the Cocoa Beach and both Port Charlotte properties, all paid for or nearly so and quite valuable. I was left with the North Carolina lot, newly bought and with no equity, and the low-value Bahama properties. I suggested that Barbara keep the business, also paid for and increasing in value daily (offers to buy the restaurant-bar had reached $75,000 by then). Keep the business and give me the Florida properties, I urged. She remained resolute, however, and I finally figured out her motive. She would rather take the Florida property in order to punish me than accept a more beneficial arrangement. Those properties were useless to her, but she enjoyed destroying my old dream, even at her own expense.

The divorce agreement required that I pay child support at a fair rate, and there was no provision for alimony, which I would have never agreed to or, I believe, ever been required by the court to pay. When signed, the divorce would be final in one year. Visitation was more than fair.

The lawyer finally ground to a stop and looked up at me with dead eyes; this guy had all the charm of a Grand Inquisitor waiting for the irons to heat up. I asked for a few minutes in private with my soon-to-be former wife. The lawyer became a bit nervous, glancing between stoic Barbara and me, wondering if it was safe to leave us alone or if he should call security. Finally he nodded and drifted silently away on carpeting that was definitely noncommercial.

Once we were alone, I reminded Barbara that my retirement was six months away, which also meant the end to my part-time employment as a spy. She seemed not to have thought of that. Since neither of us planned to remarry, I suggested she withdraw the divorce action and we separate. If so, I would assist with her support contingent on her getting a job. The days of big spending were over for her. I would earn a simple living as a self-employed commercial pilot and private investigator. She barely pondered the offer before refusing.

I moved to a second issue, her health insurance. As the wife of a retired serviceman, she had free health insurance for life. Again, she seemed not to have considered this point, thought for a moment, then insisted she wanted the divorce regardless.

I moved on to the topic of real estate, pointing out that it represented the inheritance of our children, and I worried that she would sell off her share. Further, the split was wrong, she should take the business and sell it if necessary. I would execute a trust of the Florida property for the children as part of the divorce settlement. She remained firm, no compromise. Further attempts at persuasion fell on deaf ears, and as usual, she enjoyed my frustration. "I will deal with the agreement as is," was her final word. "I'm a survivor." She had taken to calling herself a survivor within the past couple years, a strange term indeed. A survivor is one who prevails in spite of adversity. Barbara was actually the opposite. She was self-destructive and created her own hardships.

I summoned the lawyer and signed.

The divorce rate among military personnel is higher than the national average, and it didn't take long for word of my own divorce to spread rapidly. It did not help that I projected an aura of dejection; my spirit was in the gutter. Everyone erroneously deduced that the loss of my wife was the cause of my depression, and my friends rallied to assist. I needed a *woman*, they reasoned. Dates were contrived by the dozens. I had no idea there were so many divorcees available. Even my WAVES fawned over me, trying to cheer me up. All of the attention was quite pleasant, but it was my fear for the future and the well-being of my kids that depressed me, not the want of a woman.

My job was also boring me to death, and I spent more and more time in Plans and Operations just down the hall. It was always amusing to become involved in the next war game, to calculate how we would destroy godless communism once it finally invaded the free world.

I was wandering back from Ops one afternoon and past the office of our department secretary, Bunny Russ, when I noticed her consoling a sad and sobbing woman. I slowed down, attracted to this tall, graceful young woman with a wounded look in her hazel eyes, a shock of auburn hair damp from tears. Bunny was one of those tough secretaries who actually ran the department, and everyone sought her advice on personal and professional matters. Everyone loved her.

Back in my office, I decided that I had to meet that girl and dialed Bunny's number. Bunny was very protective of her friends but eventually agreed that she and her friend would meet me at the officers' bar.

Bunny entered the bar in her usual august manner, with Pat Marsee in tow, and joined me at a table. I was immediately captivated by this alluring country girl, and once we were past the introductions and small talk, and with Bunny's approval, Pat agreed to join me for dinner.

Pat and I shared amazingly similar marital difficulties, and it was those problems that had her crying in Bunny's office. Pat had reached a level of incompatibility with her husband, and life had become unbearable under the same roof as him. They had two daughters, about seven and nine, and her husband had no intention of leaving his home. So Pat defied the norm: she packed her things and moved out. She got a small apartment and later a small house less than a mile away from her daughters, who ended up spending most of their time with her.

The coincidence of our analogous marriage problems aside, Pat and I became instant friends and lovers, our relationship lasting for several years. We would be inseparable pals, sharing everything together, and were it not for my criminal life, I would have asked her to marry me.

Visitation with my kids remained at a deadlock. I tried to arrange visits several times, but was continually met with claims of bad timing, conflicting plans, and abrupt cancellations. The few times I made successful arrangements, the kids would be gone when I arrived.

It became obvious that court assistance would be necessary to break down Barbara's barriers. My attorney client—with whom I was becoming close friends—gave me ample advice on how to proceed with the least amount of difficulties. I procrastinated, however, even though I knew Barbara would not relent until forced, and while I dithered, Barbara moved along with her usual pernicious behavior. She called me at the office, and in her usual haughty manner, informed me that she was moving to Maine to live with her sister, Annie. I had a million questions, but while I stuttered in astonishment, she hung up.

I knew what she had done and immediately called the mortgage company to confirm that she had not made a single payment on the house since I turned the bills over to her. Foreclosure was well under way. On a whim, I called the real estate agent who sold us the house and asked how much she thought the house would sell for. We had paid about $50,000, and the agent was sure she could get $70,000 for it then. That was an amazing appreciation in value in just two years. Barbara, the "survivor," was going to simply drive away from the house, leaving an ecstatic mortgage company $20,000 richer.

Barbara initially refused to talk and only did so when I offered her $10,000 in cash just to meet with me. Persuaded by the money, she met me at the house later that day, the kids conspicuously absent. As I expected, she had no idea that the value of the house had appreciated. I offered to prepare the house for sale and to conduct the actual sale for half of the equity. Further, I would make up her lost mortgage payments from my half. All she had to do was sign the house over to me and I would hand her $10,000.

I knew that she would deplore giving me a cent of her money, and while she pondered her decision, I sweetened the offer. Retiring servicemen who do not plan to live in the city of their last duty station are entitled to a free government move of their household effects. Barbara did not qualify for this, but I could apply for a move in my name if she transferred the house to me. Moving on her own would cost hundreds of dollars, and worse, she would be forced to pack, carry, and load everything herself. She agreed that the arrangement was more than fair and also agreed to leave all the utilities functioning.

My plan was to move into the empty house for as long as it took to get the house ready to show, perhaps thirty days. I asked her to leave my den furniture, which consisted of my recliner chair and mini-refrigerator from the ship, plus my desk and chair. I would basically live in the den on an old cot, and she agreed to leave me those few items and the drapes for privacy. A few days later, my lawyer prepared the papers transferring the house to me, and I handed Barbara a package of two hundred fifty-dollar bills.

It was June of 1976 when Barbara was ready to drive north. The movers had departed, and Barbara planned to leave the following morning. I arranged to be at the house an hour before departure so I could visit with my kids. I arrived at the house as scheduled and found her car gone, the house empty. Not even slightly surprised, I could only look to the north and wonder what nightmares were in store for my children.

Chapter 26

A NEW LIFE, A NEW COLD WAR

W ith retirement approaching, I had been working vigorously toward my own living accommodations. I wanted waterfront property and finally settled on a six-unit apartment in Ocean View's Willoughby Spit. It was a rundown two-story house that had long ago been converted into shoddy apartments. The spit itself is a narrow strip of sand, created a hundred years earlier when a hurricane ripped the sand from Ocean View and stretched it a couple miles into Hampton Roads. A single street extends up the center with typical beach houses jammed on each side, faded by weather and salt amid heaps of sand. The charm of these beach communities is captivating to lovers of the sea, and I thoroughly enjoyed my new neighborhood.

My new property was on the Willoughby Bay side, and boats had to pass under a short bridge beneath I-64. The sailboat mast was too high to pass, and while it broke my heart to do so, I sold my beloved Yankee Dolphin. I had been shopping for a houseboat, however, and settled on a used thirty-six-foot Drift-R-Cruise. It cost under ten thousand, and after the owner, Pat, and I took her out for a shakedown cruise, I fell in love with her. The retired airline pilot took the payment in cash, and we motored away from her old home in Virginia Beach, out Lynnhaven Inlet, into Hampton Roads, under the two bridge tunnels, and moored at her new berth in Willoughby Bay. It is considered bad luck to rename a boat, but I changed the name from an awkward mix of the ex-owner's wife's and kid's names to my basic initials: JAWS (close enough to John Anthony Walker Jr.). The boat was in splendid shape, and everything worked except the central air conditioning, which was easily repaired and almost never used.

The pier was a useless shambles, but with the help of the local craftsmen, we sunk new pilings and installed planking in an L-shaped pier, fifty feet out and fifty feet parallel to the shore. I tapped into my apartment water and electricity for shore service and had a phone installed. The boat became my new home, and while I had but one small closet and sparse accommodations, I was thoroughly happy living on the water among the colorful natives.

In the landlord-tenant scheme, the tenant definitely has the upper hand with respect to local law and in the ability to create grief. The rent was low and the apartments appealed to a low strata of renters. With only one apartment vacant, I would just break even in mortgage and utility payments, but the building stayed mostly full and actually earned income. To relieve the hassle of dealing with the tenants, I designated a competent tenant, Roberta Puma, as manager. She earned a reduction in rent and totally relieved me of the burden of landlord. One of my newly married WAVES moved in, and other navy personnel from the base helped keep my vacancy at zero.

The new pier was spacious enough for several boats and earned even more income as a mini-marina. Those renters were mostly smaller ski-boats and day sailors, and the friendly and gracious company of local boaters was most welcome.

Small aircraft is an ideal way to mask one's movements, and my Sky-hawk was a perfect adjunct for spy travel. The miserable four-hour drive up interstates 64 and 95 was replaced by a comfortable hour and a half in the air. Once I'd loaded my flight bag and a small tote, I would quietly fly off without a flight plan, telling the tower I was going to the student training area west of the airport. Pilot practice includes low work, so it was normal for such aircraft to go below radar. In my case, I would turn off my transponder and head north.

There are many quiet and nearly deserted airports in the DC area, but car rental can be impossible. My normal procedure was to reactivate my transponder on the VFR (visual) code of 1200 when clear of Norfolk and land at Dulles International. I would then tie-down overnight and blend into the hundreds of car renters. Many of my drops and pickups were along the small roads in that area of Route 123, Leesburg Pike, Lee

Highway, Arlington Boulevard, and Gallows Road. On the other hand, aircraft of suspects are easily tracked by an FBI installation of a hidden transponder sneaked aboard in the dead of night.

The routine nature of my spy drops was causing less and less tension, and I worried that I might fall into dangerous complacency. Indeed, instrument landings in severe weather and icing conditions would bring me closer to an aneurysm than a spy drop behind some trees.

This drop did generate substantial anxiety—not from fear of capture but worry over Jerry's acceptance and his payment for services by the KGB. The drop exchange was uneventful, but my uneasiness grew as I hurried to my motel where I would read the verdict. The package was heavy with cash, a good sign, and the enclosed note could not be better. Jerry's material was acceptable, photo work satisfactory, and the financial terms were agreed upon. Jerry and I were in business, and with my retirement just a few weeks away, I breathed a sign of relief.

In my drop note six months earlier, I asked if the Soviets would prefer a more frequent exchange schedule since I was completely available for such an arrangement. Their answer was to continue with the six-month schedule, the next drop set for the winter of 1976–77. To this day, I am perplexed that they would not want more-frequent drops and therefore more-current material. The biggest surprise came, however, when I was asked if I was agreeable to a face-to-face meeting overseas in the summer one year hence. I would answer yes six months later.

I wandered through my last couple weeks of active duty in desolation, wearing a crown of gloom. Military retirement is normally a time of joy, a transition to a more relaxed life, a cause for celebration with happy family members and shipmates. In my case, I hated to leave the life I loved, I was a stranger to my absent family, and I did not want a more relaxed life.

Retirement is a major event ashore or afloat and always includes a formal ceremony. At COMNAVSURFLANT, the retiree's department would assemble in inspection uniforms in a ceremony officiated by the admiral. The honoree is generally awarded a medal of some sort, the admiral delivers a short speech describing his distinguished service, and he is handed a national flag folded in the traditional triangle. A final hand-shake and a last salute, and the new retiree usually proceeds to a party, with wife and children attending the proud event. As the end drew near for me, I told my department head that I did not desire a ceremony. He passed on my wishes, and I was quickly called to see the admiral's chief of staff. He was visibly annoyed by my decision but accepted it. My department head later told me that my medal would not be awarded if I chose to forego the ceremony, but I would not be swayed.

On my final day of service, I casually strolled to the personnel office and surrendered my active duty ID card; the yeoman handed me the stan-dard envelope containing my transfer orders to the Fleet Reserve, a copy of my service record, and my retired ID card. After less than five minutes saying good-bye to my division personnel, I shook hands with my boss, who handed me my flag, and I quietly slipped away. I cannot describe my depression. My friends seemed to understand that the retirement cere-mony would have been too painful to endure.

My résumé had "naval officer" deleted and "landlord" added. My military pension was half of my basic pay. In today's dollars, a chief war-rant officer earns about $4,000 a month and would draw about $2,000 a month in retirement. Rental income helped greatly and included a couple hundred from the restaurant-bar, about the same from the apartments, and even more from boat slip rentals. My plan was to increase flying and PI income and make up the difference. Barbara was sent $1,200 to $1,500 per month (I forget the exact amount) in cash, always in fifties.

Communications with Barbara were sporadic and lacking substance on her part. She remained unemployed and seemed unconcerned that she had no short- or long-term goals. Did she plan to live on child support for-ever? I wondered. I finally reminded her in the strongest terms that I had retired and the extra money from my part-time (spy) job had come to an end. I could not afford the extra child support she now received, and she would have to become self-sufficient. She seemed sobered by the lie, and while I would never have let her or my kids suffer, I needed her to believe that my criminal activity had ended as a means of protecting myself.

Six months after Barbara moved to Maine, she finally found a job with Dexter Shoes and moved to her own four-bedroom house in

Skowhegan. It was a production-line manufacturing job, but I was actually proud of her for finally becoming employed. Maine was one of the most depressed states in the country, and the numerous shoe factories in the region were fast disappearing to low-wage offshore competition. Luckily, she was no longer a total dependent, but she still received my monthly envelope of twenty-four (or was it thirty?) fifty-dollar bills.

As the glorious days of summer gave way to the first hints of winter, I had done nothing about preparing the house for sale. The job was not appealing: interior painting, shampoo carpeting, replacing a couple window casings. Barbara's dirty trick had simply demoralized me. I rallied, however, and spent the money on utility deposits and bought a full-size refrigerator and a cheap bedroom set. Drapes for the den and one bedroom followed, plus curtains for the kitchen and baths. Pat's ex-husband, experienced in every phase of the building trade, helped me with the task for a few under-the-table dollars. I was falling into a trap, however, making the house livable and not just camping out while doing repairs. There was nowhere to sit so I purchased a kitchen table set. I found myself living half on the boat, half in the house, and half at Pat's.

My daughter Margaret was an eighteen-year-old adult when she traveled to Maine with Barbara, and she finally left the cramped living conditions that winter. She moved in with her Uncle Frank in Boston and found work at the Tupperware factory. When I heard about it, I immediately phoned her and asked (practically begged) her to come back home. I sent the airline fare and paced the airport arrival area like a thrilled father in a maternity ward. I was so delighted to see her, I still remember how beautiful she looked, exactly what she was wearing.

Margaret's return combined with Barbara's sabotage ended the plan for selling the house. Pat, Margaret, and I finished furnishing the rooms and covering the nearly thirty windows. It was worth it just to have my girl home and to at least get to know her. We did everything together, usually as a threesome with Pat.

I avoided pressing Margaret for the details, but slowly she related the conditions in Maine. Barbara's sister's house was the same one Barbara and I visited many years earlier, the one with the bellowing carpet when the wind seeped in between the floorboards from under the house. Annie had seven children, four of whom were still at home when Barbara arrived with our four. The house had only four bedrooms for eleven people, which forced most of my kids into a roughly converted attic. Conditions were far below anything my family had ever experienced, complete with chickens wandering through the house and even into the attic. Indoor plumbing was totally primitive. I do not wish to criticize Annie, for she was kind enough to offer her humble and cramped dwelling to a sister she thought was in need. I do criticize Barbara, however, for imposing herself upon that family for no valid reason.

Barbara squandered her ten thousand dollars in six months by foolish spending, such as on extravagant restaurant dinners for the eleven-member household. In a positive step, she did pay a contractor to completely renovate and modernize the plumbing, but that totally depleted the funds that should have been used to buy a house. When she moved to Skowhegan, she had difficulty in paying the rental deposit, but at least she would draw a paycheck to augment the child support.

Unencumbered by a work schedule for the first time in my life, I casually flew to California and picked up Jerry's material in preparation for my winter drop. Commercial airlines were at a high level of service and convenience in those years, even in cattle class. Jerry and I quickly completed our exchange—secrets for cash—and it was even possible to catch a red-eye flight right back to the East Coast without spending a night in California.

In all of my contacts with the Soviets, I never experienced the slightest difficulty in executing the drops or meetings. Their maps and instructions were meticulous and actually overdone. The winter 1977 drop would present the first problem ever. My package was missing.

The drop exchange was otherwise unremarkable. I made my signal, a dropped 7-UP can, and observed that my counterpart had done likewise. My package was delivered at some obscure point, and I moved slowly to my pickup spot, lagging as necessary to maintain our separation. The pickup was in a desolate area far from any dwellings and located behind the last post supporting a guardrail. It was easily located in the glare of my headlights on a night that was as dark as a hole in space. No package. A bullhorn announcement at that point would not have been a surprise:

"This is the police! Hands up! You're surrounded!" But there were no cops, and, tension aside, I searched the twenty-five feet of guardrail on both sides, but I did not find my package.

The next step in the procedure was to observe the KGB agent's signal that he had recovered my delivery, and the signal was present. In the worst-case scenario, my contact had been arrested before he made his drop, perhaps with my package still in his possession. In the best case, one of us had made a simple mistake in the drop location. The alternate plan was to try again one week later and continue doing so until successful. I went home.

One week later, we both signaled our presence and readiness to proceed, but still my package was missing. I crawled over every inch of the guardrail and beneath where a small creek passed under the road. Totally baffled, I again cancelled and went home.

A third attempt would be made one week later according to plan, and I pored over the maps, scrutinizing every detail. I was making a mistake but could not identify it. Extraordinary methods would be necessary. I knew the area thoroughly by that point and decided to covertly go on foot to my pickup site and observe the KGB agent as he exited his car and hid the package. However, there was no place to safely park a car within a couple miles of the bridge and, thinking militarily, I needed a driver to assist with my "insertion" and "extraction." Police on patrol always investigate cars parked in remote areas. My plan was to have a driver drop me off about a mile or more away, have them wait in a public area, then pick me up at a designated time. Since all of my friends were associated with the military, my apartment manager, Roberta, was the perfect choice.

Roberta was happy to make a couple hundred dollars for an evening's work, and we drove off for my third attempt to recover my drop. To make my signal, I simply had her pull over while I pretended to relieve myself. My explanation for the trip was that I had to meet someone involving a PI case and I did not want either me or my car to be identified. She seemed satisfied, and I left the car as she drove off to wait. I left the road and, concealed in the brush, I shifted to black clothes, cap, and gloves. I held a flashlight obscured with electrician's tape save for a tiny point and paralleled the road in the bush at about forty yards. No cars used the road during my hike.

The road to my right would eventually meet an intersection where the procedure called for me to turn left and proceed to the first guardrail. My path followed a stream that would pass under the road at that guardrail about a mile away. I had by then rejected the idea of FBI surveillance of the site, but I proceeded with caution anyway. If surveillance were in place, I would likely approach them from behind, so I moved with extreme stealth. Lightning bugs were in abundance, and my rarely used light seemed no brighter than their bioluminescent flashes. There was no moon or stars, and I was a bit surprised when the bridge appeared out of the gloom. I settled in a spot of maximum concealment that still gave me an unrestricted view of the guardrail and approaching cars. There was a buzz of excitement to my adventure, but not nearly as high as that experienced when hitting a seventy-five-degree bank while spiraling toward earth in a jump plane.

I had arrived over an hour before the drop, and on schedule, a car appeared and turned toward the culvert. He should slow and stop but he just continued on to my left. As he passed, I glimpsed the license plate as the type issued to the Soviet embassy. I was obviously in the wrong place, but I was close. The drop had to be farther up the road to my left.

Dropping most of my caution, I ran in the direction the car had gone, angry at the mistake. Then, after about fifty yards, I came to *another* guardrail, mostly covered in brush, a short span of about twenty feet, protecting cars from a dangerous drop-off. My package was at the last post, exactly where it should be. They were wrong in saying it was the *first* guardrail, and I was wrong because the drop point was the exact distance from the intersection, a distance I should have measured.

Package jammed into my backpack, I stripped off the black shirt, ski cap, and gloves and slipped into a red shirt and red Cessna ball cap. Red is the perfect color for night work since it appears as black in the shadows but shows as innocent red in the lights of a car or spotlight of a cop. I marched in a quick pace down the center of the road and only jumped into the bush one time for a passing car. Roberta showed up on time at the extraction point.

The buzz generated by this dangerous game slowly ebbed once it was clear that all had gone well and, as always, was followed by a totally drained feeling. I was ready for a motel, but Roberta wanted to go home. Fine, I told her, you drive, I sleep.

The above vignette is mentioned for one reason: upon my arrest years later, Roberta and the news media would make much of her involvement in my spy mission. She would be the classic example of Andy Warhol's fifteen minutes of fame as she enhanced and elaborated upon my "using" her as part of my dark world of espionage. She was never in the slightest danger and made a few hundred dollars to hang around a mini-mall for a couple hours. Regardless, the press loved it.

The director of central intelligence in 1976 and 1977 was an unknown to me, a cipher, by the name of George Herbert Walker Bush. His résumé included naval service in World War II followed by involvement in the oil business in his home state of Texas. He lost in a bid for US Senate, did two terms as a US representative in 1966 and 1968, then lost a second Senate race. Rewarded by his party, he spent the next four years as ambassador to the UN and headed the US Liaison Office in Beijing, China. He seemed an odd choice to head the CIA.

As DCI, George H. W. Bush presided over one of the most enduring intelligence groups, code-named the B-Team. President Ford and the congressional leadership decided in mid-1975 to audit the CIA's intelligence data by a committee of independent experts and scholars.

I was still on active duty and highly cleared when the B-Team was formed, and my first impression was that it would do much to temper the exaggerations of the Soviet threat. My hope was reversed, however, when I recognized some of the B-Team members, hawks all, including Paul Wolfowitz, Richard Perle, William von Cleve, General David Graham, and others. These characters, I concluded, would make matters even worse.

I recall sitting in on an intelligence briefing in which the B-Team was mentioned, and we all wondered who constituted the A-Team, an unknown group to us all. Eventually, I learned that the A-Team was the entire US intelligence apparatus: CIA, DIA, NSA, NRO, the intelligence of the State Department, and all of the armed forces. These organizations all dump their intelligence data to the CIA where it is compiled, analyzed, and presented to the president. The function of the B-Team was to "audit" the results. As CIA head, George H. W. Bush should have screamed in protest, but he remained silent as though he was part of the arrangement. I feared the worst.

By early 1978, the B-Team issued its review of the CIA's procedures and programs. Its voluminous report was harshly critical of nearly every finding US intelligence had made in previous years about Soviet military and its intended use. It dismissed intelligence analysts who held that Moscow would not start a nuclear war unless attacked by the doomsday weapons of the United States. The B-Team stated that the Soviet Union was planning all-out war. They further stated that Moscow was secretly developing a "first-strike" capability because Soviet strategic doctrine concluded that such a sneak attack on the United States would make them winners in a nuclear exchange. This was a stunning reversal of the analysis of all other intelligence organizations that correctly concluded that the Soviets had neither the intent nor the capability to successfully strike the United States. To illustrate the reaction to this preposterous conclusion, a White House security staffer was reported as saying that the B-Team's finding was grossly wrong and laughably exaggerated.

For the B-Team to sell their nonsense, it was necessary to create convincing lies for a war scenario. One of the B-Team's secret reports erroneously warned that the Soviets were running out of energy. They forecast that by 1980, Soviet oil production would suffer critical shortfalls, forcing Moscow to import as much as 4.5 million barrels of oil a day. Starved for oil, Moscow would soon invade the oil-rich Gulf nations, even if it meant a nuclear conflict with the United States. This astonishing conclusion was accepted, even though the Soviet Union has one of the largest oil reserves in the world.

The B-Team theories were sheer disinformation, but under President Reagan, they would harden into official doctrine. A new era would begin, that of an even more menacing Russia, the evil empire. Yet, anyone with a modicum of Soviet understanding, including myself, recognized that a long period of stagnation prevailed since Leonid Brezhnev's ascent to power in 1964. By the late 1970s, economic and political stagnation expanded as the Soviet Union entered its death throes. The future vice president and forty-first president, George H. W. Bush, had to know this.

It should come as no surprise that many B-Team members would rise to key posts in the Washington bureaucracy. At least two of them, Perle and Wolfowitz, are making war in the Middle East as I write these words.

The B-Team managed to intimidate and subvert the CIA and other intelligence organizations, but one man fought back. He was John Paisley, a senior national intelligence officer who was assigned to provide liaison and guidance between the CIA and the B-Team. Paisley quickly concluded that these cosmopolitan intellectuals were discrediting the CIA and creating alarmist views of Soviet intentions. He decided to expose them, but, as expected, he got no support from Bush's CIA. The fix was in. What amazed me was that the tens of thousands of professional intelligence experts, except for one, were cowed to silence by the B-Team elitism.

Paisley stubbornly carried on his one-man fight, talking to congressional investigators and newspeople. In the summer of 1978, he got his hands on a secret copy of the B-Team's final report and began writing a detailed critique that would destroy their distortions, exaggerations, and disinformation. He was still writing that exposé, battling the B-Team, when he was shot to death and dumped into Chesapeake Bay. The B-Team's only critic was silenced.

An interesting footnote to this story is that a few years later, I would be accused of murdering John Paisley. The reports implied that Paisley had detected my spy activity and I had somehow learned of this and killed him. The story is completely ridiculous since Paisley was not engaged in counterespionage activity at all, and I could not possibly know if any CIA agents had detected me. Indeed, if I had known about John Paisley and his anti-B-Team mission, he would have been one of my heroes. But the story had "legs," and the press loved it.

Chapter 27

AROUND THE WORLD

My winter spy exchange had fallen into a familiar pattern. I purchased an airline ticket in cash at an obscure travel agent for an unannounced trip to California. Arrangements were made through pay telephone calls, and Jerry met me at the Oakland airport, blending in with the other happy passengers meeting friends with cheerful hugs and handshakes. We moved to an unused waiting area across from a food kiosk, where Jerry grabbed two cups of undrinkable coffee.

Alone with our backs to the glass, the kaleidoscope of humankind wandering the concourse before us, I passed Jerry several thick packets of cash, several thousand dollars, in a small flight bag. He handed me a plastic bag containing a half dozen Kodak 35-millimeter film boxes, each containing about ten rolls of Minox spy film. His access to classified material had improved: this delivery contained some top-secret cryptographic keying material. Those would earn him a raise in pay.

I quizzed him at length concerning surveillance, warning him to stay off the phone to me and to share his spy activity with no one, even his most trusted friends. Jerry felt sure that he was not being watched, even though I knew in my heart that as amateurs, neither of us was likely to detect a skilled surveillance team.

Our meeting ended in fifteen minutes with a good luck handshake, and I watched carefully for a tail as he strolled toward short-term parking. I tailed him for a distance and saw nothing suspicious. I followed this with my own seemingly erratic wandering routine characteristic of a bored traveler but actually designed to frustrate anyone tailing me. After several minutes of zigs, zags, and course reversals, I, too, seemed free of suspicion. Confirming my return flight by telephone, I joined the throng and ambled to the departure gate for my all-night return flight to Virginia.

My winter spy drop with the Soviets was a few days later, and I flew my Skyhawk to Dulles without a flight plan or comments to family and friends. Following the mix-up of the summer drop, I had memorized the procedure completely, and the KGB maps and instructions were flawless.

To describe a spy exchange and a major crime as "routine" would seem contradictory, but my heart rate elevated only slightly as I deposited Jerry's film behind a tree stump on a dark gravel road. Picking up the KGB package an hour later in a similar setting produced a second increase that would scarcely be noticed on an EKG. I had been in the spy business for ten years, however, and had made at least twenty dead drops by that time. I did maintain a cool professionalism and keen alertness, but one becomes more relaxed with experience, even toward the most dangerous activity.

"Be careful what you wish for," says the old adage, and that pithy saying would ring in my mind as I read the note and instructions enclosed in the KGB payment package. I had advertised myself as the courier who would travel anywhere between Jerry the spy and our KGB handlers. Accordingly, I was instructed to meet my Soviet contact in Casablanca, Morocco, for our summer exchange. They wanted a face-to-face meeting, probably to admonish me in person for my impetuous behavior in recruiting Jerry. Casablanca seemed an odd choice. It was hardly a Soviet stronghold and carried that old stigma of being a hotbed of spy activity in the 1960s. Still, traveling five thousand miles to Africa was no problem.

I quickly checked Jerry's operating schedule, and discovered that his ship would deploy months before that date. Jerry would head *west*, the opposite direction of Morocco, and I would have to chase him down somewhere in Asia before my meeting in Africa. I groaned aloud in contemplation of the miles and days of travel involved.

I became a grandfather in the winter of 1977. Unaware of the pregnancy, Barbara informed me after the event that Cynthia had given birth to a healthy son, Thomas. In a sense, it came as no surprise that the most abused child, both physically and emotionally, would seek love in all the wrong places. The irony was that this child tried to escape from an abusive mother, and now she was an unwed mother herself, trapped with the tormentor from whom she sought escape. Now Cynthia was handcuffed to her miserable mother. I could only wonder how I could ever help, if I would ever get to know my daughter or my grandson.

As my Casablanca trip loomed ever closer, I pondered Jerry's operating schedule with dismay. The USS *Constellation* was deep into East Asia, visiting the usual liberty ports infrequently. I shuddered at the expense but arranged to travel halfway around the world and meet Jerry in Manila. Within a couple weeks of picking up Jerry's spy film, I would have to be in Morocco, but the question was, what direction should I go? Spinning the globe, it was shorter to continue west, or to travel completely around the world for my spy pickup and delivery. Now that would be courier service stretched to the maximum.

Flying commercial to Asia was fast and comfortable, even in coach, but as I peered over the vast expanse of the Pacific Ocean six miles below, I would rather have been driving a ship or even a slow sailboat.

Manila airport was stifling in August, the humidity impossible to measure, the air like steam. Even though my clothes hung wet on my body, I grinned with remembered pleasure of the taste, smells, and busy activity of South Asia. Why didn't I retire out here, buy a big sailboat, anchor it in Manila Bay, and cruise the ports I loved when the notion struck? I should have retired from the spy business as well and lived like a king on just my retirement check. My children could visit me or come to live here in Asia just as well as Virginia. I did not know the answer then and still cannot answer that question today.

Spies know to stay off the phone, and without preamble or needless confirmation, Jerry traveled from Cuba and met me at my hotel as arranged months earlier. I greeted my old friend warmly, and while we would have enjoyed dinner and the exciting nightlife together, we limited our meeting to an hour. I passed several thousand dollars to Jerry, he passed dozens of Minox rolls packed in Kodak boxes. He was as relieved to be rid of the incriminating file as I was dejected to receive it. I would now carry a life sentence on my person for the next few weeks. It was always best to keep the film in the open, to call no attention to it. Casually tossed in the camera bag was the best method, but Asia was well known for thieves who snatched such items and ran. Taping the film to my body would prevent theft, but a simple pat-down by a cop or customs inspector would reveal my secret. For this trip, I carried Jerry's film on my person. For future trips, conditions would dictate the manner of carrying the film.

Filipinos are friendly and hospitable, and it is impossible to have an unpleasant night in Manila. I could not resist taking a bus to Subic the next day, however, just to visit old friends from the war years. Everyone was shocked to see me as a civilian, and all of the young women made attractive marriage offers. One old friend assured me that a relative in Hong Kong could build just the boat I wanted. Her offer brought me face to face with my old dream. We could easily fly together to Hong Kong and have her uncle start the construction. I was forming the idea of transferring ownership of my house to my kids, which would be a perfect alternative for Cynthia and her new baby. The girl making the offer was a happy and sensuous Pacific Island beauty, long hair as black as raven's wings, sparkling anthracite eyes. The only drawback was her obsequious nature; it would take a lifetime for her to learn how to be a partner and not a servant. That damn file of stolen secrets burned a hole in my reasoning, however, and I left behind one of the best offers of my life.

The next day I was wandering Tokyo, marveling at the progress since my first visit there in 1961. Starved for land, the city was expanding into the bay at a frantic pace, building apartments, industrial centers, and recreation areas everywhere. The Ginza district outdid Times Square but was too expensive even for a well-paid spy. I stayed one day.

I planned to spend most of my time in just two places, and one was Bangkok, Thailand, formerly called Siam. I had visited Bangkok during the war and positively loved the erotic, natural charm and rare warmth of the Buddhist people. There is something about their calm poise that makes Westerners seem like uncultured barbarians.

Then on to Casablanca and time to put the vacation behind me and get serious. I checked into a midlevel hotel and immediately began reviewing the complex walking procedure that would precede my meeting. The process started at a specific time in the evening: I would stand facing a shop window from exactly 9:17 p.m. to 9:22 p.m., then walk away following a precisely timed route for about an hour. Once my contact and his security team were sure I was not under surveillance, my contact would approach me using a prearranged code exchange. It was necessary to familiarize myself with the locations, to get into my spy mode.

A flaming orange sunset filled my room, the seacoast hotel giving me a perfect view of the Atlantic Ocean. I had started this trip on the shores of that ocean, beyond that burning sun, forty-six thousand miles away. I taped the film to my body for safety, secured my passport and emergency cash in a money belt, including several hundred dollars in the local currency to satisfy any potential robbers.

Casablanca generates an exciting mystique, probably because of the famous film by the same name. It was like entering another world with curious sounds, tantalizing smells, old neighborhoods with a mix of French and Arab-Berber. The religion is Islam, the language Arabic, the people friendly and helpful.

The start point and meeting spot were easily located, and I casually strolled the route in segments, estimating the walking times, trying to look like a tourist, purchasing trinkets. Searching for a tail was impossible due to the crowded streets, but I went through the drill anyway.

Somehow I ended up in the Casbah district, which seemed to attract the majority of tourists. In a Muslim country, one never knows what to expect in terms of the popular vices, but alcohol was available in some sections and the prostitutes were exotic and plentiful. I tried a local restaurant and found the cuisine to be quite good. The entertainment was right out of *The Arabian Nights*.

Even though I was faced with the most difficult part of the journey, the KGB meeting, I was not ready to go home. I had the urge to bum around Europe for a week or so and thought of Pat and the unused vacation time she had accumulated. Back in the hotel that night, I sent a telegram to her, asking to meet me in Casablanca in forty-eight hours for romance and a vacation. She wired back her flight number and arrival time.

Not having seen a single Russian in ten years and worried how I would be treated for my recruitment of Jerry, my apprehension was unusually elevated. The meeting was twenty-four hours away, so I decided to travel a bit and search for a tail.

The hotel desk was helpful in obtaining a round-trip ticket to the capital city of Rabat, and I strolled touristlike to the bus terminal. A few abrupt turns and reversals revealed nothing suspicious, and I slipped quietly onto a bus to Marrakech. Rabat was about thirty miles north of the coast; I was heading one hundred miles south. Converting the ticket was easily accomplished. If any of the passengers behind me were US agents, they had achieved perfection in the art of disguise.

The trip was slow and the stops frequent, but I thoroughly enjoyed it. It became desert-hot; the sun was dazzling. The passengers all carried bundles, which added a lusty scent of strange herbs and fruit to the smell of country dust. At each stop, children sold strange foods and drinks, but the fear of food poisoning limited me to bottled drinks.

Marrakech is inland toward the Atlas Mountains, and Mount Jebel Toubkal was visible at 13,500 feet. I snapped my tourist photos and wandered the bazaar, sure that I was not tailed. Boarding the next bus to Casablanca, the round trip took the entire day.

Dusk was filling the streets with a purple haze as I stepped to the storefront window. A *Time* magazine clutched in my hand as part of the signal, I seemed to be eying the toasters and blenders within but I was actually studying the scene behind me in the glass. Nothing seemed amiss. After exactly five minutes, I walked off, following the detailed procedure. It called for a zigzag pace through a mostly commercial area, the path designed so that one or more people could weave back and forth along my path watching for a tail or fixed surveillance. It was a timed event, like a sports car rally, requiring me to be at specific spots at exact times. After nearly an hour, I stopped at another shop window at the precise time, butterflies in full flight, when a man walked past and quietly asked me to follow. My KGB contact.

The event was relaxed and less formal than I had imagined; he seemed like a nice guy, one I would enjoy sharing a beer with. He explained that we would follow the procedure of "walk-and-talk" and falling silent when other people were near. That rule acknowledged, he asked if I had a delivery. I patted a bulge taped under my shirt, and as we barely slowed on a dark street, I ripped Jerry's film loose and passed it to my contact. He instructed me to follow a simple left-and-right pattern, stated that he would catch up with me in a few minutes, and disappeared into a dark alley.

I moved slowly along the route, aware that he would pass the file to a confederate before joining me. I felt that same wave of relief that Jerry must have felt weeks earlier in Manila once that damning file was out of possession.

He was back at my side a few minutes later and drilled me at length about security, the situation around me, passing on tips to detect surveillance. His next subject was Barbara, recognized by all as the weak link. I assured him that she was amply compensated and would remain silent. I was personally less than confident in my assessment. In the movies, the KGB would have "sanctioned" her, eliminated her as a problem. This was not Hollywood, however, and they would not kill her just to protect one of their operatives.

Discussion of my unorthodox recruitment of Jerry was mild, and my arguments for doing so were vigorous. I pointed out that if I were still on active duty, I would be stuck halfway around the world from Washington and unable to make a DC drop. What could he say? I agreed not to recruit again, to leave it to the professionals.

Our final topic of discussion was politics, world events, and the cold war. It was enlightening to hear the perspective of the Soviet side, the poorer and weaker of the cold war combatants. He described Russia as the victim of worldwide US aggression in a conflict in which economic warfare created everyday problems and armed attack from the United States at any moment was a valid concern. It was like listening to a short-wave radio broadcasting an English-language news service from a foreign country. There was little similarity to the news we were fed by the US media. I took a pro-American stance, one that I did not really believe, just for the enjoyment of the discussion. It would have been pleasant to continue over a couple glasses of vodka, but he signaled an end with a glance at his watch.

Our final discussion before shaking hands regarded future meetings. He asked if I would agree to meeting once a year on a rotating pattern between DC drops and foreign meetings. I agreed but objected to Casablanca, where I stood out too sharply. We discussed a few Western European cities and I chose Vienna. It was agreed. He handed me a white envelope containing the Washington drop procedure for six months later and a package of cash. We departed in opposite directions, quickly fading into the night.

It was just past midnight, and, strangely, I felt in the true milieu of the spy. I walked among shuttered shops along deserted streets, wet from an ocean mist, feeble streetlights barely moving the gloomy shadows. A lone car crossed a murky intersection far ahead. The incriminating film had been delivered, but I was again tense as I carried the new deadly items: spy instructions and a large sum of cash.

A taxi would be nice.

My spirits rose with Pat's arrival, and I quickly moved from my spy mode to that of a simple tourist. We spent a couple of days in Morocco, then meandered across the Mediterranean Sea to Spain. Much like my trip through Europe with Barbara years earlier, we just bummed through Spain, France, and into Northern Europe in honeymoon style. It was a delightful ten-day finale to a long and often dangerous trip. When our return flight touched down in the United States, I had surely recorded the most miles for any spy mission.

Chapter 28

DRUG SMUGGLERS

My winter drop is hardly worth mentioning. Jerry returned to the United States in November 1977, and I flew to California to exchange his film for cash. A few weeks later, I drove to the hinterlands of Washington and dropped off his package of film on some dark road.

Laura, the child I knew and understood the least, did not consult with me before making a major life change. She had joined the army. With my wide military experience, the army would be the last service I would recommend for a woman. My first choice would have been the coast guard, but this was a time when they actually guarded the coast and helped mariners—before they became drug cops. Second choice would be the air force.

To my surprise, Laura called to say she had orders to Fort Jackson, South Carolina, for basic training and asked if she could visit before reporting for duty. I agreed, of course, and quickly picked up a bedroom set for one of the two empty bedrooms.

I could hardly remember seeing Laura laugh, perhaps only on an amusement park ride or on the back of a pony. Dour or just serious, I could never tell, but she displayed her usual lack of expression when I picked her up at the airport. We had three or four days before she would check in for duty in Columbia, South Carolina, and since I was self-employed, I was thrilled by the opportunity to get to know my youngest daughter.

I positively doted over her the entire time. We shared dinners in the better restaurants, enjoyed boat rides, night clubs, and general entertainment, often with Pat, Margaret, and her friends. We had ample time alone, however, and I patiently waited for her to ask about me, my position in the family, the reasons for my actions. I swore to myself that I would not argue my side, but she asked nothing and remained characteristically withdrawn, cool, and distant. I do not recall that she smiled even once during our short time together, nor would her icy veneer ever crack in the future. Perhaps her mother had thoroughly poisoned her toward me. She never asked a single question about my point of view, then or ever.

Laura graduated from recruit training and moved to Fort Gordon, Georgia, for advanced infantry training (AIT). I did not attend her graduation since Barbara was present and tension would surely have resulted. I did visit her during AIT, however, and saw my daughter in uniform for the first time. She looked small among the swaggering male soldiers, but she sported temporary sergeant stripes, moved confidently, and held herself like a queen. She gave me the tour, but I sensed a sorrowful spirit within her. The army, in my opinion, had declined sharply since the Vietnam War, with drug use running rampant and recruiters reaching into the lower rungs of society to fill the ranks. It would improve with time, but it was no place for my daughter. The Woman's Army Corps (WACs) had been dissolved; all servicewomen were now integrated into the regular branches, their special jobs and much of their isolation gone. Many of the men resented the women joining the ranks of "ground warriors" and made life miserable for them. My confidence in her success was low, not because of her, but because of the army.

No one flies a 140-mile-per-hour Skyhawk six thousand miles across country and back, but it was time to visit Jerry again and I just felt like flying. It was the winter of 1978, and ferry flights were virtually stopped due to the treacherous weather and eternal night of the arctic. Pat gladly took vacation time, and we escaped the snow-chilled misery of winter by flying south until we reached the sweet, warm air of Florida. It is impossible to cross the continent without encountering serious weather at least once, but so what? We turned right, aimed toward Texas, and cared not if we were forced to spend a rainy day somewhere ahead. Weather did force us out of the sky for a day at a backwater airport in Texas, but to our surprise, we were close to Mickey Gilley's, then featuring the longest bar in the world. Pat was in country-girl heaven, and while I was totally out of my element with pseudo-cowboys everywhere, I had to enjoy the beer-commercial environment.

It took two more days to reach San Diego; at one point nose winds slowed us to the point where cars below were passing us. Jerry met us at the airport, and we concluded our spy business in less than thirty seconds. After a couple of days enjoying the sights, we hugged the warm Mexican border on the return trip, not turning left toward Virginia until reaching New Orleans. Jerry's film spent most of its time taped to my leg at the spot I usually wore my ankle holster for my .38 pistol.

It is almost embarrassing to admit that the Washington dead drop had become so routine that I remember none of the details. What I do remember was the enclosed procedure for our Vienna meeting in the summer. I was anxious both to visit that old historic city that I so loved and to quiz my contact at length about the Soviet Union's position in the insane cold war.

The aircraft ferry season opened slowly for me, but remarkably, I secured a contract that would put me in Europe at a time to coincide with my summer meeting. My customer beamed when I set down in Shannon, Ireland, with his Cessna 182. The next day, I was on the Continent, heading for Vienna on a fast and comfortable train.

I found myself on the shimmering Danube River at the foot of the Weinerwald. I had not been to Vienna in years and smiled as I entered the enticing city. Many find the stone buildings drab and cold and the Austrian people too rigid and controlled. I personally love the skillful stone architecture of the cultured city and enjoy the total lack of neon crudeness. In fact, while strolling along the Ring Strasse shortly after my arrival, I noted with pleasure the nearly complete lack of color—even the people's clothes were dark and subdued. Then in the distance I saw an unusual flash of color. As I neared, I was aghast to see a familiar orange sign with yellow arches, "McDonald's" spelled in German, the inharmonious clashing with the natural ambiance of elegance. As for the people, I enjoyed their ordered minds and utter competence, although they can be a bit lacking in their sense of humor.

There are two upscale cosmopolitan hotels in the city, the Hyatt Regency and the InterContinental, and I would alternate between the two over the next several years. I would have preferred something more domestic, but they fit my tourist persona well.

The procedure for the meeting was very similar to that of Casablanca, but I felt much more comfortable in a civilized Western European city. I rented a car as instructed but found it an unnecessary burden in a city with a superb rail and bus system. The KGB provided excellent maps and photographs, which led me to the Meidling district east of Schlosspark where the stately Palace of Schönbrunn is located, a baroque masterpiece.

The route was reviewed the day before. Sunset found me standing at a ski shop window in the Altmannsdorf neighborhood for a precise five-minute interval. Undetected behind me, the KGB also timed my presence, and the game started as I strolled away on my memorized route. The hour-long walking route was quite clever; it followed a long looping path that allowed a single person to weave behind and check me for a tail dozens of times. The route ended at yet another closed shop where my old contact from Morocco breezed past—I fell in beside him.

I passed him Jerry's film with little fanfare and, like before, followed a simple route until he caught up again, five minutes later. We would walk-and-talk for a couple hours, but first, I could enjoy a few minutes as a lawful tourist, free of the condemning spy film.

The neighborhood consisted exclusively of apartment buildings, built close together and rising up several floors. The area seemed to be middle class, and I was impressed by the cleanliness and lack of clutter; large and small parks were in abundance. Unlike in some US cities, people strolled in the evenings, married couples of all ages walked together, often towed along by a pet. Most were well dressed, women in dresses, men in ties. There was no waste from the dogs to be seen. How unlike America, I reflected, where neighborhoods are devoid of people, the only sign of life being the ghostly glow of a TV in a darkened room. In Vienna, one was more apt to see young adults in tuxedos and gowns walking to the opera house or the theater than youth wearing bizarre clothing and listening to offensive music.

My KGB friend returned, and it was back to business. We discussed the usual topics, the security around me, Barbara as a threat, and the advantages of socialism. The obligatory conversation completed, I moved to the subjects that had long bothered me. First, since I had provided absolute proof in the form of actual war plans showing that the United States had no intention of invading the Soviet Union, I wanted to know why the USSR would continue to engage in the wasteful cold war? He replied that intentions change, and that was my value as a spy, allowing them to develop social programs in Russia with the assurance that America was not poised to invade.

I pointed out that after eleven years of dealing with the KGB, America's intentions had never changed. Wasn't that ample proof that the United States would never launch a preemptive invasion? The point of national security, he replied, is to maintain eternal vigilance. Intentions can change.

My second question involved the six-month span between exchanges, why they were not more frequent. "I've already answered that question, John," he replied. "Our chief concern," he continued, "centers on the intentions of the United States, and since the mobilization and deployment of massive offensive forces take much more than six months, our meetings are frequent enough. Also, more-frequent exchanges would be more dangerous for you." He went on to note that a carrier battle group could sail for deployment from San Diego to Asia and return again to the United States, all in the time between our exchanges. "Such routine deployments are of little or no concern to us," he said. "We want to know the big picture: if and when your military will try to kill us."

I was sobered—his simple and straightforward explanation made perfect sense. Dejected, speaking aloud to myself, I said, "My God, the United States will never stop its aggressive behavior; the cold war will go on forever." He stopped and looked me in the eyes for the first time and said, "Friend, it will end if both sides change." "Or if just *one* side changes," I countered. "What if the Soviet Union just quit, just stopped participating in the cold war? You already know the United States will not invade—you have the war plans, they're all in response to a Soviet attack."

We walked in silence as he pondered my statement. Finally he volunteered the following: "Our leadership might consider such a thing, but what would America's new strategy be if we were to lie prostrate before the might of the United States?" A good point, I silently answered.

I could not end the meeting without mentioning Afghanistan and the fact that the United States had been active for years in destabilizing the country. (I detected a quick glance, probably in surprise that any American citizen was aware of America's misadventure in that part of the world.) Between the Muslim resistance to Marxism and the US effort in arming the rebels, I asked about Moscow's plan. My friend could only say that Afghanistan posed a serious problem on the Soviet border and that military intervention would be avoided if possible. I said nothing, but I knew in my heart that the United States would press on the Soviet Union's underbelly until they responded militarily.

Back to being illegal again, I stuffed the procedure for my next Washington drop in a pocket and bid farewell to my friend. I walked alone to the north, the streets deserted of people and vehicles, the hour well past midnight. The darkened buildings were as gloomy as my mood, for I always envisioned an end game somewhere in the near future. Now it seemed possible that this cold war could go on for decades.

Chapter 29

RESCUING CYNTHIA

I had gotten to know my daughter Margaret very well since she returned home. Tough-minded but warmhearted, she was alive with activity, usually working two jobs and taking college courses on the side. She also maintained contact with her mother and siblings in Maine, and while she was loath to criticize her mother, she was a conduit of information about her. According to Margaret, Barbara continued to drink to excess and complain at length that she was forced to work for a living. In a positive reversal, however, she had stopped battering the children as each became old enough to resist her physically. One by one, they all stood up to her, prepared to strike back, announcing, "No more!"

Still, beatings aside, I worried greatly about Cynthia, trapped with a new baby in the clutches of her abusive mother. Psychological injury can be just as damaging as physical, and I could not resist the urge to rescue her.

Fierce winter weather brought in 1979, as one bone-chilling front after another swept past, with a day or two of moderate weather in between. I had very few flying jobs or private detective work, which left me more time to consider Cynthia's hopeless plight. At twenty-two—too old to live with her dad—Margaret had moved out. A rough plan evolved of converting the upstairs of my house into a separate apartment for Margaret and letting Cynthia and her son have the downstairs. I would be happier living on the houseboat anyway.

The Flight Service Center predicted a day of storm-free weather before the next polar blast, and on the spur of the moment, I phoned Cynthia. "I'm flying up to Skowhegan tomorrow to pick up you and Thomas," I blurted. She reeled off a few problems and objections, but I assured her that I would buy all the furniture and baby equipment she would need, all she had to do was pack a couple bags with clothing and essentials. In the end, all difficulties overcome, she agreed to be ready.

I lifted off at dawn, the runway dry and clear, plowed snow heaped beyond the runway lights. Skowhegan was about six hundred and fifty miles away, beyond the range of my Skyhawk, and I refueled in Connecticut. I maintained VFR (visual flight rules) a bit dishonestly, dove through a hole in the clouds, and found the Skowhegan airport white with snow. The tower informed me that the snow had been cleared except for a light glaze and advised me to use caution. With a little slipping and sliding, I made it to the tie-down area.

My four-wheel rental awaited me and, using Cynthia's hastily drawn directions, I located her small apartment. I had arranged to arrive when Barbara was at work. Cynthia and Thomas were ready to go, bags packed, and standing by the door. Cynthia was clearly sick, at the midpoint of a bout with the flu, but she was my beautiful daughter, complete with red and runny nose, whom I had not seen in over two years. Thomas looked even worse: fighting the same virus and swathed in blankets, he looked too sick to even cry. I had become so distant from my daughter that I actually felt slightly awkward giving her a hug. I felt even more clumsy when I held my handsome infant grandson for the first time. I did not feel like a grandfather and certainly did not act like one, yet I felt a wonderful sense of pleasure as I looked at his wary little face. He looked back with wise eyes, bright and bemused. I was going to like this guy.

We spoke little on the snowy drive back to the airport, but our relationship would improve with time as would our interaction. I was already planning the house renovation, converting one upstairs bedroom to a kitchen, another to a living room. With steps up the rear from the driveway, Margaret would love the two-bedroom upper floor. After the renovations were complete, all I had to do was sign the house over to my four kids so they could all share in the equity. The mortgage payment was under $400, an amount I could easily afford to continue paying.

Cynthia and Thomas sat in the small waiting room at the local operation that was as tiny as Cavalier's. I spent ten minutes loading the luggage and performing the preflight. Back at the office to fetch my family, I was faced with Cynthia's expression of pain, as though she had been wounded. "I can't go," she said simply. I had already turned in the rental car, I explained, but she had phoned a friend to pick her up. I tried to persuade her to just try it out for a few days, and I would fly her back wherever she wished. Her mind was made up; it was futile to argue. Luggage hauled back to the terminal, blocks kicked from beneath the wheels, I throttled across the icy runway alone. The psychological bond with her mother was too strong for me to break.

I had taken a college course in psychology somewhere along the way, an easy course just for the semester hours, and I remembered something about abusive relationships. The parent and child fall into a weird symbiotic association, the abusive parent keeping the child under total control while withholding love; the child always striving for the parent's love that will never come. This could go on forever. I would try something later, I promised myself, but for now, it was up to Cynthia. My mood was as black as the cold winter night as I touched down in Norfolk.

My memory of drops and meetings are hazy as the 1970s came to an end. Jerry transferred from the USS *Constellation* in the summer of 1978 to the USS *Niagara Falls*, a strange coincidence in a navy of four hundred ships. His access to crypto-material and other highly classified material increased, but he would transfer again in just a year.

The pattern of winter meetings in Vienna and summer drops in Washington were somehow reversed. One winter drop in Washington was nearly aborted due to a massive snowstorm. I drove north in worsening weather, my snow tires becoming less useful as I neared the Beltway. The District lacks both the equipment and expertise for snow removal, and while the Beltway was passable, the lesser highways were nearly blocked. On Route 214 heading east toward Birdsville, I stopped and had a service station install chains. Thanks to my driving experience in the north, I already had a shovel and sections of carpeting in my truck.

Following the procedure was impossible, but I made my signal and drop, only having to dig out of one drift. Stuck again fifty yards from my pickup site, I walked the final distance and dug out again. The Russian, whoever he was, must have been raised in Siberia, for he seemed to have no problems with the weather.

I had questioned the logic of the summer/winter rotations for years, recommending a spring/fall scheme to avoid the foul weather of winter.

My recommendation went nowhere; perhaps the Russians *like* the blustery blizzard environment. I do not recall how it happened, but the meeting-drop schedule was reversed a year later.

Those who know me best would correctly say that I essentially believe in women's rights. As a professional serviceman and war veteran, I had one exception to that conviction: women should not be in the military service except during dire national emergencies, and then they should absolutely be excluded from war-zone assignments. World War II was a good example of making the most of women's skills: the Woman's Army Corps (WACS) and Women Accepted for Volunteer Emergency Service (WAVES) allowed women to work at desk jobs behind the lines, thus freeing the men to fight on the front. At the end of the emergency, the female forces should be drawn down by natural attrition and eliminated.

The women's movement of the 1970s resulted in the wrongheaded decision to eliminate the WACS and WAVES entirely and to integrate women into the regular services. Women in the old auxiliary branches were already resented to some extent, and that acrimony increased greatly when they were incorporated into combat units. First, consider the old auxiliary services after hostilities ended. The women *stayed* at all of those plum jobs, leaving the men to vie for the less-desirable and less-available positions. The WAVES filled all of the best shore billets, which disrupted the men's shore rotation. For example, when I finished my sea tour on the *Johnny Hutchins*, I should have rotated ashore. As a newly married man with a baby, I needed that assignment, but instead, I went to even worse sea duty on an aircraft carrier. It was then that my morally weak wife went to bed with my uncle and got caught by the entire family. I often wonder what twit enjoyed *my* shore post while I served *her* tour at sea. My life may have been far different had she not "played sailor" at my shore duty assignment. Real sailors go to sea.

Hostility toward women in the military actually grew after their integration, principally in the army and marines, and it is deeply embedded to this day. These services train young men to become ground warriors, and the men quickly recognize that the women are not up to the task. But worse, the women continue to grab the best assignments because, as in the marines, women cannot be assigned to jobs "coded for combat." I am more familiar with the marines (a branch of the navy), in which women entering boot camp were told that only "bitches, lesbians, and whores" enlisted in the USMC. The term "WM" for woman marine is said to mean "walking mattress." In the most derogatory terms, male marines state that women should not go into combat since they smell so bad when they menstruate that they attract the enemy. As a father, I could not imagine any of my daughters stuck in a three-man fighting hole, under fire, and just having to urinate, much less endure the difficulties of menstruation.

The aversion to women in the service naturally—though wrongly—leads to sexual harassment and rape. There are about eighteen hundred female marines at Camp Lejeune, North Carolina, and in 2001, a civilian rape counselor off-post got one complaint a month from women marines. This number is probably inaccurate, however, since most women do not complain for fear of reprisals, and few would seek out a civilian counselor. One only has to think of the rape scandals at the military academies, where officers are trained, to understand the depth of the problem. If the system could not prevent female officers from being raped, what chance did a private have?

It was into this hostile environment that my daughter Laura had thrust herself. I took it as a personal insult that she would not avail herself of my lifetime experience. But the die was cast, and I could only hope that she would survive. My expectations dropped when she informed me of her transfer to Fort Gordon, Georgia, where she would participate in a program in which men and women soldiers would train together for the first time. So she would be among the first to integrate with the men, and among the first to endure the abuse common to so many women in the military.

Thanks to Margaret as an intelligence source, I found out that my son, Michael, was experimenting with marijuana and having problems in school. In fact, he had been ordered into a work-farm program as a result, an assignment that seemed just short of juvenile hall. I called Barbara, and since she admitted to having little control over Michael, she suggested he move in with me. I solemnly agreed while suppressing a shout of joy.

My fourth-born was coming home, and again, I paced the arrival terminal like a new father waiting in the maternity ward. And in fact, there is more reality in that description than metaphor, since I did not know Michael at all, and he would be "born" to me at last.

I watched the passengers make their way off the Jetway, and then saw the sunshine break across Michael's face, shining on a bright smile of eagerness and happiness. His eyebrows rose in pleasure when he spotted me, and he crossed the lounge with his usual vigor and grace and his light and earth-sprung athlete's gait. I did feel as proud as any new dad, thrilled to meet and get to know my son. Michael was seventeen years old.

Michael had two problems, one academic and one involving marijuana use. I suspected that both were the result of his mother's stern management style that was short on love, guidance, and assistance and long on demeaning lectures and draconian discipline. One of marijuana's effects is to create apathy in the user. If one was scheduled for execution in five minutes, the drug would eliminate all anxiety—the victim might well laugh all the way to the gallows. I suspected that Michael was using marijuana to escape from Barbara's tirades; however, in addition to not caring about being yelled at (or beaten), he had also stopped caring about his schoolwork. I therefore decided upon a strategy of treating him respectfully and like the young adult that he was. In other words, I would just be myself.

It was a glorious summer. Having Michael around gave me every reason to revisit all the sights and participate in every activity available in the area. Pat was our constant companion, and Michael enjoyed her company. The boat burned hundreds of gallons of fuel as we explored every inch of the bay.

Michael quickly found a local marijuana source, but instead of the manic condemnation that he expected upon my discovery of it, I calmly instructed him on two points. First, he should use it responsibly, never while driving or during classes. Second, while it was, in my opinion, no worse than alcohol, it was illegal and could cause his arrest.

He followed my advice scrupulously. In fact, with no further prodding, he stopped the habit completely after a few months.

People quit bad habits only when they choose to do so. My only contribution was to provide him a comfortable and nonstressful home environment. I was very proud of the strength he displayed in overcoming that damaging habit.

The year 1979 started as a benign year for international difficulties with President Jimmy Carter at the helm. In June, Carter met with Soviet premier Leonid Brezhnev in Vienna to sign the second Strategic Arms Limitations Agreement (SALT II). This was a significant achievement that would slow the arms race in general, and if on-site verification could be worked out, I sensed real movement toward ending the cold war. The treaty limited each side to twenty-four hundred missiles and set other ceilings on ICBMs and SLBMs (submarine-launched ballistic missiles).

The world looked a little better, and with two of my kids back home, my spirits were at a maximum high. I had planned a European vacation for my mother for the last few years, and the summer of 1979 seemed like a perfect time. She had been raised in an Italian household, spoke the language, and always wanted to visit her homeland. Both her parents were immigrants from Italy, and she hoped to see the towns and villages of their youth.

Michael had charge of the house, including my finches (one hatching two new eggs) and a slightly injured cat that had allowed us to be her foster parents (I belonged to an animal rescue organization). Margaret moved back in during my absence, plus she managed the apartments and marina. I felt not the slightest apprehension as Mom and I flew to Rome, totally confident in my kids' ability to handle everything.

I had rarely seen my mother so excited, the blush of pleasure rising in her cheeks, as we touched down in Rome's Leonardo da Vinci Airport. That wonderful sense of coming home put a glint in her eyes. She reveled in every sight, sound, and smell, from the airport to the taxi ride, practicing her Italian on everyone. I had reservations at a small hotel near the Palazzo Venezia that probably never saw a tourist—there would be no Hyatt or Holiday Inn for us. The Tiber River was in sight from the small porch of her room, winding its way through the Eternal City and into the Tyrrhenian Sea to the east. She was in heaven.

Visiting all the tourist attractions was necessary, however, so we strolled a couple blocks to the Pantheon, built in 27 BCE. The Colosseum and the relics of ancient Rome at the Forum were less than a mile away. The Vatican was high on Mom's list, so we traveled by taxi to the Piazza San Pietro. It seemed to me that the huge piazza was unusually crowded. A tourist informed me that the pope was to perform his weekly blessing within minutes. I quickly caught Mom, who was heading for the Basilica, and pointed to a window with the symbol of the papacy hung from the sill. It was dumb luck on my part, but she always thought I had planned our arrival to coincide with the Holy Father's blessing.

We enjoyed three busy days of luxury living and splendid food, interlaced with hectic tours of the sights: a blur of palaces, churches, and museums. The relaxing train ride to Naples gave me a needed rest, but my mother, at sixty-seven, was still running in high gear.

"See Naples and die," goes the old proverb, and its meaning became clear as we lunched at an outdoor restaurant on a bluff high above the city. The golden sun dazzled on the busy harbor below, as Vesuvius, towering forty-two hundred feet in the distance with her base cloaked in mist, surely inspired that pithy saying. Our Naples hotel was even more provincial than the one in Rome, and Mom again had a perfect view, this time of the harbor and the lights of Capri twinkling across the gray sea. We trod every tourist attraction and walked every inch of destroyed Pompeii. A boat ride to the old home of Emperor Tiberius, the Isle of Capri, and the Blue Grotto was a must.

I learned something interesting about my mother. We had an early dinner one evening, and after wandering the shopping district, we were back at the hotel at about 11 p.m. She could not relax, however, and dragged me back outside to explore. Naples has several economically deprived areas, and while it is a safe city, there were neighborhoods I would avoid. Mom was interested in the local people, those not found in the tourist areas, and we were soon strolling those narrow streets with apartments and doors touching the cobbled streets. She spoke to everyone, thoroughly enjoying herself, and finally stopped at an even smaller street, perhaps fifteen feet wide. There was a small light in the distance, music and laughter danced in the air: she was drawn to the sound. Then I realized she was doing exactly what I did in foreign lands, avoiding the cosmopolitan areas, the tourists, and mingling with the real people.

The place where we ended up could hardly be called a restaurant: two tiny tables outside under a single light, three tables inside. About a dozen locals lounged about, sipping wine, laughing, enjoying the warm summer night. These were working-class people, probably poor. Mom greeted everyone, and they invited us to sit and offered us wine. Then Mom noticed a simple galvanized pail on the ground containing a large fish, alive in the clear water. A short conversation ensued, and soon the fish disappeared to the kitchen—an open cooking area behind a narrow counter. Shortly, two plates were brought out, piled high with linguini in clam sauce, plus the fish, now fried and seasoned to perfection. The meal could compete with one served at any of the four-star restaurants we had visited, and the company of these happy and friendly Italians was a high-light of the vacation.

Our itinerary took us back north to Florence, the cultural and intellec-tual center of Italy in the Renaissance. Our last stop was Milan, Italy's second-largest city and the area where her parents were born. Mom had done some research, and we drove around the small towns in a rental. While she did fill a notebook with data, no close relatives were located.

We left Italy heading north by train, climbing into the towering Italian Alps, their majestic peaks topped in snow. First-class European trains are an elegant form of travel and this one furnished an exquisite view of the unblemished countryside. It was summer, of course, and we were heading for Vienna. I was traveling with a dozen rolls of Jerry Whitworth's spy film taped to my leg.

I would endure considerable criticism in later years for taking my mother on a spy mission. In fact, I was unfairly accused of using her as a "mule" to help transport money back to the United States. In reality, nei-ther Pat nor my mother ever carried my illegal material or money, and I insisted (and they will confirm) that they wore money belts to hold their vital papers, credit cards, and passports. I also gave each a packet of sev-eral thousand dollars as emergency money in case I was arrested and they were forced to travel home alone, although I told them it was in case we were robbed. Still, the scandal-oriented press liked this version much better, the truth being too boring.

We had adjoining rooms at the Hyatt Regency, and while Mom missed the more earthy hotels of the other cities, she did enjoy the great rooms with massive moldings, ornate furniture, and the rich gilt overlay. When it was time to shift into my spy mode, I had to wonder if I was starting to run out of adrenaline when exposed to repetitive excitement and danger. Just the anticipation of a spy exchange had once stirred the senses like a tonic, but lately, it generated no tension at all. Perhaps my adrenaline tank had run dry.

I was able to slip away for a couple hours to review the meeting procedure, but I had real difficulty convincing Mom that I had business to attend to for an entire evening. The concierge obtained an excellent box seat at the opera house for Puccini's *Madam Butterfly*, and that seemed to appease her. He also arranged transportation from the hotel and back, and while Mom was a bit miffed about going alone, she finally decided that I had met a woman and wished to be alone with her. I encouraged that thought, and she felt much better.

So, while Mom headed for the opera, I climbed aboard the subway at Karlsplatz and rode to the Meidling station. Joining the gathering of strollers in Schlosspark to check for surveillance, I then crossed into the residential streets of Meidling. The meeting was in the Favoriten district, and the procedure was similar to previous ones, involving different shop windows and slightly different times. About an hour later, my contact bid me a good evening.

It was a quiet year, and after going through the usual film transfer and security discussion, I turned to the promising success of SALT II. We discussed the opposition to on-side verification, and I had to admit that the United States would resist inspections as strongly as the Soviets would. I had hopes nonetheless, but my KGB friend was far less enthusiastic than I was. He seemed to know something that I did not. Indeed, world tensions would become much worse in just a few months.

After my brother Arthur retired some five years earlier, he became a partner in a wholesale distribution company that handled a vast range of products, from food to auto parts. Eventually he set out on his own as a distributor of high-end automotive products, mostly automobile sound systems and air conditioners. Operating from his home garage, he aspired to expand as space at home became scarce. Arthur needed capital, and he came, naturally, to me.

I had absolutely no interest or experience in the business, which essentially comes down to sales. Arthur was a factory representative for several product lines, and his long workdays consisted of sales calls to automobile dealers and auto parts stores. In my view, the market was glutted with too many competitors chasing a finite number of buyers. Arthur seemed to have the energy, though, and since he was in need, I lent him several thousand dollars.

Arthur rented a small warehouse with three small offices near his home, bought a delivery van, and he was in business. It was a struggle, and to both help my brother and protect my investment, I begin spending more and more time at his office. My input consisted mainly of making sales calls to new businesses, and while I am a good salesman, I totally despised the work.

The business never generated any real profit, it just paid the bills and produced a minimal income for Arthur. By 1979 it was showing no growth and seemed doomed to failure. I saw little hope that my loan would ever be repaid. My money had helped not at all, and indeed, it would lead to my brother's destruction.

Chapter 30

ANNUS HORRIBILIS

America and Britain will never learn. Both countries seem to find it necessary to illegally meddle in other sovereign governments, and the United States' record of overthrowing the wrong government is well known. One American misadventure would come back to haunt us in late 1979, signaling a horrible year, indeed.

In September 1979, Jerry was transferred to shore duty at the Naval Telecommunications Center at Alameda, California. His new job gave him excellent access to classified material, but he experienced difficulties in photographing material on the job. We discussed the various techniques I had used over the years to overcome similar problems, one of which included carrying the material outside and photographing it in my van. I had done this in the parking lot, curtains closed for privacy, with a simple plug-in lamp for illumination. Jerry concluded that the method would work for him, but he owned a small sedan. Lacking the proper vehicle, he felt that the Soviets should buy him the van as necessary spy equipment. On my next drop note, I informed the KGB of Jerry's need for a suitable vehicle and asked for a $10,000 "expense" payment, the cost of a van in those days.

Shortly after celebrating the New Year holiday of 1980, I found myself trudging through a near blizzard in Vienna. I never knew why the KGB had reversed our summer/winter rotation, since Vienna's winters can be brutal. The city is on the same latitude as Ottawa, Ontario, or St. Paul,

Minnesota. But then, the Russians probably viewed Austrian weather as positively balmy compared to Moscow, which is in line with southern Alaska.

The meeting was similar to the previous ones, with only slight changes in the time and neighborhood. I was dressed for the elements, including new boots from a local ski shop, since I would be exposed to the wind and snow for four hours or more. The snow slowed my progress between points in the timed procedure, and thankfully, my contact met me halfway through my walking routine.

Case officers for intelligence agencies are well attuned to thinking at a national level, and my KGB friend's depression probably reflected the Soviet sentiment of both the Politburo and the military. A year earlier, we were buoyed by SALT II and a less threatening world. Now the Olympic winter games in Russia were boycotted by the United States, the Middle East was in turmoil, and Russia was drawn into an Afghan war created largely by the United States. I was quizzed at length regarding any further US hostile intentions, but Jerry's film delivery would reveal a basic status quo on the part of the US military, and Jerry perceived no heightened alert as a prelude to something new.

Jerry's intelligence was as important as ever, and it was a good time to broach the need for a $10,000 van. My friend quickly agreed that the money would be provided on my next exchange and even offered Jerry large bonuses for an uninterrupted flow of crypto-material. The Russians have always been worried about US aggression, but this willingness to part with more money for intelligence revealed a heightened sense of alarm on their part.

The year 1980 would also start badly for my brother Arthur. His business oscillated between small gains and small losses; he essentially broke even. He finally accepted defeat and closed the doors, but with his maritime engineering experience, he quickly found employment with a local naval contractor specializing in ship repair and overhaul. Arthur should have sought such employment when he retired—in fact, he should have not retired early at all.

Arthur may well be the most likable person I have ever met, agreeable to a fault, the guy that would actually give you the shirt off his back. That he could not repay the thousands I had loaned him was obvious, and I will admit that it angered me. That money could have been better used helping my children. Arthur was absolutely crushed by his inability to repay the loan and offered several plans of small monthly payments or working off the loan somehow. He even obtained his private detective license and worked hundreds of hours for me at no salary to reduce the debt. His near obsession for repaying the loan would eventually lead to a dangerous offer on my part.

Jerry informed me by letter that he had purchased the van and that it solved his difficulties in photographing material. His production of spy material and earning power was at its peak. I did not know it then, but Jerry had married his long-time girlfriend, Brenda, almost immediately after receiving his first spy payment. For some strange reason, they chose to keep the wedding secret, perhaps to allow for a quiet divorce in case the marriage failed.

I would learn years later that, at about the time he bought the van in February 1980, he violated both the confidence of our blood oath and the basic principle of any professional criminal: he told his wife that we were spies. The man who worried at length if my wife knew of my activity and therefore sensed the innate dangers in revealing such information to a spouse had done that very thing to himself. And even worse, he would tell at least one other person: Myra Barns. Jerry had a penchant for never losing track of an old friend and had kept in touch with Myra. As she would explain from the witness stand at his trial years later, Jerry had revealed his spy persona while trying to woo her into bed.

November 1980 found me on a dark, freezing street in Vienna meeting with a very unhappy KGB spy. Ronald Reagan had won the election, and from the Soviet point of view, their impoverished country would soon feel the boot of America upon its throat.

Chapter 31

FAMILY PROBLEMS

My source for family information was the grapevine. The four children and their mom maintained contact, but Barbara was the chief distributor of bad news, seeming to take perverse pleasure being the arbiter of gloom. Margaret was my main contact on the vine and she informed me that Laura had suffered a series of sexual assaults since entering the army. The details were spotty, but apparently the first attack occurred when she was an AIT trainee sergeant at Fort Gordon, Georgia. While on night guard duty in an office, she was assaulted by an NCO who was also on duty. A second attack took place while she was on a military convoy near Fort Polk, Louisiana. She was riding in the rear of her communications van when the driver pulled off the road and let his passenger out to get in the back with Laura. The driver then continued on his way while Laura was attacked.

In addition to the civil suit I intended to finance for Laura, I also planned to demand to the general that the army investigate Laura's claims and court-martial the offenders. This would not be brushed under the rug, I vowed. I would force action by appealing all the way to the army chief of staff and through my congressman.

Laura met me at the small airport. She was a forlorn figure who looked like she had never enjoyed a single day of happiness in her life. On the trip back to her trailer home, she revealed that her situation was much worse than I had expected. First, she was pregnant, and according to regulations at that time, she could not remain in the service. Second, she had gotten married, and third, she had already been discharged from the army. She was now an out-of-work dependent wife of a drug-addicted corporal.

It is hard to describe the flood of emotions I felt, alternating between depression and anger. Misery at my failure as a parent was the worst. I

293

hated the fact that she would make so many more poor choices in life without seeking the slightest guidance from her dad. Then there was the anger at her joining what I considered to be the worst of the services for women, followed by the even greater mistake of searching for a solution from a drug user. Finally, she chose to get pregnant by selecting a "sperm donor" (as Doctor Laura of radio fame would call it) as a means to terminate her army contract. That caused the greatest ire. And whom did she select to produce her son and my grandson? Mark, a pothead who had probably wrecked his genes with drugs.

By the end of 1980, Mark was discharged from the army, out of work, and with no job prospects. In another act of poor planning, they climbed into Laura's car and drove to Barbara's rented house in Maine, increasing that household from three to six. Mark could not find work—not surprising in a state with the highest unemployment rate in the country.

Ever since she was a child, Laura's established pattern was to run away from life's problems and, so, in 1981, she ran away from Maine, traveling alone to California, where she moved in with her childhood friend Dorie. Her husband (an inaccurate title for Mark) and her baby were left behind. Since she had gone to Louisiana in the Mazda, I had no communication with her. My information came later in pieces through the grapevine.

As I write these words, my brother Arthur is in his eighteenth year in federal prison, a man innocent of his charges yet doomed with little or no hope for release in his lifetime. I am directly responsible for his situation.

Arthur's personal difficulties were minor compared to Laura's, but he was deeply troubled by his inability to repay his loans. Arthur's nature demanded prompt restitution, and while I was ambivalent on the subject, he was haunted by his perceived failure. Moreover, he knew of the difficulties of my daughters Laura and Cynthia, and he tormented himself for borrowing many thousands from me that could have gone toward my kids.

To help repay me, Arthur worked many long hours as a PI on complicated tails and utterly miserable surveillances and always tried to refuse payment. I had mentally written off the loan, and though I will admit to being miffed at the loss, Arthur was nearly obsessed by his futility to repay the money.

Perhaps I was suffering from Pandora's box syndrome. At one time, I had asked my daughter Laura about spy work. However, she had not advanced sufficiently to gain access to any classified documents. As long as I had opened the box of problems by making the offer to Laura, why not make a similar offer to the infinitely more reliable Arthur? Laura, I hardly knew. Arthur, I trusted totally.

Arthur worked for a small defense contractor whose function was to coordinate repairs and overhauls to naval auxiliary and amphibious ships. They possessed some classified material, but I considered it to be very low level.

We met at a small restaurant for lunch as we did every couple weeks. It was in the parking lot that I presented the subject, walking-and-talking, using good spy-craft. Employing the same method I had used earlier with Laura, I went through the steps: (a) I was going to make an offer to solve your financial problems, (b) it is illegal, (c) if you do not wish to hear it, say so now and it will be dropped forever, (d) by going further, I am putting my life in your hands, and (e) you must pledge that you will never repeat our conversation to anyone.

Arthur was sincerely surprised by my revelations and quizzed me at length concerning my initial involvement, years of activity, and general procedures—his astonishment grew with each answer. Once past the shock, he finally said that, first, he was not inclined to participate, and, second, his company had no classified material of any value anyway. I respected his decision but asked him to keep it in mind and to make a closer evaluation of the classified material present.

I will admit that I mentioned the offer several more times and made the mistake of mentioning his possible involvement with some low-level maintenance material. Some time later, I picked up Arthur at his job for lunch. He had a large envelope, and before I drove off, he dumped out the contents for my inspection: the most sensitive classified material at his company.

Arthur had been correct: the material was unimportant, should not have been classified at all, and was of no espionage value. One piece was a sheet of computer paper of about a dozen pages listing all of the maintenance defects on a ship preparing to enter overhaul. The list ranged from the most mundane failures—such as a leaky valve or squeaky ventilator fan—to the most important—such as a broken radio transmitter or ammunition hoist. From a security point of view, it did reveal the limitations of that vessel to wage war. While that could seem valuable to a prospective enemy combatant, I knew from years of experience that the Soviet Union did not want such data. The sheets were not even stamped confidential and were degraded to unclassified due to their age.

The second item was a confidential damage control book for a ship, essentially a blueprint of its compartments and location of damage control equipment. I flipped though the one-inch-thick booklet, which was similar to those of the eight ships I had served aboard. Again, I couldn't find anything valuable or classified, regardless of the stamp on the cover. As an import officer of the deck, I had used these very books when directing the damage control team in fighting small fires. At sea, the books were used as training for simulated combat. The Soviet Union was not interested in the location of fire extinguishers and piping diagrams. This ship was built by thousands of shipyard workers with no security clearance at all, so nothing in the booklet could possibly be classified.

Humbled, I admitted to Arthur that he was correct. I should not have beleaguered him; the information was worthless. Then I realized that I had spoken too quickly. I had told the Soviets that Arthur might be willing to participate. Rather than try to explain the worthlessness of the material, it would be best to show them. It took me only a few minutes to photograph the computer sheets on the spot with my plug-in light and always-available camera. Later, I would photograph the damage control book. In our hearts and minds, Arthur and I knew that the material was not in fact classified or of any national security consequence to the United States.

As 1980 gave way to a new year, the world became a much more dangerous place and my own security had been compromised. I had revealed my criminal activity to two more people, and while I trusted my brother completely, Laura was a stranger to me, and I could only rely on the hope that a child would never destroy a parent. She had by then, of course, informed her estranged husband, adding a third person to the mix. Meanwhile, and without my knowledge, Jerry had informed his wife of our activity. And, as mentioned earlier, Jerry had also told Myra Barns that he was a spy in order to impress her into bed, James Bond–like. I was in far worse shape than I knew with two more people in on the secret.

To make things worse, Jerry was not the reliable partner I had thought he would be. I would learn later that he had applied for release from active duty in 1980 but cancelled his request at the last minute. So, unbeknownst to me, Jerry nearly ended our partnership without having the decency to warn me.

Meanwhile, the Soviet Union went into a frantic defense posture as Reagan's anticommunist vitriol increased and he became president. As a candidate, he caused panic in the Soviets by stating that the USSR had achieved a "definite margin" of military *superiority* over the United States. This absurd claim caused amused scorn in the military and among the few well-informed citizens who knew better, but the Soviets were aghast. They saw his monumental lie as the first step in the propaganda campaign to justify the long-awaited invasion of their country. The second step came with Reagan's first budget request for $1.6 trillion in military spending over the next five years to "rearm America" after President Carter had allowed the military to decline (another lie). The Kremlin's response to this unprecedented increase in military spending was called *rakento yadernoye napadeniye*, or "nuclear missile attack"— RYAN for short. The world was pushed to the brink of a nuclear holocaust as the Soviet Union braced for a nuclear missile attack from the United States. The American public, always kept unaware by our national security state, yawned throughout the entire crisis, not knowing that the panicked Soviet military had their finger on the button, wondering if they should just shoot first and hope for the best.

Chapter 32

RYAN AND REAGAN

At Lubyanka Square in Moscow stands a yellow-stone prerevolution building of Italianate style called the Lubyanka Prison, due to its location on the square. It is also the headquarters for the *Komitat Gosidaratvemmoy Rezopasnosti*, the Committee for State Security, or the KGB. The organization was founded in 1917 by Feliks Dzerzhinsky, whose imposing statue stands before the building. The KGB emblem was the shield to defend the Revolution and the sword to destroy those who would oppose.

In 1981 KGB chairman Yuri Andropov assembled his staff for a top-secret briefing to announce that, based upon intelligence analysis, the new United States administration was actively preparing for a nuclear attack upon the Soviet Union. As a result, the Politburo had ordered that the KGB's primary mission was to collect intelligence on the nuclear threat from the United States and NATO. To illustrate the seriousness of the impending danger, he ordered the KGB and the GRU (Soviet Military Intelligence)—organizations that were normally in conflict—to cooperate in this worldwide intelligence effort. He named the project Operation RYAN.

How could this happen? The threat of nuclear war had declined sharply over the years with the test ban treaty, SALT I, and SALT II. Leonid Brezhnev had renounced nuclear superiority as an objective of Soviet policy years earlier, and a crumbling Soviet military was spending 70 percent of their GDP just to maintain their status (as opposed to about 9 percent spent by the United States on its military). Communism was already an anachronism, in the final years of dying a natural death, its threat to the world deteriorating. Surely the United States had no intention of invading the ever-weakening Soviet Union, but somehow the KGB had concluded otherwise. How was that possible? In a word: Reagan.

In its quest for communist world domination, the militarily inferior Soviet Union had more than ample reason to fear invasion by the West. From the moment World War II ended in May 1945, Winston Churchill drafted an Anglo-American invasion war plan against the Soviets. By September 1945, the US joint chiefs of staff issued Directive 1496/3, in which the United States adopted a "first strike" policy to overwhelm and destroy the enemy in the event of a crisis. Thus, the Soviet Union could hardly be called paranoid during the cold war, given that it was economically isolated, militarily weaker, surrounded by hostile Western powers. In addition, their air and sea space were being endlessly probed, and the United States had strike-first invasion plans. Still, the Soviets understood US politics well enough to view Reagan's bitter denunciation of communism to be mere campaign rhetoric. Reagan did not mellow after the election, however, and by 1981 the Kremlin finally understood that Reagan's hostility toward the Soviet Union derived not from campaign tactics but from his obtuse sense of conviction.

It is easy for Americans to accuse the old Soviet Union of suffering delusions of persecution every time the US government made an anticommunist remark. But it is not paranoia when a weak country takes seriously the threats and antics of a powerful adversary. Take, for example, Reagan's comment on Jim Bakker's PTL network that "[w]e may be the generation that sees Armageddon." While the average American viewed that remark as nothing more than bombastic rhetoric, the Soviets' intelligence services regarded it with alarm. Armageddon is the final battle between good and evil, and when articulated by the US president, it had to be seen as an open threat of a coming war. To make the message clear, Reagan would later identify the Soviet Union as the "evil empire."

Jerry Whitworth traveled to Virginia that summer, saving me the miserable trip to California, and we discussed the Soviets' concern at length. We had pored over the operations plans and orders and could see no changes. Even sneak attacks take considerable preparation in moving supplies and troops, and this was simply not happening. Still, we had to accept the fact that the KGB had infinitely greater sources of intelligence, and something serious had increased the Kremlin's nervous tension. Jerry agreed to stay alert, and as he departed for the West Coast, he seemed both concerned at the increase in world tension and anxious to confirm its validity. We carried the $10,000 van bonus promised a year earlier plus his monthly compensation.

In January 1982, Jerry was still on shore duty and assigned to a communications unit in Stockton, California. I met him there to pick up his material in preparation for my meeting in Vienna two weeks later. Jerry's material was particularly extensive and revealed no changes to the old existing war plans that so troubled the Russians. If he detected a change in our war footing, we had arranged a simple signal to summon me to California early. I always had a contingency plan to make a Washington dead drop for such eventualities, but the past six months had been quiet.

Laura was living in San Leandro at the time, and I had arranged to spend a few days visiting her. When I phoned her from Virginia, I was surprised to hear that Mark had traveled to California to join her. Unsuccessful in finding adequate work in Maine, he talked Barbara into cosigning for a car loan and, with my grandson in tow, drove cross-country to California.

Laura's apartment was small and neat, and I doted over my grandson like any fatuous grandpa. Laura's disposition was as gloomy as ever. She frankly admitted that her marriage with Mark was over, and it was clear that she resented him joining her in California. I was sincerely concerned for her welfare, since she seemed to have no clear plan for her future. She was operating a small one-woman business called Solo Signs, in which she contracted display signs for local businesses and subcontracted them to professional sign painters.

I saw Mark just once during the visit. Laura and I sipped coffee in the living-dining room while Christopher dozed in my lap, and despite her moodiness, we had one of the few real conversations we'd ever had; she actually bordered on cheerfulness. Mark strode in the front door, cheerful as usual, and waved hello. Laura began viciously berating him for, I believe, not finding a job. Mark's smile crumbled and he silently climbed the stairs. I thought her attack was completely unwarranted, and I felt some real respect for the young man. He obviously loved my daughter and, regardless of his faulty work record, he wanted a happy and secure family. Once Mark was out of sight, Laura reverted to her more charac-teristic brooding and downcast personality. There was something else going on in her life that she would not discuss.

Laura and I stole away a couple of hours before my return trip east while Mark watched the baby. I drove to the San Leandro park where we could enjoy a glorious day strolling under a peaceful white-blue sky, a breeze skimming across San Francisco Bay. As we meandered along, I reminded her of my offer to join me in the spy business. She asked about the money, and I honestly explained that it depended upon the quality of her material, but as a radio operator, she could expect a minimum of a couple thousand a month. She would need some income during the sev-eral months it would take until she could reenlist and be posted, she coun-tered. I offered to cover her expenses at a thousand a month (this was when minimum wage was under seven thousand a year) if she truly wanted to join me. She agreed, we exchanged our vow of silence, and I left her with a thousand dollars.

I had scarcely returned to Virginia before I was headed back to JFK on another cramped trans-Atlantic flight of bad coffee and two-Rolaids meals. Perhaps I needed the Rolaids because I had Jerry's film packet secreted between body and camera bag.

As a result of their increased level of security, the KGB had asked me to avoid the Hyatt and InterContinental hotels and suggested the Regina Hotel near Karntner Ring. It was a quaint structure in the style of Vienna and more in keeping with my taste, but I seemed to be the only American guest. The Russians did not understand that I drew curious glances from the staff at such a place, whereas I could easily blend in with the mass of international guests at the big hotels. Also in a weird coincidence, the Regina had recently been used for the movie set of a James Bond film.

In February 1982, Operation RYAN was at full force and its effects were obvious in the attitude of my handler. Although he remained profes-sional and alert, he was tense, haggard, and displayed an unusual abrupt-ness. We immediately went into my assessment of the threat to the Soviet Union by America. I reviewed in detail the material contained in Jerry's film, plus Jerry's thorough review of existing operation orders and oper-ation plans. In essence, there were no changes to US war plans, logistic preparation for war, or any secret increase in DEFCON. My case officer pointed out that combat and logistic forces increase readiness in preparation for routine exercises, thus a real invasion could be masked by a fake exercise. Personally, I knew that was a tactic of Soviet military doctrine, to invade under the pretext of an innocent exercise, and the United States could be expected to use the same strategy. He was correct, and I agreed that we would study future exercise build-ups carefully.

Over my many years of dealing with the Soviets, I had for the first time experienced a true sense of dread that the world was genuinely on the verge of war. President and secretary general Brezhnev had years earlier established the Brezhnev doctrine of détente, a policy to lower tension between the United States and USSR to achieve peaceful coexistence between our different social and political systems. This threat, then, was coming exclusively from the US side, specifically from President Reagan. Now, crunching through freezing snow on a bitter cold night, I would hear the word RYAN for the first time and comprehend the staggering workload Andropov had imposed upon his KGB. My own case officer had himself only arrived from London hours earlier, where he was stationed every night at the government buildings where nuclear preparations were conducted. There he recorded lighted windows of the various offices and the vehicles in the parking lot. A great deal could be determined if senior staff officers worked late or all night. It would be cause for alarm if, for example, the operations and plans crew worked all night on a Sunday and the chief of staff himself was present. I, too, had experienced long surveillances in harsh conditions, but the RYAN-imposed surveillance my case officer described was particularly bitter. I could imagine this poor guy standing a miserable winter watch in a wet doorway all night, counting fish and chip deliveries to a military facility.

Watching military bases was a valid function of spies, but Operation RYAN pressed the intelligence agents into areas of vague importance as well, such as the increased stockpiling of blood by hospitals. Even subtle increases in animal slaughter and the stockpiling of food were considered valid precursors of impending war. The ever-present disinformation against the Soviet Union was closely monitored in addition to holocaust warnings from religious leaders and major bankers.

My case officer's weariness was best illustrated by a most unusual act during my long debriefing: he asked if I would like some soup and a beer. We were about one hour into our talk, with about an hour to go, and I agreed. It was bitterly cold, and I had started wearing those battery-powered heated socks for these Austrian winters. The Russian was not motivated by the blizzardlike conditions, however, but by sheer fatigue.

Before entering the tiny neighborhood café, he instructed me not to speak once inside. I agreed, only if he promised to order me anything but borscht, that beet soup so popular in Russia. That got a grin, the only one from my usually humorless friend on this night.

Once back out in the cold, we finished my debriefing, which later amounted to a clear judgment by both Jerry and me that the Soviet fears of a US invasion were unfounded. I pressed the point, but his silence indicated that his bosses thought otherwise. I ended our meeting with the bombshell information that my daughter Laura would reenter the army and expand my intelligence gatherers to two. He hung his head in dismay as he struggled for words to explain my mistake. Finally, he pointed out that, first, the Soviet Union *never* used women in espionage because of their inability to keep quiet: They always reveal their secret life to girl-friends, spouses, and lovers. Women agents are used only to sleep with someone as a means of extracting intelligence. And second, I had unnecessarily jeopardized my future and my life.

Properly castigated and sobered, I realized how correct my KGB friend was. As I reflected upon his comments, he moved smoothly to my biggest risk and weak link—Barbara. As usual, I lied and discounted her as a problem, but my case officer stopped and whispered a strange remark. I had earlier referred to Barbara by using a fractured version of the Russian word *pyanniy* for "drunk." Thereafter, we jokingly referred to her as Yonnie, a close approximation of the Russian word. My friend asked if I had the emergency procedures for a special drop in Washington or a meeting in Vienna. I assured him that I did. He then stated that if I ever had the need to nullify Yonnie as a difficulty, I should simply draw a circle around the "R" on the back of a stop sign in a Washington suburb. His instructions and the result seemed clear—by circling the "R," something would be done to prevent Barbara from revealing my secret life. I said nothing in return, assuming the worst. But regardless of the danger Barbara posed to me, I knew that I would never harm the mother of my children. Machiavelli would be ashamed of me.

It was near midnight as we concluded our business, and I yearned for my warm hotel room and a steaming cup of coffee. We stopped, and as I faced him, I was ready to shake hands and tell him I would see him next year. He was strangely silent, seeming to stare into space when I realized he was looking at something important, something behind me. I froze. "I'm not sure what this is all about," he finally said, "but I want you to trust me. See that parked car behind you, about a half block away, two men nearby?" I slowly turned to see two large men in dark clothes standing next to a black car parked in the distance. He continued, "Someone wants to speak with you, someone very important. Those men are our people and will take you to a meeting." I reminded him that in America when you are asked to get into a big black car with two strangers, you are about to be killed. "Who are those guys and what is going on?" I asked. He assured me that the men worked for his organization and he could vouch for them. Unconvinced and growing more nervous, I asked, "Okay, you come with me then." Impatiently, he informed me that he was not invited. Then, more sternly, he stressed that I was in the hands of friends, I was perfectly safe.

It was an ominous scene: deserted street, dim street lights making a slanting bluish glow in the glazed snow, two brutes waiting at the black sedan, exhaust fumes wafting upward in the still air. Maybe I had seen too many gangster movies. I asked what would happen if I did not go. "If you refuse the meeting, probably nothing will happen," he replied. "Friend, we've talked often of world events, the military and politics. Perhaps someone wants to hear from you firsthand rather than listen to me repeating our conversation from memory."

I shrugged and muttered an "okay" as I walked to the car.

I thought that they should be delighted with my performance, and Jerry's material had been excellent since he started in 1974. Jerry had just been paid $50,000 last May for quality material and received that $10,000 bonus. *Christ*, I thought, *these guys should be happy with us.*

I was completely unarmed and thought back to one of my first visits to Vienna when I had purchased a cheap .25-caliber pistol in Italy. It was foolish to carry the weapon across the border to Austria, and the scant protection it offered was more than nullified by the danger of being arrested for carrying an illegal weapon. Nevertheless, that tiny Beretta automatic would have been comforting in my pocket right then. I never carried a weapon to meetings and wondered how insane I would look shooting it out with KGB Department KII hit men on a quiet Vienna street.

The closer I got to the car, the more menacing the men looked. Big, serious, no-nonsense guys, they spoke not a word as one opened the rear door for me. I sat with one in the rear while the other joined the driver in the front. I relaxed a bit at not being squashed between those monsters in the backseat. We drove the nearly deserted streets heading east toward the Danube River, a black ribbon slicing through an icy landscape. No one spoke. I had to urinate.

We finally stopped after perhaps ten minutes on another deserted street in what I believe was the Simmering District. The silence was finally broken when one of my escorts said, "We must move you to a more secure form of transportation, for your safety." We got out of the car and walked a few paces to a small, windowless, European-style delivery truck. I entered through the rear door and sat facing the back in a van-type seat with one escort alongside. The door closed and we were shortly on the move. A very dim dome light barely illuminated the otherwise empty rear, and we braced ourselves as best as possible on the bumpy, swaying ride.

I had been outside and on the move since about 7:30 p.m., or about five hours, and my need to urinate had reached crisis proportions. That beer at 11:00 p.m. added to the problem. So, after about fifteen minutes in the truck, I finally told my escort that I needed to use the toilet. He brusquely told me to hold it; we could not stop. We went back and forth for several more minutes, but he provided no information or resolution for my problem. I finally got angry. "You either stop this truck," I said, "or I'll piss on the goddamn floor." He ignored me, so I stood up and, hanging on as best I could, I let loose behind the seat toward the front. But like a moving buckboard, it went everywhere, including on me. My escort found this hilarious—the only time any of my guards ever expressed any emotion.

Stopping at last, the door opened to near total darkness in a snowy wooded area. We walked to a small white cottage of about four rooms. Once in the frigid air, I realized that I had splattered myself worse than I thought in my emergency relief stunt. My apprehension was completely replaced by anger or, in the vernacular of the street, I was totally pissed off.

Only my three escorts were present, but I sensed security personnel in the darkness. After walking through the front door, my escorts vanished behind the closed door as I faced a small table with four men sitting in a semicircle. I recognized none of them. They wore suits and ties, but they lacked the fit and good tailoring of the West. Bottled water and glasses were scattered on the table. One man motioned to an empty chair facing them and said, "Sit, friend. Would you like coffee, tea, water? Vodka?"

I accepted coffee and was surprised that it was served in a delicate china cup and saucer. A detailed debriefing was expected and began before I swallowed my first sip of the strange brew. The questions, revealing a high order of intelligence, came quickly from two of the officials. I was tasked to the limit, having been out of the service for six years, but held up to the deep and clever questions. Could the operation orders and plans be fake plants while the real attack plans received limited distribution? Could STOP (the nuclear release war plans) be implemented only among the nuclear triad units without the knowledge of the conventional forces? Jerry's aircraft carrier was not even part of the nuclear triad—would he know if STOP was planned? There are logistic and personnel build-ups in preparation for large exercises. Could not that disguise war preparations? Deployed ships and troops are relieved on station, doubling the military presence for a short time. Would that not be a likely moment to attack? My answers were thorough and specific, but as my coffee became cold and my pants stuck to my legs, I finally interrupted with a slap to the table and a sharp retort. "I have been supplying you with the highest level of classified material for the past fifteen years. Is anyone reading this stuff? The United States is not planning a sneak attack against the Soviet Union. You are being drawn into this stupid cold war to the detriment of your economy. Why not just quit the cold war— you have nuclear missiles to protect you from any invader."

Silence fell, except for some whispered Russian to one or two who seemed to speak little or no English. Then I focused on one older man and realized with a start that I had seen his picture, his distinctive non-Western glasses. It was Yuri Andropov himself, chairman of the KGB, personally sitting in on the debriefing of a major spy: me. I looked away quickly and tried not to blanch, hand a little shaky on the fragile cup.

The silence lingered until an official intoned, "Are you aware, John, that President Reagan plans to deploy a missile defense system that he hopes will render useless any missile attack against the United States?"

"No, I did not," I replied and understood just how vulnerable the Soviet Union would become, and knowing in my heart that Reagan would enjoy raising the nuclear stakes of the cold war.

The debriefing seemed to be at an end when, with a flair, one of the officials produced a small black box. Holding it before me, he snapped a slide to reveal a single button, and with a grave voice informed me that if I pressed the button, the Soviet Union would be immediately informed that the United States had increased DEFCON. He paused to emphasize the seriousness of the matter, then asked if I would agree to push this button if and when the United States went to a higher DEFCON.

I was stunned by the dire consequences of activating the device, which I dubbed the "DEFCON box." As they solemnly waited for my answer, I understood that the Soviet missile officers throughout the USSR were prepared to "launch on warning," their fingers poised at the launch controls. My heart pounded as I stared at the tiny DEFCON box, about the size of a deck of cards, probably satellite-linked directly to the Kremlin war room. By pushing that small button from my home in Virginia, I could very likely bring about a Soviet missile launch to preempt the coming American launch. Could I push it? Could I directly participate in killing millions in a nuclear war? Could I give the Soviet Union a slight advantage in that war by allowing them to shoot first?

In my heart and soul, I knew the questions were moot, since Reagan was not going to invade the Soviet Union. I did not refuse the DEFCON box, but I did at least delay receiving it by pointing out that it was far too dangerous to transport it through customs to the United States. Also, it would go to Jerry, not me, since I had no direct way to monitor increases in DEFCONs. I suggested a simple signal in Washington to inform my handler that I was ready to accept it. One of my signals was a small lightning flash to be drawn on a residential wall. Drawing a square around the flash would signal a drop exchange where I would pick up the black box. They seemed satisfied, and that being the end of our business, we warmly shook hands and I was soon back in the distasteful interior of the truck.

Once I'd returned to the safety of the Regina at 4:00 a.m., I was able to deflate from the tension of a long night and reflect on the strange journey. First, I felt certain that the silent man was indeed Andropov, since I had seen a recent photo of him. He wore distinctive glasses with wide gold stems and dark plastic arcs above the lenses. Andropov was in his mid-seventies and had the gray complexion of a man in poor health. This description matched the silent leader at my interrogation. That the KGB chief would personally attend the debriefing of a common Soviet agent illustrated the sheer gravity of RYAN and the danger the Soviets perceived. Andropov would never leave the confines of the Soviet block, but the Czechoslovakian border was just twenty-five miles from Vienna. My strange ride then became clear—I had been shuffled across the Czech border.

Cramped in a KLM seat on my return flight a couple days later, I had time to consider my Russian friend's reference to Laura, and I knew he was right. My daughter *was* a stranger to me, and I had failed to carry out the vital second step in spy recruitment: spot, *assess*, and recruit. I had never assessed her propensity to commit the crime of espionage, to maintain secrecy, and to protect her team players. I had relied solely on my hope that a child would not willfully harm or endanger a parent. Yet, any street cop would point out that most violence occurs between *family* members, not strangers. Still, I had confidence in her and would not have believed that she had already told Mark, a man she neither loved nor liked and would soon divorce.

I also thought about the KGB's apparent offer to have Barbara killed. At that point in my life, I had finally come to realize the meaning of Jesus Christ's teachings about "turning the other cheek." As a child, I thought that if one did not fight back when being beaten up by another, that he was a coward or a fool. Later I understood Jesus' meaning: that when you injure another, you really injure yourself. To kill another is the worst crime because you have killed yourself *spiritually*. Thoughts, too, are real, so to even think of harming another will cause injury to one's self. (Once in prison, however, I would be severely criticized for not arranging Barbara's death to save myself; my critics failed to see the paradox.)

Something good happened in 1982. Cynthia had endured Barbara's abuse for twenty-three years, and now that Barbara was unable to torture Cynthia physically, she finally found her own apartment. Cynthia's recovery from years of torment would begin at last.

I would think again of the danger that Barbara posed as I drove through the Washington hinterlands in preparation for my summer 1982 drop. My practice was to check my emergency signal sites to ensure that urban sprawl did not plow them away, to be replaced by strip malls. My stop sign stood sentry on Johnnycake Road, the faded red backside ever ready for my signal. A simple chalk circle around the letter "R"—a three-second effort—would put an end to the threat Barbara presented. I drove on to my drop location with the chalk unused.

Jerry's photo material was at the highest level, and my lengthy debriefing of him in California left me convinced that the Soviet Union's appraisal of the United States' intentions was seriously flawed. My written report that accompanied the delivery was unambiguous—there were no logistic preparations or movements of combat units to support a RYAN attack. My return note from the KGB emphasized that we should strive harder, however. Andropov and his KGB estimates were already wrong, I surmised, since Jerry's material was of prime quality. The only information he lacked was that of special intelligence, but even if an attack on the Soviet Union was formulated at that level, it would be revealed first in massive logistic support, then in well-planned movements of major combat units, including his own ship. This simply was not happening.

When I picked up Jerry's material in California, we discussed the DEFCON box in detail. He did not like the idea at all, and I did not press the issue. To push that button when other events were aligned could be tantamount to pressing the Soviet launch button itself.

Then the worst would happen relative to Operation RYAN on November 10, 1982, when Brezhnev died. He was replaced by none other than the KGB chairman himself, Yuri Andropov, the architect of Operation RYAN.

Chapter 33

MICHAEL

Nearly every boy wants to be like his dad, to enter the same profession and even master the same hobbies and other talents. I was fascinated by my father's skill as a radio personality, which drove me into amateur radio as a boy and certainly led to my military profession in radio communications. When my son, Michael, came back home, it was not surprising that he would become a proficient pilot and a skilled sailor at the helm of a sailboat.

Michael had heard all of the private detective tales of dare-devilry from my friends, and it was only normal that he would want to be a part of that sphere of my life, too. Michael struggled to overcome some poor grades at the start of high school, and to improve himself, he enrolled in college courses during the high school summer breaks. In 1980, he completed the state private investigator course at age eighteen, the youngest allowable age for a license. We used him sparingly at first, usually in three or four car tails where we would take turns as the prime tail car and switch off every few blocks. Michael was very successful as a tail since no one suspected that the yellow Mazda pickup with accent stripes and a surfboard affixed to the roof could ever be the vehicle of a PI on the job. He quickly graduated to long overnight surveillances, which were always dangerous but especially so for Michael since he was too young for a weapon permit. But he still spent many a night alone in the van with cold coffee and the shotgun for company.

One of Michael's greatest assets was his youthful appearance. At age nineteen, he could easily pass for sixteen or even younger. Surveillance always entails situations in which it is simply impossible to park a vehicle near the subject's house. On one such occasion, Michael solved the problem by riding his Beach Peddler Bike to the street in question and "hanging out" with the local kids on the corner. No one notices two or three kids sitting on the curb; surely no one would believe that one kid noted every event and had a two-way radio in his backpack to alert the rest of us when the subject moved. Michael invented the concept of "bicycle surveillance" and even shot decent photos from concealed cameras while engaged in conversations with neighborhood kids.

In short, Michael was the perfect son who never caused his dad the slightest grief. He had his own friends, but he and I still hung out together frequently. And, finally, he was an important business partner at Confidential Reports, always willing to engage in the dangerous work, even though it scared me enormously. Due to our special relationship, it seemed only natural that I would eventually talk to him about the spy business, an act that I am ashamed to write about, to even think about. That I had gone to war against my government was one thing, but to encourage my son to cross that line into the danger zone was unforgivable.

The attempted recruitment of Arthur and Laura was done for altruistic reasons; they were both in trouble. The prospect for either of them taking the path I offered was always considered to be slim, and neither really seemed to possess the willingness for so perilous a journey. Michael, conversely, had the aptitude for success in the field, and I had seen him coolly work the street in dangerous situations. He was a real recruit, and indeed, the only one who could carry on after me to play out this counterfeit cold war drama.

I spoke to Michael about the spy business in the summer of 1982, when Jerry and I were at the top of our game. Michael had already planned to enter the navy after graduation and was slated for the yeoman rate, a prestigious job in which he would run the ship's office. The job has access to classified material.

I explained that I had been a spy for the Soviet Union for the past fifteen years, and why. He listened with his usual amusement as I interpreted my psychology of the cold war, how it drained our blood and national treasure to enrich the elite, and how there was a good chance that the Soviet Union would soon end it all by quitting the expensive game. He asked several questions, including what might be the hazards of the job. It was among the worst of crimes, I pointed out, but the prospect of arrest was very slim, as my fifteen years without the slightest hint of detection proved.

That Michael knew of my spy profession was obvious, just as it had been with Laura. Barbara had told the kids my dark secret, but I felt she had done so to demean me rather than to cause trouble. Thus, Michael had many years to think about my activity and wonder if we would eventually discuss it. After we finally did discuss it, he considered his choice only briefly before agreeing, with his usual élan, to join me. He had only one request, that I not tell his mother of his decision. His request prompted a question on my part: Would Barbara be a risk to our new arrangement—did Michael think she would eventually have me (us) arrested? Michael felt that her main motivation was to degrade me to my kids and would never go so far as informing the authorities. His view was a little reassuring, but we both recognized the danger she posed.

Michael entered the navy as planned and was assigned to a fighter squadron as a yeoman. He began producing useful classified material, which I photographed for delivery.

My winter meeting in Vienna was scheduled for January 15, 1983, and I flew to California just after the New Year to pick up Jerry's material. We performed the usual exchange of money and film, but Jerry displayed less than his usual lively interest as we discussed the ever-increasing dangers resulting from Reagan's aggression and Andropov's RYAN response. He was growing tired of the sea duty, and I could sympathize with the pressure of seemingly endless deployments. Jerry had entered the navy in 1956 and could have retired seven years earlier; indeed, his thirty-year mandatory retirement would be in just three more years. In our initial agreement, Jerry had consented to remain for the full thirty years, but I had urged him to consider a civilian communications job with the government if he chose to leave the service early. Former servicepeople frequently continue at the same job as civilians, assigned to a nice communications center for a second career and second retirement. I would have been perfectly happy for Jerry to take a civilian job at Alameda or Stockton, but if Jerry felt more daring and sought a larger income, there were always job openings at the CIA, DIA, NSA, and other government agencies where higher-level classified material was available. In short, a young but retiring senior chief radioman would be actively sought by any government communications facility. The issue was left unresolved, but Jerry assured me that he was in for the next three years and very likely beyond as a civilian government employee.

As I flew back east with Jerry's film, I was only slightly concerned that he seemed to have lacked his usual zeal. In fact, I would have been startled to learn that Jerry had not only lied to me but that he had embarked on a most destructive course of deception.

I expected my KGB friend to be in a panic as a result of the KGB boss's ascension to the leadership of the Soviet Union. As head of the KGB, Andropov's apocalyptic vision of a nuclear attack by the United States was not shared by all at Moscow Center. There were those in the Soviet military hierarchy who did not take the Western threat seriously, and some experts in Moscow Center regarded Andropov's assessment as seriously alarmist. Andropov's critics could harbor such opinions while Andropov was the KGB head, but as president and secretary general of the Soviet Union, Andropov would face very little criticism. Operation RYAN went into overdrive.

I was thankful for my electric socks and huge fur cap as I followed the procedure on Vienna's frozen streets. My contact approached me earlier than usual as I slogged through the snow on Gudrun Strasse. The four hundred thousand KGB officials and officers were worked even harder to confirm Andropov's worst thoughts, and my friend was hollow-eyed and haggard. We exchanged material, and he recited from memory the material he was most interested in receiving. A specific US exercise was mentioned, Able Archer '83, which was to take place later in the year. Jerry had not mentioned it, indicating that he had seen nothing in the plan to cause alarm. I agreed to seek more information on the exercise, correctly assuming that President Andropov viewed Able Archer '83 as a feint to mask the real invasion.

My contact recited a long list of items that they were interested in receiving plus a list of items they did not wish to receive. Since the list was a bit long, I fished a scrap of paper from a pocket and wrote it down with frozen fingers. One column was listed under "Y" for yes and included the usual desired items: cryptographic, operation orders, operation plans, and DEFCON changes. The second column was listed under "N" for no, and since the small note survived my arrest and is now held as evidence, the list is repeated here exactly as I wrote it:

- Intelligence
- KY-8
- Authentication Systems
- Key Squares
- SAS
- 30 Series
- KG-14

The "no" list had some surprises for me, but the reaction to the list by the FBI and NSA (the people who make the codes and ciphers) was positively stunning. That a major spy would be told to avoid obsolete material was to be expected, but to disregard the current and newest material and equipment suggested the unthinkable—that the Soviet Union already had a reliable and uninterrupted source and didn't want to put Jerry and me at risk by trying to get what they already had.

Here is the explanation of my "no" list and some opinions.

- Intelligence. On the one hand, US intelligence is merely an exaggerated assessment of Soviet plans and power. But it should be valuable in revealing US sources and methods. The Soviets obviously had better sources in the intelligence community than Jerry and me.
- KY-8. A crypto-device to encode voice messages on a tactical level. Probably of little or no value when up to six months old.
- Authentication Systems. A code system to ensure that tactical messages are sent by a legitimate station. Useless when old and was sent by Jerry in error.
- Key Squares. Part of an obsolete crypto-system.
- SAS. Sealed Authentication System, the code system used to verify our war messages. You have seen those plastic envelopes snapped

open in movies where six or seven letters match those on the war message; if they match, turn the keys and release the missiles. They are of no value to the Soviets.

- 30 Series. Among the next of the crypto-systems to include the KG-36 for high-data-rate satellite links and secure voice circuits. It was implausible that these latest devices were not wanted and surely suggested that the Soviets had a separate source.
- KG-14. A current crypto-system used to decrypt different channels of a multichannel circuit; also suggested a separate source.
- No spy should be so arrogant to believe that he is the sole source of secrets, so I accepted the list calmly. During debriefing after my arrest, the NSA was quite agitated by my list. I can reveal no more than I have here, which would seem to show significant success by the KGB in obtaining America's highest secrets. Keep in mind, however, that the purpose for spies and intelligence is to create transparency, to preclude a country from planning a surprise war-like act. As long as the US plans were known to the Soviet Union, a "launch on warning" by Moscow would be prevented.

My film delivery that night also contained the first items assembled by my son. Since my case officer was well aware of my lack of reverence to KGB rules, he accepted my information about my new team player with grace. I explained the contents of his material and what we could expect in the future. In light of Operation RYAN, he could hardly be angry at my success in expanding upon my source of intelligence.

The inclusion of Michael's material unknowingly saved me from severe problems with the KGB since my friend and crime partner, Jerry, had embarked on a most cunning scheme to trick the Soviets into paying him more than he was owed. Jerry had lied to me about retiring in 1986 and his plan to seek work as a government civilian employee for years to come. In fact, Jerry secretly planned to retire in just eight months and work as a stock market consultant. His ruse would involve selling a large cache of secret material over the next couple years while appearing to remain in the service. His stunt was already in effect. He had purposely "fogged" the majority of his film, which I had just delivered. His idea was to pretend it had been an accident and draw out the sale of his material for as long as possible.

Poor Jerry. Didn't he know that the KGB invented the concept of deception? Did he seriously believe he could play this chess game of intrigue with a spy organization that had been playing it since 1917?

When a spy is detected or suspected, that person is always transferred to a new job with less sensitive access, or else something is done to stem the flow of secret material. The poor dumb spy goes to his new job unaware that the authorities are either building a legal prosecution against him or planning to convert him to a double agent. Spy bosses are thus alert for any change in a spy's access or the quality of his deliveries. Jerry's fogged and mostly unusable film surely alerted Moscow Center that Jerry and I were compromised. In the movies, some loathsome and humorless killer would travel circuitously into the United States and quietly assassinate Jerry and me. In real life, we would be scratched from the spy roster and any material supplied would be disregarded or at least considered highly suspect. But in any event, the money would be stopped.

The KGB must have wondered which American came up with so sophomoric an idea as fogging the film. Perhaps because it was such an unsophisticated pretense, they concluded that it had to be foul play by Jerry. A further complication was the material from Michael, which would seem to disprove the suspicion that we had been caught. In spite of Michael's useful material, there was obviously something unsavory going on. As a form of discipline, the KGB stopped our payments until we proved ourselves useful again.

As I flew back to the United States, I knew nothing of Jerry's treachery. A couple years earlier, I had suggested to the KGB that I stop receiving payments in Europe, since transporting undeclared money into the United States was needlessly dangerous. They agreed, and payments were made only in US dead drops thereafter, our payments coming but once a year.

The worst part of Jerry's deceitfulness was the impact it had on world events. The Reagan-RYAN–generated prospect of creating a nuclear exchange had reached its peak in 1983, and our flow of information to reduce the hazard was now disregarded. Just eleven months earlier, my role was so important that I had met personally with the future president of the Soviet Union. Today, I was fired.

As we moved deeper into 1983, I could not help but wonder how the United States had failed to detect the enormous danger poised by Operation RYAN. Surely the CIA had detected the increased readiness and Soviet threat to launch on warning. What happened to the CIA-KGB back channels? But Reagan seemed absolutely giddy as he routinely referred to the USSR as the "evil empire," taunting Moscow like a schoolyard bully. Then he announced the Strategic Defense Initiative (SDI) missile defense system that quickly took on the name of the popular movie *Star Wars*.

Star Wars called for developing technologies for a layered "shield" of weapons based primarily in space that would destroy incoming ballistic missiles before reaching the United States. Listening to the Reagan proposal, it did sound more like a George Lucas movie than a valid weapon system. In space, it called for the creation of "homing overlay devices" to shoot down ICBMs in their ballistic phase in the stratosphere. Satellites containing "smart pebbles" would launch small rockets at the offending ICBM. Also in space, particle-beam weapons would fire high-energy subatomic particles at the ICBM. Finally, other satellites would direct lasers at the missiles.

It all sounded quite impressive, but when I'm faced with what I consider to be outlandish bombast, I turn to the experts for their opinion, in this case, the American Physical Society (APS). This prestigious group of physicists severely criticized the Reagan administration, saying that the space-based missile shield was far beyond the technical ability of the United States.

Star Wars would go through many mutations over the decades: most of the space nonsense was dropped as ground-based interceptor missiles and aircraft-borne lasers were emphasized. And what was APS saying about the current Star War schemes by 2003? The latest incarnation of intercepting the descending warheads is still a pipe dream beset with major technical problems.

The squandering of citizens' wealth on such a ridiculous project made me think of a pithy quote from a US senator: "I believe in the division of labor. You send me to Congress; we pass laws under which you make money . . . and out of your profit, you further contribute to our campaign funds to send us back again to pass more laws to enable you to make more money" (Senator Boies Penrose [R-PA], 1896).

In July 1983, Jerry returned from a western Pacific deployment aboard the USS *Enterprise* (CVN-65), and I was there a few days later to pick up his material for my summer drop. Jerry seemed normal as he reacclimated to family life after months of demanding sea duty. As we strolled and reviewed my "yes-no" list, he was unusually introspective. He made two comments, both of which I found a bit troubling. One had to do with our years of success as spies and that no one would ever know of our accomplishments. He speculated about writing a book from his deathbed. In his second comment, he lamented how married life and that of a spy did not mix. The only way to succeed as a spy was to remain single and to avoid any serious relationships.

Had I known then about his fogged film and his secretive retirement plans for three months hence, Jerry's disturbing remarks would have made perfect sense. He was retiring from the spy business, and no one would ever know. His second comment about remaining single revealed that he had not only told his wife but that she was also causing him some grief. Indeed, she was probably the reason for his decision to retire.

On a brighter note, Jerry had assembled a sizeable quantity of Able Archer '83 material, which revealed that US and NATO forces would test the command and control procedures for the use of nuclear weapons. My stomach sank as I flipped through portions of the operation order and various messages relating to the test. Able Archer was to examine our war plans for a preemptive nuclear strike against the USSR and Warsaw Pact countries. No wonder the Soviet Union was alarmed; this would be the perfect ploy for a *real* launch.

Still, the overall exercise did not reveal any of the other necessary preparations for war, and while Jerry and I felt confident that it was a mere exercise, we could appreciate the anxiety and dread Moscow was experiencing. In fact, I would learn later that Moscow Center had issued a flash alert for all information indicating that the United States was preparing for an imminent nuclear attack. The Soviets had already increased their military alert status as nuclear-capable aircraft were readied to launch and Soviet forces prepared for a retaliatory nuclear strike.

I was just days away from my Washington drop and I knew that the

Able Archer material in my hands could be vital in averting a global war. I reminded Jerry that the prevailing Soviet nuclear doctrine held that in the face of impending nuclear attack, the Soviets would avoid disaster by launching a preemptive nuclear attack first.

Later in July, I would drive to the dead drop in the DC suburbs, where an uneventful exchange was made. Back in the motel room hours later, I would learn of Jerry's duplicity and the KGB's response. The film was "fogged," to use their term, and as an experienced photographer, I knew that there were a number of ways that such a thing could be done. Under-exposing, overexposing, or deliberately taking out-of-focus photos were just a few. Jerry could even have opened the film cartridge and exposed the film to light. Perhaps he hoped that it would appear that airport x-ray scans had fogged the film, and I thought of his wife, Brenda, a postdoctoral biologist. I had toured her lab at the University of California at Davis, where she radiated mice using a radioactive isotope. I could picture Jerry lowering the film behind the lead shield so he could blame it on airport security. No, it was highly unlikely that Jerry, a superb photographer, would make so serious a mistake.

There was no money included at the exchange, and according to the enclosed note, the KGB followed their usual deceptive means to explain its absence. Not wanting to accuse Jerry and me of some ruse, they simply claimed that they were "temporarily lacking the funds to pay us at this time." The reason was so preposterous and clever that I had to smile. A country with a GDP in the trillions of dollars could not find a few thousand in change to pay its spies? They suspected that we were toying with them, and they were toying with us in exchange. I wanted to strangle that idiot, Jerry, but it would be more enjoyable to inform him later that his pay was zero.

The ramifications of Jerry's act went deeper than our being disciplined and at least temporarily fired. The critical Able Archer material would be disregarded as "suspect" from agents who were probably turned into double agents for the CIA. As I crawled into bed in that seedy, backroad motel, I had a melodramatic thought of my location in relation to the Soviets' primary target. What weapon would hit DC first? Probably a submarine-launched missile fired from under the Arctic. Due to the United States' success in tailing Soviet missile submarines, they were now patrolling under the ice and beyond US detection.

The problem with creating the aura of impending war is the decline of rational responses by those who are threatened when danger looms. When one expects an armed attack at any moment, circumspect behavior is abandoned and replaced by a survival reaction. Reagan had put the Soviet Union into a survival mode that would cause a tragic accident: the downing of Korean Airline Flight 007 and the loss of 269 people.

Shortly after, a major tragedy would occur in Lebanon, a tiny country smaller than Connecticut. That country had been involved in a civil war since 1975, chiefly between Christians and Muslims. The war went through many phases, including Arab peacekeeping forces that kept the combatants separated. Lebanon's neighbors, Syria and Israel, were also drawn into the country that was fragmented into sectarian communities. For some unknown reason, President Reagan dispatched a contingent of US Marines to the country, housing them in a hotel at the Beirut International Airport. In October, a suicide bomber driving a TNT-laden truck smashed into the headquarters, killing 241 marines and sailors. This act effectively chased the United States from Lebanon (as well as Israel).

Reagan was furious and sought a target upon which to extract revenge against the communists. A perfect victim was quickly located, a sleepy island in the Lesser Antilles: Grenada.

Philosophers tell us that we make few real friendships in our lives, and I would lose a true friend early in 1983. Carl Baker—the son of the Cessna dealer for whom I flew an air taxi—was returning from a charter flight in the company Tiger when he decided to fly over the wedding party of friends at Virginia Beach. The celebrants were assembled on the oceanfront and cheered Carl's low pass. Carl proceeded to perform an aerobatic maneuver called Cuban Eights, which involved a series of dives close to the water. After several passes, he failed to pull up and crashed to his death in the lazy blue waves of the Atlantic Ocean.

If things were not going badly enough, my daughter Laura disappeared. We had stayed in phone contact, and she informed me months earlier that she had fallen in love with a guy, Steven (I will mercifully omit his last name), and she had moved out of the apartment she and Mark shared. Mark in turn picked up his son at day care and returned east, making the long drive to his mother's home in Maryland.

In a rare phone conversation with Barbara, I passed on what I knew. Barbara was truly concerned. I suggested that Laura was just angry at us for not supporting her and that she would show up eventually. The baby was fine, living in Maryland with Mark, and I maintained contact with Mark's mother. Regardless, a missing child is agony for parents and family members. The worst is always possible.

Jerry expected at least $50,000 for his services and traveled to Norfolk to collect. Amusingly, the money had been earned and would have been on hand had he not formulated his silly plan to collect twice on the same material. I picked him up at the airport and broke a spy rule by explaining the lack of money while driving to my home (cars are easily and often bugged). Jerry went pale and denied profusely that he had caused the problem. Controlling my anger, I had one key question: "Do you still have the material; can we shoot it again?" He answered yes, the material was composed of secret messages, a stack about two feet high, and it had not been destroyed. I knew then that he had lied and purposely fogged the film since there was no reason to retain the incriminating documents once they had been photographed. I could hardly control my anger when I told him to keep the material and that I would personally travel to California and film it prior to my winter meeting in Vienna. I let him know that he had cancelled my income as well, but I did not mention Michael.

Michael was naturally miffed by the lack of payment, and while I avoided the detailed explanation of Jerry's sorry stunt, he accepted the news graciously.

Jerry retired from the navy in October 1983 without informing me. He did not seek civilian government employment in the field, and as best I can deduce, he had honed his skills in the stock trade and invested his spy income in the market. His wife, Brenda, had a state-of-the-art IBM computer for her postdoctoral research, and Jerry worked from home on his investments; he had no other job.

As for Michael, he stayed busy all of 1983 as a navy yeoman, including several cruises aboard aircraft carriers. In November, he deployed on the *Nimitz*, probably to participate in Able Archer, an odd coincidence.

He supplied a considerable amount of classified material, but it lacked the quality of what Jerry had produced.

Operation Able Archer did not start World War III.

Chapter 34

THE END DRAWS NEAR

Somewhere during 1983, I had the last good offer of my life. I had met Rena Banks at Wackenhut security services back in 1980 where she was employed as a private detective. We worked several cases together, and I was impressed by her intuition, which often bordered on the psychic. Rena was a very spiritual and enlightened woman who was a member of the Rosicrucians, an esoteric movement dating back to 1614 in Germany. Its founder, Christian Rosenkreuz, had gained spiritual and mystical knowledge that his followers practice to this day. Perhaps this association was the source of Rena's psychic ability.

Rena was divorced from a navy chief and lived with her daughter in a large house in rural Chesapeake. We were very close for over a year, and Michael even dated Rena's daughter; often the four of us sailed the bay together. Our relationship cooled as I became buried in Confidential Reports and Rena took a job with the Chesapeake police department records section.

But then one day, Rena invited me to lunch and made an offer that I should have accepted on the spot. She proposed that we sell our respective houses, pool our money, travel to Florida. We would easily have $200,000—more than enough for a slightly used cruising and live-aboard sailboat.

There are cruising couples from every nation living the idyllic life, cruising the world in sailboats. The uninitiated believe that only a few hundred eccentric vagabond couples spend their lives in the Caribbean or the Polynesian Islands, but in reality, such couples number in the thousands and sail to every corner of the world, even the Arctic and Antarctic. They even have their own magazine, *Cruising World*, and seem to know or have met all of their fellow sailing enthusiasts.

I had subscribed to *Sailing* magazine for decades and salivated over the classified section every month. There was a cornucopia of used sailboat bargains in Florida where retired couples who had reached the age where sailing was no longer possible spent their final years. With our combined funds, we could afford a splendid forty-foot yacht.

We could actually live aboard a boat forever on my retirement check, but Rena was a skilled artist and felt certain she could contribute by selling paintings. Why not exchange all of that expensive bug and tap sweep equipment for a well-equipped electronics shop, she suggested, and earn extra money repairing electronics for our fellow sailors?

I was ready for a major change, and her proposal for the charmingly simple and carefree life was the perfect offer. But it came right at the time that Jerry had created turmoil in my life and my son's life, and until it was resolved, I was trapped. I told Rena that I could not accept at that time, but in one year, we had an agreement.

In January 1984, I traveled to California with my Minox spy camera plus my Canon 35-millimeter. My mood was cantankerous when Jerry met me at the airport, and my ill temper grew as Jerry finally informed me that he had separated from the service. There was then no question that he had fogged the film, but I still hoped to reestablish my credibility with the KGB. The entire stack of secrets was in the trunk, and since Jerry did not wish to photograph them at home, we rented a motel room for the task.

The stack of secrets was huge, close to two feet high, and I insisted on shooting the film myself. Jerry had at least brought a professional light, and I stretched the Minox cord to the eighteen-inch bead and started the process. My Minox had an abnormal feel, like there might be some sort of malfunction, during the past few months while filing Michael's material. Worried about a real accident, I switched to the Canon with the close-up lens attached. The film would be more bulky to transport, but I at least knew that the quality would be excellent. Jerry nervously paced the room, conscious of my anger and no doubt hoping that I could save his $50,000 that he had so foolishly lost. As I worked through the stack, I pointed out to Jerry that this material should have been delivered a *year* earlier and that some of the material was older than a year and a half.

Despondent, he sat on the bed looking defeated. The only sound in the room was the steady click of my camera and the zip of the auto-advance. Even in my anger, I did not have the heart to tell Jerry that they were unlikely to pay for such ancient junk.

February 4, 1984, and another Vienna winter. My old KGB friend met me early in the walking procedure and accepted my larger-than-normal film package. He quickly disappeared for several minutes, and when he returned, I noticed an uncomfortable and even pained look on his face. He had been transferred, he explained, and I would be working with a new case officer. I knew exactly what that meant. I was still deemed unreliable and suspected of being a double agent.

My old friend was taking me to meet my new contact, a face-to-face introduction to prove he was legitimate. I tried to plead my case, but there was no time. We rounded a corner where my new case officer stood. He made a stark contrast to my Russian friend of eight years. This guy was big and tough looking, a charmless individual with Marine Corps sensitivity. I knew his function—he was a troubleshooter. His mission was to determine if I was compromised or still a team player. For the first time in my spy career, I sensed mortal danger if I failed this test. I shook good-bye to my friend, who slipped quietly away with a wounded look in his eyes.

My new contact and I strolled in the shivery darkness as I described the contents of my delivery, starting with Michael's material, which was extensive and of good quality. I did Jerry a favor by giving him some benefit of doubt regarding the fogged film, but I made it clear that Jerry was out of the service and no longer had access to classified material. Further, he had not made any effort to continue as a government employee. Thus, in my view, Jerry was out of the game until he made a move to rejoin. My only asset now was Michael.

Jerry had provided me a two-page note describing his plans, which I copied and included in my delivery. It listed his future plans and clearly stated that he would "get a position at NCS [Naval Communications Station] Stockton, hopefully in near future, most likely that would be a GS-5/6 crypto-operator in the Tech Control Division." He would also try the air force in security. He went on to write, "I plan to make myself known to the larger segment of government and civilian organizations just to see what is out there. An example: CIA." His note ended with the implication that he was still a player and he would not "cut off his nose to spite his face."

He mentioned Brenda's scheduled graduation in December 1984 as a PhD and that he would give her first choice on job location. I pointed out to my new handler that Jerry's wife's schedule gave him ample reason to delay his plans and wait a year until applying, but my handler gruffly mentioned that Jerry should have simply delayed his retirement plans for that year. (I still have a faded copy of that note to this very day.)

The Russian was, of course, correct. I stressed that Jerry's strong wanderlust had driven him into long vacations of unemployment in the past. Moreover, if the CIA had turned him, they would never allow him a year sabbatical before pressing him to work. My handler seemed to agree but stressed that a decision regarding our future arrangements would depend upon the material I had just delivered. This guy did not inspire confidence, and I left him at the witching hour in bitter cold with the feeling he would continue withholding the money. If he did so, that KGB troubleshooter would likely drive Jerry away permanently.

The raison d'être of spy case officers is to recruit spies and to encourage operatives to continue supplying information, not to drive them away. The KGB was making a foolish decision by prolonging Jerry's punishment.

Secretary General Andropov would die just three days after my Vienna meeting, an event that would end the RYAN hysteria. The new head of state was Konstantin Chernenko, the Communist Party's chief ideologist who was seventy-four at the time and in ill health. I was personally not happy with the choice; he was another elderly bureaucrat from the Central Committee who would maintain the old ideology of the Marxist revolution. The cold war would continue unabated.

An unusual fact would emerge years later that would show that the position of secretary general should have gone not to Chernenko but to Mikhail Gorbachev. Andropov was Gorbachev's mentor, and before Andropov became seriously ill, he told Gorbachev that he should prepare to assume the responsibility of secretary general. Before his death, Andropov sent a written message to the General Committee recommending that "Gorbachev should be entrusted with the leadership." A few years later, it was learned that Chernenko cut off that portion of the message in a clever move to become secretary general himself. Chernenko would live only thirteen months after his election, and would eventually be succeeded by Gorbachev, but in the meantime, the cold war was extended for another thirteen months.

President Reagan's reckless behavior came to an end when the CIA finally came to understand the calamitous seriousness of RYAN. This had a sobering effect on Reagan, and he notably reduced his anticommunist rhetoric during his second term. Among the members of the Politburo who followed the crisis created by the US vitriol and Soviet paranoia was Mikhail Gorbachev. He, too, had been reading my material and, in thirteen months, he would make a bold move to change the world.

A Washington drop was scheduled for just sixty days later where I dropped Michael's material; I had nothing positive or new to report on Jerry. The delivery had little more than my expense money and a couple thousand for Michael. We were all on unpaid probation, and I had to wonder at the illogical and stubborn stance by the KGB. But what did I know? Those people had years of experience and perhaps this inflexible position would compel Jerry to act.

Jerry was coming to Virginia for his money since I had informed him that I would not travel west using my personal funds. He arrived within hours of my return from DC, and I let him read the message enclosed with my pickup package. Jerry was furious, his not-so-clever trick had failed. Not satisfied with collecting $50,000 over a year ago, he had turned in fogged film in an attempt to cheat the Soviets out of another $50,000 while concealing the fact that he had actually quit. I carefully explained that his sorry performance had placed us both on unpaid leave and we were now forced to reestablish our bona fides. The discussion became heated, and Jerry loudly announced, "You should find a new partner." I responded with equal intensity, "I already have!"

Jerry stormed out and returned to California. His $100,000 dream, which could have been at least $50,000, had turned out to be nothing.

Laura had been missing for about a year, and I wondered if there had been any communication between her and Barbara without my knowledge. A typical PI will develop many contacts over the years, and I had one that would provide me with ninety days of telephone billing information for just fifty bucks. I had him run the bills for both Barbara and Mark's mother that would show all of their long-distance calls plus any collect calls, which are common from those in hiding. Mark's numbers revealed nothing, but Barbara had a very familiar number belonging to Jerry in California! I stared at the number stupefied, bewildered that Barbara and Jerry would have any reason to communicate. Jerry had tactlessly met with her years earlier in what I considered an attempt by Jerry to evaluate Barbara as a psychological threat. Quickly I ran a ninety-day check on Jerry's number, and there it was, one call to Barbara during that period. Normally I would have confronted my old friend, but after our earlier altercation, the atmosphere was not right.

Meanwhile, every long-distance number on Barbara's and Mark's bills was carefully checked, but none of the calls were to Laura.

Back home in California, Jerry was no doubt seething at both himself for his imprudent attempt to double his money and the KGB for failing to compensate the $50,000 he had earned. So, just over two weeks from our meeting in Virginia, Jerry did the unthinkable: he betrayed his long-time friend and crime partner and broke his blood oath. Jerry wrote the first of a series of anonymous letters to the FBI. Specifically, he asked for immunity from prosecution and a reward in exchange for revealing the identity of an active and long-time spy for the KGB—me. I am stunned by Jerry's conduct to this day, for it is one thing for an arrestee to rat out his crime partner to save himself, but it is conspicuously egregious to initiate the process when one is in no danger of arrest whatsoever.

It is impossible for me to know what Jerry was thinking, but Jerry did tell his wife of our spy careers, and somehow I felt the hand of Brenda in those FBI letters. It was more an emotional act than one of logic, and I could see Brenda urging her man to save himself by burying his best friend.

The phone calls between Jerry and Barbara remain a riddle to this day. But it would seem that Jerry, and perhaps Brenda, had combined forces with Barbara to divulge my activity to the authorities.

Stuck in the van on an all-night surveillance, I listened to the November 1984 election returns. Reagan was elected for his second term, and since he seemed to realize how close he had brought all of humankind to the edge of extinction, his second term would be much more temperate. Seeing the extent of Soviet preparations to preempt an American preemptive attack had a moderating effect on Reagan, who showed self-restraint in his anticommunist behavior for the next four years. In fact, Reagan came to fear nuclear war with the same intensity as Gorbachev (who was soon to become the Soviet leader). In her book *The Reagan Reversal*, Professor Beth Fisher wrote that "Reagan was visibly shaken by the Soviet misinterpretation of the NATO drill (Able Archer)." Thus the Reagan administration began pursuing "cooperation and understanding with the Soviet Union in 1984 because it sought to avoid inadvertent nuclear exchanges."

You may wonder about the progress of Star Wars at this point since its original purpose was to build a missile shield around the United States. If such a shield were actually constructed, couldn't the United States attack the Soviet Union without fear of retaliation? There is a military axiom that for every weapon developed, a countermeasure is simultaneously created. So it was that in 1985, a Soviet *protivodeistvie* (counteraction) project was launched to develop a weapon that would defeat Star Wars. The result was the Topol-M ICBM, a weapon that will penetrate any national missile defense the United States might deploy until the year 2025. Star Wars was therefore nothing more than corporate welfare and should have been cancelled immediately.

Laura returned in November 1984, healthy and unharmed, having been missing for over a year. She telephoned her mother on her birthday from Buffalo, New York, where presumably she had been living with Steven.

It is difficult to speak of one's child in a derogatory manner. I would rather go no further and end this here, since my life for all intents and purposes came to an end in November 1984. Laura played a major role in my downfall, however, and I must continue my story, as painful as it is.

In her usual acerbic manner, Laura informed her mother that she had remained in hiding to "show her what it is like to have one's child missing." The statement confused Barbara, as well as it should. Laura had convinced herself that Mark had "kidnapped" her baby, and since no one would help her recover Christopher, she would show her parents what it was like to have a missing child.

My other daughters quickly telephoned, informing me that Laura was alive and well. I had always felt 98 percent certain that she was fine, that the professional runaway knew how to handle herself. But I was overcome with a flood of relief when Margaret called me with the news, and I knew then how worried I had been, that I had been in denial. My own agency's kidnap file was huge; most victims are never found. Margaret also related Laura's bizarre kidnap story. Everyone knew that Laura had left her husband and child in Maine and traveled to California to live with her unstable friend Dorie. Mark, who had little money and no car, managed to drive three thousand miles west with the baby in an attempt to save the marriage. When Laura moved in with Steven, Mark returned to Maryland with their child where he remained. Everyone knew where Mark and Christopher were; their address was in my desk Rolodex. Laura seemed to have withdrawn from reality on this point, which is a sign of mental disorder.

Laura then telephoned me, repeating the strange kidnap story, even though I explained that Christopher was a couple hours away in Maryland. I even pointed out that Mark's mother and sister visited me in Norfolk and assured me that my grandson was fine.

When it came to kidnapping, I was an expert and had personally recovered a dozen or so children by that time as a PI. As mentioned ear-lier, the FBI did not handle what they called "domestic kidnapping." They only hunted for kidnappings by strangers.

To legally recover an abducted child, the client had to produce a court order showing the client had custody. This legal document allowed me to conduct the search, and if successful, the client could then legally recover the child. Assistance could be provided and various methods were used to approach the child without frightening him or her.

In the case of Laura, she had no custody order and could have diffi-culty in obtaining one given the conditions in which she left Mark with the child in the first place. To my knowledge, neither Mark nor Laura had petitioned the courts for custody. For Laura to even use the term *kidnap* was ridiculous.

One may wonder how it was possible for me to function with the prospect of exposure by Barbara at any time. The reason I could relax was that Barbara was inert—unable to act beyond her simple world of unchanging flux. She was certainly cynical and poisonous, but also pre-dictable. She would speak badly of me among family and close friends, but she was not hateful enough to call the police. Michael shared this belief as well.

What changed everything was Laura. She came on like a Panzer Divi-sion on a mission of vengeance. She complained that I would not support her and that Barbara should "turn me in for the money." Further, she needed the help of the FBI to recover her kidnapped son. Laura was the external force acting upon the body at rest, creating the motion. As Laura persisted, Barbara's drinking increased until she eventually telephoned the FBI. But most remarkably, Barbara was so drunk that she was not taken seriously. When I was not subsequently arrested, Laura herself called the FBI, and with Barbara's story corroborated, the FBI's espi-onage investigation finally commenced.

There could have been more to the equation, since Jerry was also talking to Barbara during this period, and he may have somehow influ-enced her as well. Barbara seemed to be more a foil, reacting to the strong influences of Laura, Jerry, and Brenda. And during that very month, Jerry was writing letters—under the name "Russ"—to the FBI, which had instructed him to communicate through the classified ads of the San Francisco *Examiner*. The FBI was attempting to arrange a face-to-face meeting, perhaps in Mexico or some other neutral country.

My situation could not have been worse.

Just a couple blocks from my office was a restaurant-bar, the Pine Tree Inn, where several insurance adjusters gathered for after-work cocktails. They represented some of my best clients—Liberty Mutual, State Farm, Allstate, and others. I had quit drinking entirely by then, but since I could pick up new case files over drinks, I made a point to stop at the Pine Tree after work. These guys were hard drinkers, especially on Friday, and to fit in, I ordered a vodka and tonic—but the hostess and waitresses always knew that my vodka and tonic should be only tonic with a twist. The young hostess, Rachel, took great care of me. She was Michael's age, and the two began dating.

On December 18, 1984, Michael and Rachel were wed and moved into a nice apartment in Ghent, not far from where Margaret lived. At this time, neither of us knew that Barbara and Laura had a month earlier informed the FBI of my (our) activity.

Michael was off to sea again in the spring of 1984, flying to Diego Garcia, then on a COD flight to the *America*, which was located in the Persian Gulf area. He, too, was essentially unpaid.

The responsibility of Michael's spy education would fall upon me, but between his sea duty and new marriage, we had little time for extensive training. He was gathering a great deal of material, but he needed to be more selective, to focus on quality information. I was performing all of the camera work, and as I prepared for my January 1985 Vienna meeting, I became convinced that my Minox camera was malfunctioning. I shot some information with my 35-millimeter camera but made a serious security error. Michael's material should have been burned after filming, but I worried that if my camera was broken I'd risk delivering another cache of bad film. Thus, a mass of secret material would remain in my house to be discovered later by the FBI. Were it not for Jerry and his misguided attempt to cheat the Soviets by fogging his film, I would have burned that material regardless of the suspected camera problem.

More than a year had passed since Rena and I made our agreement. She sold her house and moved to the Tampa area of Florida. I may have been a little late, but my plan was to join her in the summer and buy the boat. My house would be signed over to my four children with the provision that Cynthia and Margaret would share residency in the duplex I had planned. To purchase the boat, I would sell the Charleston VFW Club for $100,000, more than enough to buy a quality sailing yacht of forty-five feet or larger in the mid-1980s. Rena did not know my exact plan, but I hoped she would still be willing to join me. I could think of nothing better than sailing the world with Rena during those years. My requirement to service Michael twice a year would present a problem, but I felt sure that Rena would not object to my abandoning her every six months for a couple weeks to sell her paintings in Trinidad, Saint Lucia, Montego Bay, or Aruba.

An extremely strange incident occurred in January 1985. I was scheduled to be in Vienna on the nineteenth for my winter meeting, but unbeknownst to me I had been exposed to the FBI by Barbara and Laura, and perhaps by Jerry. Phone taps and surveillance were surely in place in order to "catch me in the act" the moment I made a move to commit an act.

Law enforcement at every level follows a peculiar pattern when executing an arrest. Even when they have ample evidence against an offender, each agency will wait for a more dramatic capture at a crime scene, the more sensational the better. So, while a single cop could have knocked on my door and taken me to jail, the FBI opted for a long surveillance and spectacular arrest. The problem was, even with all the taps, bugs, and watchful vigilance, I traveled conspicuously and unmolested to Vienna for my meeting.

I have wondered why the FBI didn't arrest me in Vienna. I took very few precautions: my flight to New York was reserved under an alias and paid for in cash, but my international flight was reserved in my name using an authentic passport. To anyone watching my house, I was obviously going on a trip, bags tossed in the car. The simplest reservation watch alert would have signaled my spy move, and as a PI, I could have established a reservation watch myself.

There are only two reasons that I was able to carry out a successful delivery of national secrets without being arrested: one, incompetence by the FBI, or, two, they planned to arrest me later in Washington, DC. The FBI is certainly not incompetent, although my success may well have been the result of some small error. But is it possible that they knew about this delivery and allowed it to take place? I liked to imagine that the secrets I was exchanging were deemed to be of little value and so the FBI allowed the delivery to take place.

There are five different train, subway, and tram systems encompassing the city, and I used them almost exclusively for both general transportation and to seek out surveillance. A day or two before the meeting, I would ride the Stadtbahn or U-Bahn trains from the hotel station, then connect to any of the smaller trams into the distant suburbs, which were about twenty miles from the city center. I would then exit the tram and stroll through a neighborhood for an hour, then reboard for a return tram from a different station. Some large city stations connect up to four different lines and offer an excellent mass of confusing commuters to mask one's movements.

On the day of the incident, I had traveled for about an hour on different lines when I spotted a possible tail at Rennwag station. I changed trains at a large station and headed for the International Center, Donaustadt, the UNO City office and conference complex where some UN offices are located. The train was crowded with children and young adults bearing ice skates and excited smiles, and my tail suspect as well. The skaters got off at my stop, and I moved along with them to a large ice arena. They turned into the arena building while I proceeded straight into a sizable park with extensive walking paths. The snow was about eight inches deep, the park deserted; no one would walk in the park in such conditions. I planned to trudge a couple hundred feet and reverse course to the train stop. The tail was surely not behind me, but a casual glance revealed otherwise: he was a hundred feet behind. There was not a single footprint in the snow except my own, and I was both angry and amazed that a tail could be so conspicuous. I always purchased the heaviest possible walking cane upon my arrival in Europe, which I carried as a weapon. While such canes are usually light and flimsy, this one was stout and heavy.

The path took me to a large circle of vegetation about twenty-five feet across, brown and broken by winter, but it was thick enough to hide me as I circled to the left. Completing the circle, my boot prints met with those of the strange man. Creeping farther, he nearly stopped, looking at my tracks, seeming indecisive. His cap was a mass of fur, but a patch of skin behind his right ear made a perfect target. He went to his knees, hat flying, when I struck him again across the skull. I left him on all fours as I hurried back to the arena and then to the station. I would never discover who he was.

The meeting with my new case officer was routine, and while I suspected the mysterious tail was KGB, the incident was not mentioned by either of us. If it was a KGB agent, he was probably too embarrassed to admit it.

Our probation period had come to an end, and I was promised payment for me and Michael on my next DC drop. Jerry was out for the moment, and if he chose to come back, we understood that I would be his only contact source. I resolved to myself that I would never work with him again, and that if he did contact me, I would pass him off to work directly with the KGB through his own case officer.

On a positive note, our meet and drop schedule would change. I had recommended a spring/fall rotation for the past ten years because winter presented travel complications. The change would start at my next drop, then scheduled for May. The change would only hasten my arrest, however.

Just three weeks after my Vienna meeting on March 10, 1985, the forty years of cold war tensions would come to an end when Konstantin Chernenko died. I had spent nearly the last twenty of those years trying to show the Soviet Union that the United States had no real intention of invading. In my frustration, I had slammed the table at a meeting with a future Soviet president and secretary general, shouting, "Is anyone reading the material I deliver?" Well, someone within the power structure *was* reading it—Mikhail Gorbachev—and everything would change with his rise to power.

Upon assuming the leadership of the Soviet Union, Gorbachev stated, "The USSR has never intended to fight the United States, and does not have such intentions now. There have never been such madmen with the Soviet leadership and there are none now." He would later announce publicly the official Soviet doctrine as "one aimed simply at defending their homeland."

Probably the best quote to come out of that period of regime change was made by Georgi Arbatov, the director for the Soviet Institute for the Studies of the United States of America and Canada. He delivered the most chilling words of all to the US military industrial complex when he said: "We are going to do something terrible to you. We are going to deprive you of your enemy." The Soviet Union had tossed aside the sword, leaving the United States without even the illusion of an enemy.

As a pragmatist, Gorbachev insisted on knowing the real facts regarding his economy and industry; he refused to accept the KGB lies. He was stunned to realize that the Soviet military industrial complex and weapon production was absorbing 60 percent of GDP while the Soviet people were becoming ever poorer. Gorbachev sincerely tried to dismantle the war machine and develop trust between the United States and the USSR, but the hawks on both sides frustrated the process.

Without the theatrical stage of the cold war, the US national security state was hard-pressed to define its purpose, but the US public never seemed to understand how much money and creative imagination had been invested in the making of the communist threat. The cold war had turned the United States into a military camp.

As a result of Gorbachev's actions, the United States was left with a huge military machine without a mission. The military industrial complex could not let that happen, however. On March 19, Congress passed an appropriation to allow the construction of the MX missile, a new generation of ICBM designed to destroy a Soviet Union that had just quit the fight.

General Colin Powell, later to become secretary of state, would acknowledge this military dilemma when he said, "Think hard about it. I'm running out of demons. I'm running out of villains." The cold war had given birth to a permanent war economy, creating giant industries whose sole function was to produce goods and services for the government. I knew what would come next—the United States would invent new enemies to keep its war economy alive.

The ending of the cold war generated a wide range of emotions, starting with the prospect that I could leave the spy business at last. Everyone has pivot points in life, and I had reached the point of retirement. I did not fall into that grave danger of taking myself too seriously, but I did feel certain that I had done some good and that I could escape quietly. Years later, I would joke that they should take the 1973 Nobel Peace Prize away from Dr. Henry Kissinger, one who created and prolonged wars, and award the million-dollar prize to me for ending the cold war.

My brother Arthur called me one evening in a distressed state and suggested we meet. Following good spy techniques of walk-and-talk, we strolled in a remote area to discuss Barbara's latest phone call. Barbara had telephoned Arthur's home totally drunk and spoken to both Rita and Arthur, berating me to them in her usual manner. What worried Arthur was that she implied she had phoned the FBI to report my criminal activity. Barbara had made such drunken remarks in the past, however, so Arthur could not be sure if she was serious this time. He was upset enough that he informed me immediately.

Barbara had planned to visit Margaret during Easter, and I arranged a surprise visit so I could encounter Barbara face to face. Barbara had earlier refused to speak to me in person or on the phone, so Margaret did not tell her of my visit. Barbara was caught by surprise, and after a short but pleasant visit with my daughter, while Barbara hid in a bedroom, I cornered her and insisted that we talk privately for a few minutes.

I had not seen my ex-wife in ten years and had not spoken to her at length for many years beyond that. She was nervous and even seemed frightened by the prospect of a conversation, but I managed to usher her out the door by insisting that we had vital matters to discuss.

We drove to a nearby fast-food restaurant that was mercifully quiet—

burgers apparently are not popular Easter fare. We sat across from each other at a secluded table, scorching our fingers on cardboard-flavored coffee. She would not look at me; her poisonous phone call to the FBI had left her emotionally depressed, yet agitated. Later, I would understand her strange behavior: she had been ordered not to speak or meet with me.

The purpose of my meeting with her was to confirm her phone call to Arthur and, if indeed she had done so foolhardy a deed as to actually phone the authorities, to give me a chance to save our son and me. So I asked her flatly if she had made the call to the FBI, and she denied having done so. This was no time to be oblique, so I informed her that our son, Michael, was actively involved with me in the business. I suspected she knew that I had tried to recruit Laura while she was in the army, so she shouldn't have been too surprised that I would make the same offer to Michael. Her response was a silent thousand-yard stare over my left shoulder until she finally asked if Michael was working with me as a spy. I replied with a single "Yes." She went mute again. The last sentence I would ever speak to my ex-wife and mother to my four beautiful children was, "Look, if you did something stupid, tell me now since I still have time to save our son." She again denied exposing us, lying like a good FBI informant. I believed her at the time, simply because no mother would destroy her own son just to punish her ex-husband. Of course, I knew better, having been involved in kidnap investigations in which mothers killed their children for exactly that reason.

The FBI would enjoy a serendipitous event as the result of my Aunt Amelia's death. She was everyone's favorite and had died too young. My mother telephoned in tears to inform me that her sister had died and asked if I would take her to the funeral in Buffalo. Normally I would be in the Tiger within the hour and at her side, but I was just a day away from my Washington drop. My mind was spinning. The drop could wait for an alternative date, but after Jerry's trickery and the time-consuming effort to reestablish our reliability, I was reluctant to miss an exchange even for so important a family tragedy. I would be both inconsiderate and stupid by refusing. My stupidity was in telling my mother that I was busy through the weekend and would join her after the services. My phone was, of course, tapped, and the FBI correctly concluded that I would make a spy move.

I had seen my aunt just one time over the past years, and by a strange coincidence, the lives of Amelia, Barbara, my mother, and I had come together once before in 1957. Amelia and my mom caught Barbara having sex with Amelia's husband, and in a strange set of circumstances, we would come together again. Barbara was still the protagonist and now FBI informant, Amelia's death caused the fatal phone call by my mom into the tapped phone, and my life was again being torpedoed in the process.

The government was prepared with a seventy-five-man tail (by their own admission), both on the ground and in the air; there were probably many more than seventy-five. They lost me almost immediately, as I meandered through a residential neighborhood for fifteen minutes, but found me again on I-64. The drop was to take place in Montgomery County, Maryland, and I took a room in a Ramada Inn near Rockville.

Tailing techniques by the FBI are far different than those used by detective agencies and small police departments. For me to assemble and pay for a five-car tail was difficult enough, and we were forced to keep the subject in sight at all times. Big federal agencies have access to vast amounts of people and unlimited budgets and thus use a practice of "flooding" the area with stationary observers. They tail a suspect by watching them drive or walk past. The unwary suspect never sees a thing.

It was no doubt taxing on the FBI team as I simply drove to a motel, and since they lost me a couple times en route, they could not be sure if they had missed the exchange. But as night fell and I was on the move, their tension was again at a peak, but since I was only driving my route in segments and in reverse to check the site, they still had no reason for an arrest.

My second departure hours later would be their opportunity for the spectacular arrest of a Soviet spy and his handler. I made my signal to indicate my readiness and checked the signal of my handler—we were both ready for the exchange.

As a result of my earlier drive around the drop sites, the FBI was able to flood the areas with agents. Observing some of the arresting agents later, it seemed as if the FBI Academy had been emptied of its students at Quantico, some seventy miles to the south. Agents in the woods saw me drop my package behind a tree, at which point my life was finished. But the FBI would make mistakes that would rob them of the dramatic arrest of their dreams. First, they lost me again and for a long period of time. Then they eliminated my signal that indicated I had made my drop. The signal was a simple soda can dropped from my car window at a specific spot, and their fixed surveillance agent recovered the can. With the signal removed, the KGB agent knew something was amiss and aborted the exchange without even checking my package drop site. He obviously did not drop his package as well.

With the exchange aborted, I went to recover my package but found it gone. Since difficulties had occurred on another occasion, I did not panic and forced myself to assume that my contact had picked it up before aborting.

From all indications, the KGB agent suspected the worst and even though he had diplomatic immunity from arrest and prosecution, he left the United States immediately.

Back at the motel, I reviewed my meeting with Arthur, Barbara's denial that she had informed on Michael and me, and the exchange difficulty. At that point, I calculated my odds at 50-50 that arrest was eminent. To run was futile, since the motel would be surrounded by at least one hundred agents. Then the phone rang and my odds dropped to 95-5, against. The "desk" called to inform me that someone was seen tampering with my van. Good grief, I thought, I had used that very amateurish line myself a hundred times to lure people out of houses. My odds dropped to 99-1.

I remembered a vending machine and trash can near the elevators and decided I might be able to hide my incriminating drop procedures there, then go to the desk for my likely arrest. The hall was empty. I held my .38 pistol and the #10 envelope containing the procedure under my jacket through the left pocket. Around the corner, I headed for the trash can but was confronted by several agents lurking around a dark corner. I dropped the envelope and pistol. It was over.

People who are arrested for major crimes react in two ways. A small minority will fight to the end, regardless of the hopelessness of their situation. They may run or even engage in high-speed chases or gun battles.

Once in prison, this type of person will usually be placed under "chemical restraints," like Thorazine or other psychotropic drugs. As for the other type of reaction to arrest, psychologists use the term *decomposition* to describe the mental state of those who succumb to a force beyond their control. They regress emotionally and their mental state becomes impaired enough to require some sort of treatment. These people wander about the prison system with wrecked emotions and destroyed egos.

It is an end worse than death.

EPILOGUE

If Barbara's intention was to inflict pain, she was thoroughly successful. As I rode handcuffed in the rear of an FBI car, my only thought was of Michael; I could have saved him. Had Barbara been truthful, I could have evaded the heavy surveillance and traveled to Europe without detection. With Michael's schedule of port calls, I could have met him and saved us both. Instead, he would experience the humiliation of being arrested and dragged off the ship in shackles.

The KGB had a simple method to assist its spies when they had been apprehended. The Soviet Union's national airline, Aeroflot, had offices worldwide and their security staff would respond to an agent in trouble. The agent would be whisked to the USSR, where he would be provided for. No longer a spy, his life would be ruined, never allowed to see loved ones again and living a drab life in a sorry Moscow tenement.

I thought of an old novel in which a British spy had been captured. He was offered the gentleman's way out: a revolver with one round loaded. The other options were to agree to serve as a double agent or be thrown to the press. The United States did not use the pistol solution, and I knew there was no hope for an offer to turn double agent. The cold war was over, but the United States would prolong the illusion of the communist threat for as long as possible. My only usefulness, therefore, was in my propaganda value. My importance to the government was priceless, for they could show that regardless of Gorbachev's plea for peaceful coexistence, the Soviet Union still operated a huge and dangerous spy organization and that his peace overtures were therefore fake.

They had John Walker to prove it. I expected to be battered by the news media, but it would be much worse than I could imagine.

Immediately after my arrest, I had been thoroughly strip-searched and had every inch of my clothing inspected. As I traveled to jail, I felt an object in a small pocket at my side. Sliding my cuffed hands around, I felt the metal object and realized it was my motel room key, still in my pocket. Amazing. It was a single key, the only time I ever received a room key without a large attached marker. I remembered the story of the famous Soviet spy Rudolph Able, who was captured in the 1950s in New York. He had a spy gadget on his person, I believe it was a hollow coin that could hold micro-dot film. As Able proceeded to jail, also cuffed and sitting in the backseat, he managed to slip the spy coin from his pocket and drop it under the rear cushion. The incriminating coin was never found. (Rudolph Able would be convicted, but a deal was worked out where he was swapped for Francis Gary Powers, the U-2 pilot.) This little coincidence between Able's arrest and mine was interesting. I still have my property receipt from the Montgomery County Jail, and it includes "one key."

Jerry would pay the price for his contact with Barbara. His exact plan may never become known, but I sincerely believe that his scheme was to act jointly with Barbara or at least to encourage her to turn informant. If his "Russ" letters to the FBI were unsuccessful, why not get Barbara to do his dirty work? I do know that special agents from the San Francisco Field Office called on Jerry at his Davis home, having gotten a lead from Barbara. They had no evidence and requested an interview. Jerry could have refused; he was not arrested.

Jerry admitted to knowing me in the past but denied any contact during recent years. The FBI was suspicious since he spoke badly of me, which seemed inconsistent with his story, and he was also unusually nervous. At one point, Jerry asked to be excused for a drink of water, but, using good police work, an agent crept across the room and observed Jerry stopping first in his den, where he removed a letter from his printer and slid it under the machine out of sight. They had him. It was a personal letter to me, just written, asking to "rejoin my organization in any capacity." That letter and Barbara's statement would lead to Jerry's arrest. The "Russ" letters were later traced to him as well.

The letter in the printer could be viewed in one of two ways. First, it could have been a real attempt to reestablish our old spy arrangement. The agent who saw Jerry try to hide the letter told me later that Jerry's venture in the stock market had been mostly unsuccessful. So, Jerry may have squandered his spy nest egg in bad investments and, since he was unemployed, he needed the spy work.

The second option, and the one I believe, is that Jerry's "Russ" letters had not resulted in his immunity or any type of reward, and his attempt to finesse Barbara into action was also unsuccessful. What Jerry needed was real information on my new spy partner and my schedule for exchanges. With that information, he could reveal not just the name of a spy suspect (me) but could also lead the FBI to an actual spy exchange with a Soviet diplomat. That would surely win him his fat reward and immunity from prosecution. But, with the letter intercepted by the FBI, combined with Barbara's corroboration, he was destroyed.

Jerry went to trial and received a life sentence. He later admitted to writing the "Russ" letters.

Michael was arrested based on his mother's statement, and since he had classified material hidden away, he had no defense and pleaded guilty. He received a twenty-five-year sentence—an arrangement based on my agreement to assist the government by explaining my success over the years.

The most sorrowful story is that of Arthur, the man who had never even received a parking ticket, the patriotic naval officer, the responsible family man and citizen. As a result of a statement by Barbara, he, too, was visited by two special agents and questioned. Barbara claimed that while Arthur and she were engaged in sex in the mid-1960s, Arthur had told her that he was a spy. One reason for her disgraceful lie was that Arthur rejected her sexual advances years later after he had come to his senses, and Barbara lied to the FBI for pure revenge. The other reason, of course, was to inflict more pain upon me.

Any street-smart urban adolescent would know how to handle a situation involving cops and courts, but Arthur was the antithesis of a street kid. Arthur's aversion to lying and his utter respect for authority would spell his doom. Also, his mental state was impaired by the "decomposition"—the inability to fight or stand up for himself—that I mentioned earlier, so he sought advice from his wife, Rita. Unfortunately, Rita was as ignorant of cops and courts as Arthur, and together, they agreed that he should "do the right thing" and admit his knowledge of my activity. The material he showed me was, of course, unclassified, so he should do his civic duty. They figured that the authorities would forgive him for this minor infraction. Rita watched too much television and Arthur was not thinking right.

I had always believed that Arthur was arrested and convicted due to the geography of my arrest. Most of my drops had occurred in the Virginia suburbs, but my fatal drop and arrest was in Maryland, just five miles from the Virginia border. Since I committed a federal crime in the Maryland Federal District, the US attorney (USA) for that district had the right to prosecute me. The USA for the Eastern District of Virginia was livid and wanted me prosecuted there since I had operated the spy organization from his district for at least fifteen years. They fought vigorously over who would get to prosecute this major case, but Maryland had me, and the courts ruled that Maryland would try me.

The Virginia USA was crushed; the show trial was lost by just five miles. Worse yet, Michael had returned from Europe to Maryland as my codefendant and Jerry was in the clutches of a California USA. Virginia had nothing. Then they turned to Arthur, the overly cooperative brother.

I am absolutely convinced that if I had been arrested in Virginia, Arthur would have been ignored as a defendant or used only as a prosecution witness. Instead, a major espionage case was developed from the two items he admitted showing me. The maintenance record that was downgraded to unclassified would appear in court with a fresh, new confidential stamp. The damage control book was also presented as evidence with its classification marking, but both items were easy targets for a successful defense.

Before Arthur's trial, I was visited by a lawyer and writer who had written a damaging book about the government intelligence services. He was tried under the Espionage Act for revealing secret information, but he successfully showed at trial that the secrets were already in the public domain. That means once the government reveals classified information to the public, it loses its classification. For example, if the specifications of a weapon system are revealed to *Time* magazine, those facts can no longer be classified; the government has relinquished its authority to classify them. In the case of the damage control book, uncleared civilian ship-yard workers, dependents, and ship visitors had walked through the entire ship by the thousands. To imply that the specific location of the radio room or the ship's armory is still secret is sheer nonsense. All of the information contained in the damage control book was in the public domain, its classification surrendered by the government.

The lawyer offered to clear Arthur for a small sum of $40,000. A larger Washington law firm made the same guarantee for about $90,000. Arthur's house was worth more than that, and with their children grown and Rita living in the big house alone, it was time to sell and mount a vigorous defense. Knowing Arthur's nature, he would refuse, ever the faithful provider who would die before casting his wife on the street. Rita, the practical one, should have sold and moved into a cheap trailer to save her husband, but her greed overruled her duty.

For the cost of a house, Arthur should have been found not guilty. Rita lives alone in that big house today. Arthur lives in federal prison with a life sentence. Living together in an old Airstream trailer would have made more sense.